# A Race Redeemed

**Did God Come To Earth On A Secret Mission?**

En Route Books and Media, LLC
Saint Louis, MO, USA

Cover design by Juan Novo
and Christine Horner of Open Book Design



Scripture passages are taken from: "The Didache Bible, with commentaries based on the Catechism of the Catholic Church." Ignatius Bible Edition, 2020, and also from: "The New Catholic Study Bible, St. Jerome Edition," (NCSB), Thomas Nelson Publishers, 1985.

ISBN 979-8-88870-689-3
Library of Congress Control Number: 2025938124

Printed in the United States of America

First Edition

## CONTENTS

# PREFACE

## CAN CHATGPT BE TRUSTED WITH A CATHOLIC BOOK?

A close family member who does not communicate with me very much, sad to say, requested a copy of my book A RACE REDEEMED in pdf so he could have it summarized by ChatGPT. I had heard the name ChatGPT before, here and there, but honestly had no idea what it actually was. However, since this family member leans to the left a bit and we do not always see eye to eye, I thought, "Good news! I am glad he's interested. Perhaps this book will bring him closer to Christ." A day later he sent me a copy of the summary that also included a critique of the book. The critique was after the summary and was included as the answer to a question he sent them after receiving the summary. The question was : "does this book make any claims or statements that conflict with true catholic doctrine?" The answer was: "Yes, while *A Race Redeemed* by Juan Novo strongly promotes Catholic teachings and aligns with many core doctrines, it does contain a few questionable or exaggerated claims that either stretch or misrepresent true Catholic doctrine or established Church positions. Below are some key examples:" (The following are three points critiqued by ChatGPT followed by my rebuttals.)

Statements that conflict or are theologically problematic:

1. Rejection of Possibility of Intelligent Life Elsewhere:

The author claims it is "absurd" to think Jesus would redeem beings on other planets, and therefore intelligent extraterrestrial life cannot exist.

*Conflict:* The Church does not teach that intelligent life elsewhere is impossible, nor does it claim that Christ's redemption cannot apply universally in unknown ways. The Vatican Observatory has stated that such life wouldn't contradict Catholic theology.

REBUTTAL: On page 23 I write: "…Jesus already has a human body, and will have it forever, and He would have to abandon His human body in order to take on another one, or other ones, to complete the redemption of other beings, and this reaches the level of absurdity when you think about it. This is why I **personally, as a Catholic**, do not think intelligent life with free will like us exists on other planets **unless His sacrificial death redeemed the entire universe**…. [that is why] **personally, and strictly from a Catholic point of view, in my opinion**, I do not believe that beings with free will, like us, exist on other planets." Contrary to what this Chatbot seems to imply, I do not say the Church teaches "that intelligent life elsewhere is impossible, nor does it claim that Christ's redemption cannot apply universally in unknown ways," I very clearly state that this is my personal opinion from a Catholic perspective. Moreover, you will note, I also say: "**unless His sacrificial death redeemed the entire universe**," which, again, is contrary to what the Chatbot claims I say.

2. Exclusive Interpretation of Bible Authorship:

He claims the Catholic Church is the sole "author" of the Bible, and only Catholics can interpret it correctly.

*Clarification:* While the Church compiled and preserved the canon, it does not claim authorship of the Bible in a literal sense. Also, the Church acknowledges the Holy Spirit as the divine author, with human authors inspired by God.

REBUTTAL: Once again, I do not say that the Church is the sole author of the Bible in a literal sense. On page 11, I said "original author" simply meaning that it was the Catholic Church that created the Bible and not the Protestants nor anyone else. Just before this, on page 9, I state: "It [the Bible] was compiled by Roman Catholic bishops and scholars under the guidance of the Holy Spirit." And on page 12, I state: " Thus, **God is the actual author of the authentic and original Bible, the Roman Catholic Bible**." I believe readers will get the point I make here while the Chatbot did not. Where's the Chabot's [supposed] intelligence?

3. Over-personal theological speculation as if definitive:

He makes speculative theological claims (e.g., God placing all weird life forms only on Earth to show humans are special) and treats them as authoritative.

*Conflict:* While such views can be held privately, presenting them as doctrinal conclusions oversteps the bounds of personal theological reflection.

REBUTTAL: Wow, what nonsense! I again make it very clear that this is my personal opinion; I do not present them as "doctrinal conclusions." That is clearly a gross misinterpretation of what I actually said. Proof of this is found on p. 23 where I state: "Moreover, I also **personally believe** that all of the weird and strange life forms God could have placed on other planets He instead placed them on this planet. There are literally trillions of weird and strange life forms right here on planet Earth."

Final Verdict:

The book is passionately Catholic and well-meaning, but it contains theological overreach, polemical exaggerations, and some mischaracterizations that could mislead readers unfamiliar with official Church teachings. It does not promote formal heresy, but readers should discern its content alongside the Catechism and magisterial guidance.

REBUTTAL: My above refutations serve as enough and ample evidence that the statements made herein by this ChatGPT Chatbot regarding my book, A RACE REDEEMED, are false and erroneous intended to discredit this book, this Catholic book. In fact, as the late brilliant economist Dr. Walter E. Williams used to say, "This doesn't even pass the smell test!" Which proves, beyond the shadow of a doubt, that ChatGPT is not a reliable source of information when it comes to analyzing Catholic literature. Whether the same is true for other topics is currently unknown to me. In short, as far as this topic is concerned, evidently ChatGPT is very good at using double-talk: a mixture of sense and nonsense, employed to confuse the reader in the attempt to justify the double-talker's position. It even uses Church documents and Scripture toward that end, which reminds me, Satan did the same thing with Christ when he tempted Him in the Desert. Coincidence? I hope ChatGPT likes Crow.

So, I repeat the initial question: "CAN CHATGPT BE TRUSTED WITH A CATHOLIC BOOK?" The answer is quite obvious to me. What do *you* say?

Juan Novo

# INTRODUCTION

This book is the result of a personal research project I undertook in order to answer some serious questions I had regarding Jesus Christ, His Church, and His Mission on Earth. I also wanted to learn more about Judaism, the religion Christ was born into, the one He practiced during His life up to His Public Ministry, and the one whose followers failed to recognize that He was the foretold Messiah up to the moment of His death on the Cross, and even to this very day!

Of all things in the Universe, the human race is the zenith of God's Creation. He created us in His own image and likeness and then placed us in the world, and He created both mankind and the Universe out of nothing. We were given power – by God – over the fish, the birds, and the animals, both large and small, and this is found in Scripture, in the Bible's Book of Genesis (Gn 1:26), but we were not given power over the physical world itself. Some deluded people think they have this power, but they are wrong. Only God has this power, and He controls, maintains, and regulates the entire universe which of course includes Earth – day after day – according to His Will, not ours. We little humans can only live in the world, manipulate its contents, as well as manipulate other human beings, and we can do so for good or evil purposes. God wants us to follow His Will and do everything we can for the common good, of course, but as human history has shown, evil is frequently chosen by evil people and primarily for the power to dominate others.

Evil entered this world through Satan, more commonly referred to as the devil. His original name was Lucifer, and he was once a very powerful, beautiful and good angel created by God. The name Lucifer means "morning star" or "light bringing." Scripture tells us that at some point, Lucifer rebelled against God, and together with many other good angels who also rebelled, they were cast out of Heaven and down to Earth before humans were created. As a result of his rebellion and freely chosen decision to be evil instead of good, apart from losing an excellent relationship with God forever, he also lost his beauty and much of his God-given power. And last but not least, he also lost his name, for it was taken away from him by God Himself, the One who gave it to him personally.

From then on, this once beautiful, brilliant, and good angel became – by his own free will – an ugly, despicable, revolting and evil entity known as Satan, a name that means "adversary" or "enemy;" a name that, without the shadow of a doubt, suits him to a tee. As described in Scripture, evil entered this world through the fallen angel, Satan, because he succeeded in persuading the first human beings, Adam and Eve, to disobey God thereby committing what the Catholic Church calls Original Sin: the first sin committed by the first human beings. This resulted, of course, in the breakup of the intimate relationship they had enjoyed with God, the Loving Creator of all things. The repair and restoration of this broken relationship between God and mankind was finally achieved 2000 years ago by the suffering, death, and Resurrection of Jesus the Christ, who was – and is forever – both God and man in one Divine Person; the Son of God the Father. This astounding phenomenon and miracle, that God made for Himself a human body, entered it, and lived with it and in it until adulthood, and then allowed Himself to be brutally tortured and executed like a common criminal in front of hundreds of witnesses is not only a historical fact with plenty of hard evidence to prove it, but also the perfect way He Himself chose to save the human race from Eternal doom in Hell because of Sin. This is extremely mysterious!

The coming of Jesus into the world with this horrible salvific Mission as the primary objective and Main Mission was prophesied by Old Testament Prophets throughout the centuries, so it really should not have come as a surprise that Jesus was the foretold Messiah to those who were familiar with the Holy Scriptures; namely, the Pharisees, the Sadducees, the Essenes and the scribes. But that is precisely what happened! They not only rejected Him, but they treated Him like a common criminal and then had Him executed as well. This mysterious and stark reality, together with other curious data I found in Scripture, finally led me one day to the conclusive question:

Why didn't these "experts" realize–and therefore believe–that Jesus was the promised Messiah? After hundreds of years of prophecies about Him, including where He was going to be born and by whom; what His mission and lineage would be; what tribe He would come from; what His name would be; how He was going to be mistreated by His own people; that He would be called a Nazarene; that He would speak in parables, and many other details about Him, why didn't these "experts" in Jewish Law and Scripture recognize Him when He finally came to Earth? What more information could they possibly have needed and wanted that wasn't given to them by the Prophets, and even by Jesus Christ Himself – in Person? This kept going through my mind. One day, I opened the Bible and read: "And as they were coming down the mountain, he [Jesus] charged them to tell no one what they had seen, until the Son of man should have risen from the dead. So they kept the matter to themselves, questioning what the rising from the dead meant" (Mk 9:9-10). I then turned a few pages and read: "And Jesus went on with his disciples, to the villages of Caesare'a Philip'pi; and on the way he asked his disciples, 'Who do men say that I am?' And they told him, 'John the Baptist; and others say, Eli'jah; and others one of the Prophets.' And he asked them, 'But who do you say that I am?' Peter answered him, 'You are the Christ.' And he charged them to tell no one about him' " (8:27-30). First, "tell no one what they had seen," and then, "tell no one about him"? I asked myself, "Why the secrecy"?

These curiosities became a research project and the answers revealed not only why the Jewish experts did not recognize Jesus as the foretold Messiah, but also a little about "the secrecy" and how Jesus prepared for His Sacrificial Mission; even perhaps the steps God took in order to ensure its success. All of this information became a booklet entitled: "Who Do *You* Say I Am ?" But soon thereafter, I realized this should be a chapter of a larger book that briefly explained the origin of the Universe and how planet Earth came to be, the creation of the first human beings, how their relationship with God was broken by their sin, leading to evil, illness, suffering, and death, how – and why – God prepared a savior to restore this broken relationship, **why this Savior was not recognized when He finally came**, and how this Restoration resulted in the formation of a brand new religion; a "Universal" religion established by none other than God Himself in Person. Such a book (although a brief one), with this booklet as a chapter in it, would give a more complete picture to the reader about the **real** world we live in; a sort of "sketch of existence" in order to arrive at some level of understanding of the reality all of us are in. So, I put on my research hat once again and the present book is the result.

The researching and writing of this book has brought me much closer to Our Tender Father in Heaven; to our Lord Jesus Christ, our brother, Redeemer, and God; to the Holy Spirit, our Helper and Counselor; and to our sweet Blessed Mother, Mary, Mediatrix of all Graces, mother of Jesus and tender mother of us all. And last but not least, to a fuller appreciation of the Work God has done for all mankind through Christ, our Lord; an appreciation that continues to grow, day after day. The Redemption of Mankind by Christ is like a Big Beautiful Diamond. This humble present work is only a very tiny little facet of that Precious Gem.

Juan Novo

# A Race Redeemed

## Chapter 1

"In the beginning God created the heavens and the earth. The earth was without form and void, and darkness was upon the face of the deep; and the Spirit of God was moving over the face of the waters" (Gn 1:1-2).

### ALL IN TIME

#### The True Universal Church and The Bible

The above passage from Genesis ("Toledoth" in Hebrew) is how the Roman Catholic Bible begins. The Roman Catholic Bible is the original Bible (Fundamentalists take note!). It was compiled by Roman Catholic bishops and scholars under the guidance of the Holy Spirit. After many years of work, it was completed and approved by the Roman Catholic Council of Carthage in 397 A.D. and then promptly sent to Rome where the Pope gave it the final and official approval. [1] This means, of course, that the Church Christ founded, the original Christian Faith: one, holy, catholic, and apostolic Church, existed way before the Bible was written, almost 400 years before! The Holy Roman Catholic Church is the original Christian Church founded personally by Jesus Christ in 33 A.D. [2] This is not a subjective opinion or a Catholic "whim"; it is an objective historical fact found in trustworthy and reliable history books worldwide. Most importantly, it is a decisive fact of paramount importance for the true follower of Christ. More on this later. The original Church Christ founded was named "Catholic," which means "Universal," taken from the Greek word "katholikos," because it is open to all peoples worldwide without exception or prejudice.

The Holy Catholic Bible consists of 73 books: 46 Old Testament (OT) books and 27 New Testament (NT) books. The Bible is divided basically into two parts: the OT, originally written in Hebrew, and the NT, originally written in Greek. The former is largely an account of and written by the Hebrew and Jewish people; the latter is an account of and written by the close followers of Jesus Christ. The first five books of the OT were written by Moses, the Hebrew liberator who freed the Hebrew/Israelites from Egyptian bondage around the 13th century B.C., and the rest of the OT was written by various Hebrew/Israelite scholars over a period of centuries. The NT was written by eight different authors, six of whom were Apostles of Jesus Christ. It is largely an account of the birth, life, and teachings of Jesus Christ, Son of God the Father, the Messiah promised by God to mankind – through the Jewish people – in OT times, who came to Earth from Heaven to redeem the entire fallen human race through His Sacrificial Death on a Cross, an event that took place in Jerusalem around the year 33 A.D. All of the writers of the entire Bible were either Hebrew, Israelite, or Jewish, except one, St. Luke, a Greek (Gentile) physician, traveling companion and secretary to St. Paul.

The Bible was first printed in the 15th century by Johannes Gutenberg, a German Catholic and the inventor of the printing press. He was also the first to divide Scripture passages into verses. Before that, the Bible was written entirely by hand, year after year, by Roman Catholic scholars and handed down from generation to generation with the passing of time. It was not until the 16th century that the Bible began to be read and used regularly by non-Catholic individuals for spiritual and moral education, particularly regarding salvation attainable only through Jesus Christ and no one else. The majority of these individuals eventually became known as "protestants" like their leaders, because most of their leaders, ex-Catholic clerics, had broken away from the Roman Catholic Church, the True Church founded by Christ, "protesting" they were not going to follow such a serious and strict religion any more for personal reasons. In time, these leaders became known as "Protestant Reformers," founders of new heretical "Christian" movements, and naturally, all of them were excommunicated by the Pope. The most notable were Martin Luther, Ulrich Zwingli, Andreas Karlstadt, and John Calvin (a lawyer, not a cleric). Since the movements they established were not as strict, many were attracted to join their ranks. Interestingly, protestants continued to call themselves Christians even though they had separated themselves from the Catholic Church founded by Christ. One may therefore ask: "Can people be considered Christians if they don't belong to the original group of believers that follow the teachings of Christ, namely Catholics?" And the answer is: "Yes." Validly baptized Protestants are regarded by the Magisterium of the Catholic Church as true Christian brothers and sisters who are in an imperfect relationship with the Catholic Church Christ founded, and for a baptism to be valid, the person must be baptized using plain natural water with the words: "I baptize you in the name of the Father, and of the Son, and of the Holy Spirit" (see CCC 817-18, 838). Worthy of note, it is better to be a Catholic Christian enjoying a perfect relationship with Christ and His Church than to be a Protestant Christian who is not enjoying a perfect relationship with Christ and His Church. Since there is only one Christ, it follows that there is only one True Christian Faith, and that Faith is unmistakably and historically Catholic. It always has been, and always will be. Today, there are tens of thousands of Protestant denominations worldwide. Jesus only has one Spouse, one Bride, and that Bride is the One, Holy, Catholic, and Apostolic Church (see Eph. 5:23-32; Rev 19:6-8; 21:2, 9).

This brings up a very important point regarding the Bible. Since the Roman Catholic Church is indeed the only and actual "original author" of the Bible, a historical fact, it therefore follows that the Catholic Church is the only one that can properly explain the contents of that Bible, no one else or no other religion or religious group is better qualified to do so. However, it is interesting to note that one does not need the Bible to be saved! i.e., to go to Heaven after death, although one would be a more informed Christian in regards to the Faith and all related to it if one read the Bible and studied it properly under the guidance of the Catholic Church, its only True Author. I must also add here that the Catholic Bible and Protestant Bibles are not the same, because the Protestants removed some of the books and even edited some of the text in order to suit their agenda and beliefs. Therefore, if you want to read the original, unedited and complete version, you must get yourself a Catholic Bible. Only then will you be reading the REAL Bible.

It must be understood that the Bible does not answer all theological questions. That is not its purpose. That job belongs to the Magisterium of the Church. Moreover, although the Bible contains both historical and even some scientific data, it is not a science book or a history book and therefore many passages in it are not to be taken literally, nor should anyone expect to find perfect chronological order or historical accuracy in all of its pages, particularly in the OT. The writers of the OT, chosen by God, were not scientists or historians, and even though the majority of the 73 books were written by more than one human writer, it has one actual author and "director": God.[3] For God Himself inspired and directed the human writers to write what they wrote that is contained in those 73 books.[4] Thus, God is the actual author of the authentic and original Bible, the Roman Catholic Bible. However, in regards to Sola Scriptura: There is no actual and real proof that the Bible is the Word of God.

"The Church, which has spread everywhere, even to the ends of the earth, received the faith from the apostles and their disciples ... Having one soul and one heart, the Church holds this faith, preaches and teaches it consistently as though by a single voice. For though there are different languages, there is but one tradition. … Just as God's creature, the sun, is one and the same the world over, so also does the Church's preaching shine everywhere to enlighten all men who want to come to a knowledge of the truth. Now of those who speak with authority in the churches, no preacher however forceful will utter anything different—for no one is above the Master—nor will a less forceful preacher diminish what has been handed down. Since our faith is everywhere the same, no one who can say more augments it, nor can anyone who says less diminish it." St. Ignatius of Antioch

God gave the Bible to mankind through the Church to: (1) teach us how the universe came into existence; (2) teach us there is only one True God in three Divine Persons; (3) teach us how to live with one another; (4) tell us how our first parents, Adam and Eve, disobeyed Him resulting in suffering and death; (5) teach us there's a better life after death (in Heaven) and a worse one (in Hell); (6) and most importantly, to teach us that this life of bliss in Heaven is attainable only through His only Son, Jesus Christ, who died for all mankind. These are the main reasons for the Bible. No other religion has such a book. Ironically, Protestants are using - and relying on - a Catholic book for religious instruction to attain their salvation, but then refuse to become members of the religion that wrote the very book they so highly esteem! This is illogical, senseless and unreasonable–to name only a few. God gave us the Bible because He loves us and wants us to know the reason for our existence, and that of everything else.

The story of the relationship between God and the Hebrews actually begins with Abraham. God revealed himself to Abraham (actually Abram) to inform him that there was only one God to correct the erroneous practice of polytheism common to the people in the region and worldwide as well. Thus, the main objective of the Bible is to inform mankind that there is only one God and that Salvation (going to Heaven after death) can only be attained through Jesus Christ, the only-begotten Son of God the Father, who came down from Heaven a little over 2000 years ago, took to Himself a human nature by being born of a woman, and willingly sacrificed Himself by dying on a Cross in order to redeem the entire fallen human race.[5] Knowledge of technical or scientific data is not necessary for Salvation, thank God for that. In fact, it might hinder Salvation! For it is certain that Hell is full of disbelieving and disobedient intellectuals, while Heaven is full of believing, obedient, and repentant saints.

## Origin Of The Universe

In the Book of Genesis, the first book in the Bible, it says in chapter 1, verse 3: "God said, Let there be light," and then God separated the light from the darkness, and this He did on day one. This seems to suggest that God created our Sun on the first day of Creation, but St. Augustine believed this was a reference to the creation of the angels, because later, in verse 16, it says that God made the Sun and the Moon on the fourth day. In this light, St. Augustine believed the passage in verse 3 was a reference to God separating the good angels (light) from the evil fallen angels (darkness) who followed Lucifer (Satan) when he rebelled against God in Heaven. This view, found in St. Augustine's "The City of God," Book 11, is quite interesting and perhaps true, but the main teaching to learn about Creation from Genesis is that the universe, and everything in it, was created by Almighty God.

## The "Big Bang"

We know now that the Bible words "In the beginning" are synonymous with "The Big Bang" theory, a popular yet derogatory nickname that was coined with sarcasm by astronomer Fred Hoyle during a BBC radio broadcast in 1949 ridiculing the theory. Although Hoyle was not the person who came up with that famous and established theory–a theory he never accepted before he died–the person credited with the Big Bang Theory was a Jesuit trained Belgian Roman Catholic priest, astronomer and physicist named Georges Henri Joseph Édouard Lemaître.[6] (By the way, Hoyle was one of the most ardent Cartesian atheists in the history of physics.) Fr. Lemaître published a paper in 1927 that stated the universe was expanding and was not static as other scientists were claiming it was (including Albert Einstein, Edwin Hubble, and others), but his theory was not accepted at first by the scientific community, and in fact, it was ridiculed,[7] even by Einstein. Moreover, these scientists were quite uncomfortable having a Catholic priest telling them they were wrong about their science and remarked that it was his religion that was to blame for this ridiculous theory. At one point, Einstein told Lemaître his expanding universe theory was wrong and said: "Your calculations are correct, but your grasp of physics is atrocious." Interestingly enough, it was Fr. Lemaître's expanding universe theory that ended up saving Einstein's failing general theory of relativity thereby correcting Einstein's "grasp of physics" in the process.[8] Einstein being corrected by a Catholic priest. Imagine that! God works in mysterious ways indeed.

Two years later, in 1929, even though Hubble had been a staunch believer in the static universe theory for quite some time, he changed his mind because, using the telescope, he saw that the universe was indeed expanding due to the redshift of distant galaxies moving away from us. He jotted down a graph of what he saw and was later credited with "discovering" the expanding universe when in actuality Fr. Lemaître had come up with that discovery 2 years earlier. Continuing his research, Fr. Lemaître came to the conclusion that if the universe is expanding, it must have had a beginning, which led him to publish in 1931 "The Primeval Atom, A Hypothesis of the Origin of the Universe." [9] In short, "The Big Bang Theory" was born and the rest is history. To this very day, all serious cosmology work uses Fr. Lemaître's Big Bang as a foundation to build on even though his name is rarely mentioned by cosmologists and scientists.

Most interesting to note, Fr. Lemaître was one of the first – if not the first – to adopt a computer in 1958 for cosmological calculations, the Burroughs E 101, and he was one of the inventors of what became known as the Fast Fourier Transform algorithm. Moreover, Fr. Lemaître was the first scientist who declared that the expanding universe is actually accelerating,[10] an observation that was later confirmed in the 1990s, using, ironically enough, the Hubble Space Telescope.

## How The Earth Became Our Home

Modern science now tells us that the universe is about 13.8 billion years old and that planet Earth is about 4.5 billion years old. "Why does the Earth have to be so old?" For one, the typical life of a star is billions of years [11], and a star has to explode–a supernova–in order to release into space the elements and materials that it contained so that planets, suns and moons can be formed by gravity [12] from those exploded stellar materials. [13] Everything on Earth, including our own human bodies, came from–and were made from–the materials released by supernova stars. Stars are "factories" where elements and minerals are made, like iron, for example. (Yes, iron was–and is–made inside a star.) Earth contains 4,300 distinct minerals. [14] Without stars, there would be no planets, no Sun, no Earth, and of course, no life on Earth.

As mentioned earlier, the Universe began with a Bang, a BIG Bang, initiated by God Almighty. This primeval explosion set into motion a series of processes that culminated, for one, in the formation of stars which were going to become the factories that would produce the building materials needed to form galaxies and our own Solar System. With the passing of time, after maturing over billions of years, these stars exploded and released into space huge amounts of "debris" (elements, minerals, rock, water, etc.) from which suns and planets were formed, guided and aided, of course, by the Hand of God. Our planet Earth, initially formed from this stellar debris, passed through many developmental stages before arriving at its present stage as we now know it. Early in its infancy, about four billion years ago, Earth was continually pounded and bombarded by asteroids and comets for quite some time which resulted in the deposit of many minerals, including the majority of water that we now have. Asteroids and comets are stellar materials. Comets are mostly ice. Millions of years later, the atmosphere on Earth still had no oxygen whatsoever and life as we know it did not yet exist. As plants and trees began to emerge, multiply and cover the land masses, the oxygen they produced with energy from the Sun, together with volcanic activity and the release of interior gases combined together to prepare the atmosphere for human life and other forms of life to exist. [15] By this time, the Earth had now reached the point where God would now create and introduce the zenith of His work: the human person. Male and female He created them, and placed them in a beautiful Garden, a Garden He had created just for them, the Garden of Eden, most likely situated on top of a big mountain (see Gn 2:10-14). Creation was now complete and God rested "from all his work which he had done" (Gn 2:2).

## Timelines

Our Solar System is located in a large assemblage of billions of stars called the Milky Way Galaxy (a good name for a candy bar!). Just prior to Fr. Lemaître's 1927 paper on the expanding universe, it was thought by astronomers that the universe itself was the Milky Way, that nothing else existed beyond it and that it was static (not moving).[16] This was due to the fact that telescopes of that time were not strong enough to see any further which made Fr. Lemaître's theory so remarkable. You might say, inspired by God Himself.

In order to help us get a mental idea of how old the Universe and the Earth is, Dr. Gerard M. Verschuuren on pages 8-9 of his book "In The Beginning" uses the timeline of a 24 hour day to illustrate this. Each hour represents 600 million years. The Big Bang took place at 12:01 am; Earth begins to form at 4:17 pm; life begins at 5:08 pm; and humanity appears at 11:59 pm, at the last minute, just in time! Using a year as the timeline with a day representing 38 million years, the Big Bang took place at the beginning of January; Earth starts to form at the beginning of September; life appears during mid-September with dinosaurs around December 24th ; and mankind around December 29th .[17] God saved the best for last!

APPROXIMATE AGE OF THE UNIVERSE
13.8 BILLION YRS.

APPROXIMATE AGE OF THE SUN
4.5 BILLION YRS.

APPROXIMATE AGE OF THE EARTH
4.5 BILLION YRS.

EMERGENCE OF UNICELLULAR ORGANISMS
3.8 BILLION YRS. AGO

EMERGENCE OF MULTICELLULAR ORGANISMS
1 BILLION YRS .AGO

EMERGENCE OF HUMAN BEINGS
c. 80,000 YRS. AGO [18]

APPROXIMATE SIZE OF THE UNIVERSE
100 BILLION LIGHT YRS. RADIUS

* DARK MATTER - 30% OF THE UNIVERSE

** DARK ENERGY - 70% OF THE UNIVERSE

*The Universe's Dark Matter is 6 times greater than its Visible Matter which is 5% of the Universe.

**Dark Energy, a "field" in the Universe, is what is causing the Universe to expand. But contrary to expectations from the Big Bang effect, the expansion of the Universe is accelerating due to Dark Energy instead of decelerating because of gravity.

Although there are exploding stars, black holes, killer asteroids, and so much more out in space, the Universe is not chaotic. In fact, everything is perfectly ordered by God, the Creator. All material things change *with* and *in* time. Yet, the human soul, which is immortal and immaterial, is also subject to change, but only while it is in its living body. After death, it becomes immutable. A quick look at the above factual data and realizing how vastly long it has taken for things in the universe to develop to their present stages may bring to mind one very interesting characteristic of God, the Creator of it all, and that is Patience, with a capital "P." But this, of course, is only from a human point of view, for since God exists outside of time and space, patience (waiting for time to pass) is irrelevant and nonexistent in Him. God doesn't wait.

Most people envision the galaxies moving out through space as if space itself is standing still and everything in it is moving in different directions due to the Big Bang Explosion that started everything, but that is not what is going on out there. What is actually going on is that the space between the galaxies is "stretching," like a balloon filling up with air, which gives the impression that the galaxies are moving but space itself is not. This is what the term "expanding universe" means. What is happening in outer space is indeed mysterious and fascinating, but even more fascinating is how God continues to bring intelligent life into existence through the human race by creating–out of nothing–the immortal soul of a baby in its mother's womb. The creation of a living person. A living, breathing, thinking, and loving person! THAT's an awesome miracle! Without God, nothing would exist.

An excellent yet simple explanation of how God keeps everything in existence can be found in the roof of a house. The roof has what scientists have termed "derived causal power" which means it depends on something else to keep it up there. That is, the walls of the house, which also have derived causal power. The walls are held in place by the foundation which is supported by the Earth below it which is supported by the universe. All of these possess derived causal power, but what holds and supports the universe? God does, and He possesses inherent causal power which means nothing supports Him; He does not depend on anything or anyone else for His existence. He is the First Cause and source of all things. So, from a certain angle, God supports the roof of the house, and in fact, the entire universe.

Anthropogenic "Climate Change," touted by pseudo scientists and the originator/swindler Al Gore does not actually exist because God regulates all things on the planet according to His Will no matter what humans do on it. Planet Earth is not some "runaway train" due to man's use or misuse of it; God regulates it and keeps it in control, as well as the entire universe, whether we know it or not, and whether we like it or not. Only atheists can "technically" fall for the fallacy of climate change; believers should not and cannot for they should know God is always in control of planet Earth and the entire Universe as well (see Acts 14:15).

According to radiometric dating, planet Earth is about 4.5 billion years old. [19] After the Big Bang, at the beginning of September using a year as the timeline, Earth began to form and continued vigorously on a process of development with intense treatment received from all sides. As mentioned earlier, one such treatment was continued bombardments of asteroids and comets that deposited minerals, heavy metals, and most importantly, water on the fledgling planet. Comets can consist of up to 85% water in the form of ice. [20] After thousands of these bombardments, the deposited water eventually began to condense, cooling the exterior into a crust and creating super massive oceans much larger than the ones we presently have. This period of Earth's history, known as the Precambrian Period, ran from the beginning of September to the middle of December using the annual timeline. Surprisingly enough, this is roughly 7/8ths of Earth's complete history. [21]

The Earth continued to develop, refine and take shape in God's Hands for millions of years until the atmosphere and terrain was just right for the introduction of human life: the zenith and summit in all Creation, God's ultimate and precious masterpiece. A most important feature that continually protects our beautiful planet is the Earth's magnetic field which is maintained by its liquid iron core that surrounds its solid iron core. This field protects the fragile planet from deadly cosmic and solar radiation keeping Earth's atmosphere intact preventing it from being swept away by solar particles. [22] Earth's atmosphere is extremely unique. Nothing that remotely resembles it is present in any other observable planet. Rigorous scientific discoveries have confirmed that the presence of life on planet Earth is largely responsible for this uniqueness. [23] Perhaps the Blue Planet *is* the only such planet in the entire universe. If so, *we* are the most intelligent life in the universe. Incoming scientific discoveries keep pointing in that direction. [24]

There are ninety-two (92) natural chemical elements in nature. Carbon 12 is one of them, oxygen is another; the simplest and smallest of all is hydrogen 2. These, together with 4,500 different known minerals are the building materials of all matter that exist on planet Earth. God could have created all things, including man, in an instant, but He chose not to. Instead, everything in Creation came to be *after* the passing of time. All in time.

Scientific studies show life on Earth began as simple unicellular organisms that in time developed into multicellular organisms. Some believe these eventually became creatures, even humans. The erroneous theory that humans evolved from apes (Darwinian evolution), discarded by serious minded scientists long ago, unfortunately continues to be taught in schools, but the notion that human life came into existence by God "breathing" life/Spirit (Gn 2:7) into an already existing creature, a caveman of sort for example, makes more logical sense. One possible scenario that comes to mind is that God only "breathed" the Life/Spirit into two cave dwellers thereby making them "humans," created in the image of God, possessing rationality, morality, self-awareness, immortality, and most importantly, free will. These two, tempted by the Devil, set aside rationality and morality and committed a sin against God in order to obtain what they freely wanted; an act that was sinful but satisfied their wants. The rest of the cave dwellers that did not receive the Life/Spirit (not planned to be humans by God) in time became extinct, never becoming part of the human race. And from that time forward, the two that did receive the Spirit from God became Adam and Eve, the parents of the human race. (That is why there is no "missing link" to be found: they were both cave dwellers.) St. John Paul II, in his "Address to the Plenary Session on 'The Origins and Early Evolution of Life,'" states on par. 5: "Pius XII [in his Encyclical Humani Generis, par. 36] stressed this essential point: if the human body takes its origin from pre-existent living matter, the spiritual soul is immediately created by God.... theories of evolution which.... consider the mind as emerging from the forces of living matter, or as a mere epiphenomenon of this matter, are incompatible with the truth about man. Nor are they able to ground the dignity of the person."

## Life on Other Planets?

The existence of intelligent life on other planets is a very popular subject for discussion. Since God is omnipotent with power without limits, this is indeed a viable possibility. However, although there may be life forms lacking reason and free will on other planets, strictly from a Catholic point of view, in my opinion I do not believe that intelligent beings with free will like us, created in the image and likeness of God, exist on other planets and I'll tell you why. If such beings did exist, they, like us, would eventually sin and Jesus would have to suffer and die – on all those planets - to redeem them, just as He did for us here. I personally feel God would not permit His Son to be tortured and executed hundreds or thousands of times like that, and therefore, He did not create "intelligent life" on other planets for that very reason; and thinking that God would create perfect beings with free will that would never sin is not realistic, only wishful thinking. Jesus already has a human body and will have it forever. If intelligent beings on other planets with free will also sinned, like us, Jesus would have to abandon His human body, take on their bodies, and then willingly suffer and die to redeem them. Again, I don't think God the Father would agree to - and permit - His beloved Son to undergo hundreds or thousands of executions. This is why personally, as a Catholic, I do not think intelligent life with free will like us exists on other planets - unless His sacrificial death redeemed the entire universe. Moreover, I also personally believe that all of the weird and strange life forms God could have placed on other planets He instead placed them on this planet. There are literally trillions of weird and strange life forms right here on planet Earth. I believe God created only one universe, one Earth, one human race, and one Catholic Church.

One may then say, "Maybe Jesus could redeem these other beings some other way instead of giving His life and dying for them," and my reply to this would be, "Then why didn't He do that with us? Why did He choose to die for us?" The answer to this question was given by Christ Himself when He said: "Greater love has no man than this, that a man lay down his life for his friends" (Jn 15:13). Now, I am sure Jesus would have the same kind of love for extraterrestrials as He had – and has – for us, so it follows that He would want to show this kind of love for them by dying for them too. Otherwise, it would mean that Jesus would have more love for us than for them, and I don't think that would be the case. Therefore, knowing that Jesus said He was sent here by His Father and our Father in Heaven to save us and redeem us (Jn 5:30; 6:57; 7:28,29), I seriously do not think God the Father would ask His only Son, Jesus Christ, to go through so many cruel experiences ending in death, over and over and over, repeatedly. It would seem One sacrificial horrible Death on a Cross is enough (Rom 6:9-10; see Heb 9:24-28). Again, this is only my personal opinion from a Catholic perspective.

I imagine many atheists firmly believe there are intelligent beings with free will on other planets who perhaps also do not believe in God (like them), but they are wrong about this, and other things, because they live in their own made up world. And why do they live there? Because if they "gave in" and became believers, they would have to obey God and change their lives and they like their way of life too much to change their ways. Another reason why I personally believe God did not create intelligent life in His image with free will on other planets is because many here would then think–and say: "So you see, we are not so special," which would trivialize the human person even more. But we ARE special, especially if we are indeed the only ones in the entire universe. Since God wanted to make sure that we know just how special we truly are, I personally believe He "proved" it by creating only us on this one planet and not others.

## The Science of Religion

Some scientists can converse about science without including personal views, only objective facts, but they can't do that with religion because it concerns them personally. Many of them have a real love for research, a staunch concern for the objective truth, but when it comes to religion, they introduce and also allow prejudice, bigotry, and narrow points of view to affect their minds. They allow their personal views and feelings to influence their attitude toward objectivity in religion. It is important for all of us, but especially for these individuals and others like them, to know and accept the fact that there is more than one field of knowledge, and religion is one of them. I would say without hesitation that it is the most important one of all because this field specializes in providing answers to the most important questions about this life, and most importantly, about life after death.

Unfortunately, there are many religions that simply are not teaching the objective truths on both of these topics, and the primary reason why is because all of them – except one – were founded by mortal human beings like you and me, prone to errors and mistakes, and they pass these errors and mistakes to others: to those who listen to them. The only religion on planet Earth that can truly boast of teaching the absolute truth about life, death, and life after death, is the one founded by God Himself in the person of Jesus Christ, the Holy Catholic Church. People, even religious people, can and will lead you astray and even take advantage of your ignorance for their personal gain, either for money, power, or both, a typical human trait. But those who listen to and follow Christ are like those who build their houses on a rock foundation; it is very difficult to fool these fortunate folks. On the other hand, those who do not follow Christ and listen to His teachings through Mother Church are like those who build their houses on sand; a strong willed, smooth talking con-artist (even a religious one) can come along and sweep them away, even to ruin, spiritual ruin. By knowing the truth from Christ, a person can also come to know himself: "Faith and reason are like two wings on which the human spirit rises to the contemplation of truth; and God has placed in the human heart a desire to know the truth, in a word, to know himself, so that by knowing and loving God, men and women may also come to the fullness of truth about themselves." Pope St. John Paul II

Scientists, cosmologists, physicists, and the like who are atheists believe and proclaim that religion has no place in science, yet many important scientific discoveries in all fields of science have been made by religious scientists, including Catholic scientists like St. Albert the Great, Copernicus, Cavalieri, Torricelli, Pascal, Galileo, Lemaître, and many others. (For more, Google: Catholic Clergy Scientists.)

Some scientists even go as far as to hate God. There are several reasons for their atheism, but one that they all share is that God cannot be proven by science (according to them) because science can only verify what is "observable," and what is observable exists only in this Universe, and since God is outside the Universe of space and time, he cannot be "observed" and verified by science, thus, according to them, He does not exist. This, of course, is silly from a certain angle since scientists are not robots but human beings with reason, intelligence, and common sense, and it does not take much of these to realize that the world and Universe around us is too awesome, complex and precise (to name only a few) not to have been created by an omnipotent Person. All this around us certainly did not come about by chance! Only a fool, especially a Cartesian fool, believes that.

Believing in God does not affect true scientific work and study in a negative way because true scientific work and study involves finding the absolute truth about something "observable" using intelligence and reason–and even common sense–which have nothing to do with religion. That is to say, one can be religious and not be intelligent, or reasonable, or have common sense. On the other hand, one can use intelligence, reason and also common sense to study either religion or science without negativity of any kind affecting the results. Science is in essence the study and pursuit of truth, and so is religion, for God is Truth with a capital "T." Studying the Universe and its observable contents to achieve understanding, all of which were made by a God who is not observable, is a noble task indeed, but so is the study of theology, the "Queen of the Sciences." To note, it was the Catholic Church's scholastic elements that gave birth to the scientific process.

There is one important exception here that must be mentioned. Although it is true that since God is Spirit and therefore unobservable, we must not forget that He became observable when He came to Earth and incarnated in the person of Jesus Christ. Lucky were those people who were able to see Him, touch Him, talk to Him, listen to Him, eat with Him, and watch Him work the wonderful miracles that He performed. Here, in the Person of Jesus Christ, God was observable, tangible. Some of these scientists remind me of Philip the Apostle: "Philip said to him, Lord, show us the Father, and we shall be satisfied. Jesus said to him, Have I been with you so long, and yet you do not know me, Philip? **He who has seen me has seen the Father**; how can you say, Show us the Father? Do you not believe that I am in the Father and the Father is in me? The words that I say to you I do not speak on my own authority; but **the Father who dwells in me** does his works. Believe me that I am in the Father and the Father is in me; or else believe me for the sake of the works themselves" (Jn 14:8-11) [my emph.] (see also Jn 12:44-45).

Although Christ Ascended to Heaven 2000 years ago after He completed His Redemptive Mission, He did not abandon us.

He left us the Holy Eucharist: His body, blood, soul and divinity for our spiritual nourishment and for us to be united to Him – spiritually and even physically. The Holy Eucharist, by the way, is only to be found in Catholic churches worldwide. For those who do not believe that the Holy Eucharist is the body, blood, soul and divinity of Jesus Christ, please read "Eucharistic Miracles," by Joan Carroll Cruz, "Unseen," by Ron Tesoriero, and "A Cardiologist Examines Jesus," by Dr. Franco Serafini. These works contain credible scientific evidence of the Holy Eucharist miraculously changing into living, bleeding, even beating human flesh and remaining this way to this day.

So here's the evidence these atheists have been waiting for! (Richard Dawkins, Sam Harris, Christopher Hitchens, et al, take note!) These they can observe to their heart's content, and they can test them, marvel at them, wonder how this can be, and then drop to their knees and worship their Lord and God. God sent us this "evidence" no doubt to help our faith, but especially to help the atheists! These Eucharistic miracles have been submitted as evidence by God to prove that Jesus is God. Since this scientific evidence has been "proven" in the "court" of science, it is now considered the "science of religion." Therefore, this long standing case regarding whether Jesus Christ is God is now officially closed with this incontrovertible and sobering evidence. Sad enough to say, the atheist lives day after day without hope, but the believer has hope in Christ; hope of life after death in Heaven united with God, his Loving Creator. "It is said that an argument is what convinces reasonable men, and a proof is what it takes to convince even an unreasonable man" (Alexander Vilenkin). "And without faith it is impossible to please him. For whoever would draw near to God must believe that he exists and that he rewards those who seek him" (Heb 11:6).

After Fr. Lemaître gave a detailed description of his Big Bang Theory at the California Institute of Technology in 1933,

Albert Einstein stood up applauding and said: "This is the most beautiful and satisfactory explanation of creation to which I have ever listened." [25] Albert Einstein being instructed by a Catholic priest. Truly beautiful! If we pray and ask Jesus to give us every day the grace necessary to do His Will in order to become saints, He will do just that. And we will become saints! All in time. "There is still time for endurance, time for patience, time for healing, time for change. Have you slipped? Rise up. Have you sinned? Cease. Do not stand among sinners, but leap aside." St Basil the Great.

"The Holy Bible is like a mirror before our mind's eye. In it we see our inner face. From the Scriptures we can learn our spiritual deformities and beauties. And there too we discover the progress we are making and how far we are from perfection." Pope St Gregory the Great

"For it is always in your power to show great strength, and who can withstand the might of your arm? Because the whole world before you is like a speck that tips the scales, and like a drop of morning dew that falls upon the ground. But you are merciful to all, for you can do all things, and you overlook men's sins, that they may repent. For you love all things that exist, and you loathe none of the things which you have made, for you would not have made anything if you had hated it. How would anything have endured if you had not willed it? Or how would anything not called forth by you have been preserved? You spare all things, for they are yours, O Lord who love the living. For your immortal spirit is in all things. Therefore you correct little by little those who trespass, and remind and warn them of the things wherein they sin, that they may be freed from wickedness and put their trust in you, O Lord" (Wis 11: 21-26; 12: 1-2).

# Chapter 2

"In the first place it should be known that if a person is seeking God, his Beloved is seeking him much more." St. John of the Cross.

## THE FALL OF MAN AND NEED OF A SAVIOR

Considering human nature, the nature God created us with, I suppose it is not very surprising to find that the very first human beings God created, Adam and Eve, who were man and wife, ended up disobeying the very God that created them and thereby severed that very intimate relationship they enjoyed with Him. Although tempted to do so, they were not forced in any way to disobey God, for a distinct part of that human nature they were given by God: "free will," allowed them the "freedom" to do as they pleased. This means they were not like robots who acted according to a program they were given. Just like you and me, they were free to do whatever they wanted to do. There was only one condition however: remain obedient to God.[26]

The Bible tells us that they parted company and divorced themselves from God Almighty; their Loving Father Who brought them into existence with incredible Loving Care. How did this happen? They both committed, what must have appeared to them to have been an insignificant offense, the grave sin of disobedience.[27] As a result, their offspring, in fact the entire human race, was also affected by this very serious sin, a sin the Catholic Church calls "Original Sin" [28] since it was the very first sin committed by the very first human beings. Needless to say, it was the worst thing that could have happened to mankind.

In Genesis 3:1-13, the Bible tells us that Satan, the devil, took the form of a cunning snake and succeeded in getting Eve to eat the fruit of the Tree of Knowledge of Good and Evil, a fruit that God forbade them to eat, saying, according to Eve, that if they ate of it, or even touched it, they would die. But the devil told Eve, "You will not die. For God knows that when you eat of it your eyes will be opened, and you will be like God, knowing good and evil" (Gn 3:4-5).

After some contemplation, Eve decided to eat this fruit and then persuaded and induced her husband Adam to do the same. The devil used his favorite technique here: the half-truth technique; i.e., tell a lie, "You will not die" (physically, not right away), and then follow it with a truth, "knowing good and evil." This type of deception still catches people off guard (not knowing which is which) and it is very effective in fooling people. It is so effective that people have been using it on other people for centuries.

For untold generations, the apple is the "forbidden fruit" Adam and Eve ate, the fruit that most people refer to in this regard. But the Bible says "fruit," not apple. How the poor innocent apple got mixed up in this big mess I don't know, but this "fruit," according to theologians, is meant to be a metaphor and not to be understood in the literal sense, not unlike other passages in the OT. Since the metaphorical "fruit" of Knowledge of Good and Evil can therefore be many things, we don't know for certain what offense they committed, but one thing is for sure, the teaching here is that God was to be the only and sole judge of what is good and what is evil, not them, so anything that they did in violation of God's Command would result in "eating" this fruit, and eat it they certainly did.[29]

I once heard that perhaps the fruit was a metaphor for a Command God had given them not to go outside the protection of the Garden, for by doing so they would put themselves at risk of being injured or killed by other creatures thereby learning the difference between good: protection inside the Garden, and evil: experience of being killed. The problem with that, however, is that the animals, birds and fish that God had created supposedly lived in peace and harmony with Adam and Eve (see Gn 2:18-21; CCC 374). So maybe God's Command was indeed a simple one, not to eat a particular fruit, and not because it possessed any special powers, but because He wanted them to be obedient to Him and this was a very simple way to test their faithfulness and obedience. The fruit itself was perhaps insignificant; but the Command was not.

And, of course, there is no doubt the devil played a big part in this catastrophe, for Eve is quoted as telling God: "The serpent beguiled me, and I ate" (Gn 3:13). Eve thought that eating this "fruit" was the right road to take. The Book of Proverbs warns us regarding the choices we make: "There is a way which seems right to a man, but its end is the way to death" (Prv 14:12). After Original Sin, the human race became Satan's "property." That is why Jesus is called the Redeemer; He came to "redeem" the human race and "buy it back," and did so with His blood.

It is also true that we will never know what could or might have happened to the human race if the devil had never tempted Eve. But tempt her he did, and by using the free will that God gave her, she chose–without being forced–to believe the lies the devil told her, disobey God's Command, and commit the horrible Sin. I've always wondered: "Where was Adam when all this was going on, when his wife Eve was being tempted by Satan? Why did the devil choose to tempt Eve instead of Adam?" The original Hebrew text, and also the King James version (and others) says that Adam "was with her" when she was tempted (many Bibles omit this). Thus, both were present with the serpent, and therefore, both sinned together, one after the other – as One Flesh.

One might be tempted to think: "Why would God not want the first human beings to know the difference between good and evil?" "Isn't that a good thing?" "What is wrong with that?" But one would be missing the point. The point here is, God was to remain the Sole Judge of what is good and what is evil, not them, and God gave them a specific Command to this effect for them to obey–for their own good–and they disobeyed that Command. End of Story.

It is a fact that this human desire to be the judge of what is good and what is evil is still with us to this day. This sin continues to be committed day in and day out throughout the entire world with devastating consequences leading to conflict, wars, famines, diseases, misery, and even death.

On a personal level, the effect of this sin leads many of us to want to lead our own lives the way WE think is best. Once we get old enough to leave home and go on our own, we like to do things our own way without anyone else telling us what to do and how to do it. Many of us don't even want our parents telling us what to do anymore (thank God we're finally out of that house, right?). In fact, many of us don't even want God to tell us how to live. BIG mistake! We humans are rebellious by nature, by our fallen nature. "All we like sheep have gone astray; we have turned every one to his own way" (Is 53:6). Frank Sinatra's hit song "My Way" describes this human flaw to a tee (it became a hit because most people agree with this title), and I am sure it is also the favorite song that is sung by those who enter Hell after death. It is a lot smarter and much better to live life "God's Way" than "Our Way." The end is MUCH nicer.

All the many terrible things in life are the consequential results of Original Sin; a selfish act chosen and carried out. The result: a broken relationship with God that led to sickness, suffering, evil in the world, and death. Yes, even evil! The answer for those who ask: "Why is there evil in the world, and why does God allow it?" The answer: "Because men and women decide to choose evil over good. God is not going to stop them because He has total respect for the free will He gave them!" It is not surprising that some people get angry with God for allowing the existence of evil, suffering, sickness, and death. In fact, many lose faith in God and become atheists because of this. They think it is impossible for God to exist because if THEY were God, they would destroy evil. (I am SO glad they are not God.) God will not destroy evil. God is a Creator, not a destroyer. Satan is a destroyer. God allows evil to exist, if that is what one freely chooses, because He respects the free will He gave to all.

### The Reason For Death

Once our first parents sinned, they were expelled from the Garden of Eden and a "flaming sword which turned every way" (Gn 3:24) was placed there to keep them from entering the Garden, eating the fruit of the Tree of Life, and live forever. God's Wisdom and Love for man are shown here once again. Sinful, evil human beings who can live forever would not be good and therefore God did not allow it.[30] Can you imagine an immortal Lenin, Stalin, Mao, Pol Pot, Hitler? What kind of life would God-fearing decent people have? More importantly, God removed their immortality to prevent them from becoming immortal sinful creatures, separated from Him forever like the fallen angels who followed Satan. Once mortal and subject to the conditions and laws of "time," Adam, Eve, and all their descendants would have the opportunity and ability to "repent and change" after sinning and then be "saved" through the mediation of a Savior, Jesus the Christ. With repentance comes Hope: of a life in Heaven.

Adam and Eve were never going to die and would have lived forever (us included) if they had remained obedient to God's Command.[31] One may wonder, perhaps the death God mentioned to Adam was a spiritual death and not a physical death. The word "life" has more than one meaning to it, and so does the word "death." For example, some people can possess a lot of wealth and material goods, have many friends and good relations with family members, and all of a sudden commit suicide because life to them was no longer tolerable or worth living. So life, to them, had quite a different meaning than most of us have.

According to modern science, death was common and natural to the living things that existed before the time of Adam: the vegetation, trees, fish, fowl, and animals. In time, these died and were replaced by others of the same kind. There is plenty of archeological (fossil) evidence that proves this to be the case. The continuous cycle of life and death on Earth was in full operation when Adam and Eve were brought into existence by God in the Garden of Eden. That is, life–and death–already existed in the world before they were created, [32] and before they sinned. However, Adam and Eve were not mortal animals with only one life to live like the animals around them. Unlike those, our first parents were created with two "lives," so to speak: a "natural life": a physical body and a spiritual soul, the latter giving life to and animating the former, and an "immortal spirit" with **supernatural life.** Unlike the souls of animals and other living things, Adam and Eve's souls were indeed spiritual souls but they possessed what the Church calls "sanctifying grace" (supernatural life), given to them by God that, unlike the other animals, made them children of God with the *ability* to live "face to face" with God in Heaven.[33]

After God created Adam and "put him in the Garden of Eden to till it and keep it" (Gn 2:15) and before He created Eve, God told Adam: "You may freely eat of every tree of the garden; but of the tree of the knowledge of good and evil you shall not eat, for in the day that you eat of it you shall die" (Gn 2:16-17). As mentioned earlier, since death already existed all around them, was God saying to Adam, 'for in the day you eat of it, you will be "dead" to me,' meaning "spiritually" dead? no longer having a close and good relationship with God? In other words, did God mean a physical death or was this only a metaphor for spiritual death? Or was it for both? Let's continue with Scripture and see if we can find an answer there.

Once Eve gave in to her temptation, sinned, and then persuaded Adam to do the same, God said to Adam: "Because you have listened to the voice of your wife, and have eaten of the tree of which I commanded you, 'You shall not eat of it,' cursed is the ground because of you; in toil you shall eat of it all the days of your life; thorns and thistles it shall bring forth to you; and you shall eat the plants of the field. In the sweat of your face you shall eat bread till you return to the ground, for out of it you were taken; you are dust, and to dust you shall return" (Gn 3:17-19).

This passage makes it quite clear that both Adam and Eve were going to experience physical death, decompose, turn to dust, and then return to the ground from which they were made. Death will be a humbling experience that neutralizes false pride and self-reliance. Their physical life would indeed come to an end at some point in time. But they also incurred another type of death; one that was instantaneous. Their Sin eradicated the supernatural life and sanctifying grace God had given them that separated them from the rest of Creation, and this happened the moment they sinned. They were now left with only one natural life, just like the rest of the animals around them. The supernatural life they lost, the sanctifying grace that only they possessed, was and is a tremendous power; a power that enables a human being to live in Heaven. Just like an astronaut cannot live in outer space or a diver under water without an oxygen tank, a human soul cannot live in Heaven without sanctifying grace. Without this supernatural power, this sanctifying grace, Adam and Eve could not enter Heaven to live with God in eternal bliss.[34]

Thus, the intimate and holy "spiritual relationship" they once enjoyed with God as His children–that the other animals did not enjoy–was nullified by their Sin of disobedience because they chose to do their own selfish will instead of God's Will. That is, they loved themselves and their desires more than loving God enough to obey Him. This relational "Spiritual Loss" reveals a very special and unique link between love and obedience (a fact most parents know), and of course, this Loss was far worse than the "Physical Loss" they experienced at death at some point in time. Scripture tells us that the loss of this treasured relationship was instantaneous after they sinned:

"Then the eyes of both were opened, and they knew that they were naked; and they sewed fig leaves together and made themselves aprons. And they heard the sound of the LORD God walking in the garden in the cool of the day, and the man and his wife hid themselves from the presence of the LORD God among the trees of the garden. But the LORD God called to the man, and said to him, 'Where are you?' And he said, 'I heard the sound of you in the garden, and I was afraid, because I was naked; and I hid myself.' He said, 'Who told you that you were naked? Have you eaten of the tree of which I commanded you not to eat?' The man said, 'The woman whom you gave to be with me, she gave me fruit of the tree, and I ate'....Then the LORD God said, 'Behold, the man has become like one of us, knowing good and evil; and now, lest he put forth his hand and take also of the tree of life, and eat, and live forever'—therefore the LORD God sent him forth from the Garden of Eden, to till the ground from which he was taken. He drove out the man; and at the east of the Garden of Eden he placed the cherubim, and a flaming sword which turned every way, to guard the way to the tree of life" (Gn 3:7-12; 22-24).

The shame our first parents felt after sinning is revealed by the fact that they began to cover themselves with leaves to hide their nakedness, something the animals did not need to do. In fact, Scripture tells us that God–obviously out of love, replaced their fig leaf coverings with something more durable: "The man called his wife's name Eve, because she was the mother of all living. And the LORD God made for Adam and for his wife garments of skins, and clothed them" (Gn 3:20, 21), but there's no mention of repentance. The loss of sanctifying grace due to Sin also resulted in the loss of their original human integrity, the ability of the soul to master and control the passions and desires of the body. Therefore, from that time forward, they–and their descendants–would always find it almost impossible to control their passions and desires, something all of us still struggle with to this day.

After Adam and Eve sinned and were banished from the Garden, Adam's first born son, Cain, killed his younger brother Abel out of envy, and as punishment, God told him: "When you till the ground, it shall no longer yield to you its strength; you shall be a fugitive and a wanderer on the earth" (Gn 4:12). Cain told God that this punishment was "…greater than I can bear […] and whoever finds me will slay me" (Gn 4:13, 14). The question here is, if Adam and Eve were the first humans on Earth, and they only had two sons at this time, and one killed the other, who was Cain going to fear–that might kill him–as he wandered about the land of Nod, East of Eden? Who was he afraid of being killed by? His father, Adam, or the brothers he would later have?

Father Mitch Pacwa, SJ proposed (in a YouTube video)[35] that at the time of Adam, there were other "human-like" creatures roaming the Earth, the Neandertal (NT) for one: the "cave man" of old. He says it is important to know that NTs were not humans, not members of Homo sapiens sapiens (HSS); not our ancestors. Some "distinguished" scientists disagree. Fr. Pacwa says NT was a separate species within the genus Homo. According to DNA studies, modern humans have about 5% NT DNA, and according to the Neandertal

Genome Project, NTs interbred with HSS many thousands of years ago, and they say this is the reason for NT DNA in modern humans. But if God chose two NTs to be Adam and Eve, THAT is the reason why we still have some of their DNA. As I mention on page 18, the possibility that God "breathed" the Spirit into two cave dwellers turning them into Adam and Eve coincides with what Father Pacwa said, that Neandertal also existed during the time of Adam. Was it two NTs that God picked to be our parents? It's possible. If so, these dwellers, like all other forms of life, had a soul that kept them alive, but that soul would've died with their body at death. However, after receiving the Spirit from God, they became immortal forever. Spirit and mind were fused into one. When a modern person dies and has an out-of-body experience, he remembers leaving his dead body and floating above it; his mind remaining alive by the power of his immortal Spirit. Frank Sheed, on page 164 of his book "Theology and Sanity" talks about the soul/spirit of man: "....man's soul is spirit. It does not only the things that souls do, but the things that spirits do. By intellect and will it knows and loves as spirits know and love.... Man, having a body and soul, is an animal; but he is a rational animal, for alone of the animals he has a soul which is a spirit." Genesis describes the creation of Adam in what can be called "poetic terms" and not literally with actual details. This proves what the Catholic Church teaches, that some information in the Bible cannot be taken literally; not because they are lies, but because they were written in a style to teach a truth that could be grasped and understood by almost anyone. Incidentally, did Cain take a NT female as his wife? It's possible!

Adam's third son, Seth, was a righteous man, a man of God (Gn 4:26), but his male descendants: the "sons of God" in Genesis 6:2, married the Godless daughters of Cain and produced the "Nephilim" (Heb. "fallen ones"): individuals so corrupt that their large numbers brought grief to God's heart and He repented of having created man: "So the LORD said,

'I will blot out man whom I have created from the face of the ground, man and beast and creeping things and birds of the air, for I am sorry that I have made them.' But Noah found favor in the eyes of the LORD" (Gn 6:7-8). God then sent a worldwide flood that destroyed all flesh (Gn 6:17) except Noah and his family and made a Covenant with him in order to preserve the human race thereby making Noah the "New Adam." However, since Noah and his family were still members of the fallen human race, serious sin eventually entered their lives when Ham, Noah's second son, had sexual relations with his own mother apparently for political reasons.[36] The descendants of Ham: the Egyptians, Assyrians, Babylonians and the Philistines, became the enemies of the descendants of Noah's firstborn son, Shem: i.e., Abraham, Isaac, Jacob, and David.

It is important to remember what Eve said to the devil in the Garden: "He [the devil] said to the woman, 'Did God say, "You shall not eat of any tree of the garden" '? And the woman said to the serpent, 'We may eat of the fruit of the trees of the garden; but God said, "You shall not eat of the fruit of the tree which is in the midst of the garden, neither shall you touch it, lest you die" (Gn 3:1-3). As I mentioned earlier, this "fruit" may not be metaphorical after all. For by eating the fruit in disobedience, they acquired the knowledge of good and evil since the Sin itself made them aware of evil because sin is evil; therefore, they now knew the difference between the two and hid from God in fear, a normal human response to being guilty.

There can be no doubt that the Fall of man has been the greatest calamity the human race has experienced, and the effects have been devastating, both to mankind and to all of Creation itself. We have illness, suffering, death, deformities of all kinds, physical and mental, tendencies to sin and continue to disobey God, destroy and hate others, even ourselves!

But strangely enough, human suffering has a very positive side that is far removed from masochism. By choosing death and suffering as the means to redeem the human race, Christ sanctified suffering. As a result, if we make "good use" of our suffering for love of God, we receive graces from God through that suffering, and if we unite that redemptive suffering to Christ's suffering on the Cross, we participate in the redemption of mankind (see Col 1:24). [37]

"Many men keep the commandments in the way sick men take medicine: more from fear of dying in damnation than for joy of living according to our Savior's will. Just as some persons dislike taking medicine, no matter how pleasant it is, simply because it is called medicine, so there are some souls who hold in horror things commanded simply because they are commanded.... On the contrary, a loving heart loves the commandments. The more difficult they are, the sweeter and more agreeable it finds them, since this more perfectly pleases the Beloved and gives Him greater honor." St. Francis de Sales.

Even though Scripture does not mention this, it doesn't seem too far-fetched to believe that Adam and Eve repented for their Sin of disobedience, or at least, regretted it. But there was nothing they could do to restore that relationship they once had with God. Nothing! The qualification needed for this Super Special Job of Atonement was out of this world!

## The Need Of A Savior

Before the Fall, Adam and Eve enjoyed a state of holiness and justice, possessed innocence and immortality and were very happy in Paradise (CCC 374). But after they sinned, instead of becoming "like God," they became aware of their "nakedness," their "littleness," and how weak they were without God. They were left with suffering, pain, more sins, and eventually, death. As I mentioned earlier, Adam and Eve did not possess the "qualification" to restore their broken relationship with God, their Creator, and this is quite clear, because instead of remaining in the Garden, they were cast out as punishment for their Sin. Had they possessed the qualification, God would have forgiven them and allowed them to remain in Paradise. Therefore, we can deduce that something had to be done by someone to achieve this restoration. A savior was needed. Someone to save them from this terrible, unholy predicament. But who? There was no one else around! They were all alone, in a big world, with no one to turn to.

The need for a savior to restore this broken relationship with God is documented in the very first pages of the Bible. After Eve tells God that the serpent (Satan) tricked her into eating the forbidden fruit, God said to Satan, "I will put enmity between you and the woman, and between your seed and her seed; he shall bruise your head, and you shall bruise his heel" (Genesis 3:15). Here, God said that the "seed" of the woman, a male descendant ("he"), would bruise Satan's "head"; i.e., would defeat both him and his kingdom. This "he" would therefore defeat Satan and restore the broken relationship between God and man. "He" would be their savior, mankind's Savior. And this "he" would be Jesus the Christ, the son of Mary most holy.

The actual definition of the word "enmity" is "true hatred." Thus, from the moment sin entered the world, God placed true hatred between the human race and Satan, and also between Satan's demons and mankind. True hatred for the devil–and also evil–is therefore a natural instinct for both man and woman, and it was formed into an instinct and infused into the human soul by God Himself, and for good reason. This means that a human's normal negative reaction to evil and the devil does not necessitate the use of reason, does not involve reason at all. It is an instinctive negative repellent reaction, spontaneous! The experience of the devil and/or evil is both disgusting and offensive to the normal and healthy human soul.

## The Demonic On Earth

A person, however, can become attracted to Satan and evil through a disordered mental state which can be treated with psychotherapy. On the other hand, a person can be tormented by the devil and/or his demons and even become possessed by him/them which will require the assistance of an exorcist to remove them for good. According to Father Vincent P. Lampert, M. Div., designated exorcist of the Roman Catholic Archdiocese of Indianapolis, when a person makes contact with him requesting his assistance, the first thing he will do is have the individual with the problem tested by a competent and professional psychiatrist in order to rule out a mental disorder. If the psychiatrist's evaluation reveals that the problem is not mental, a physical examination is performed to rule out any problems there. If both the mental and physical evaluations determine that an exorcism is warranted, a decision that is only made by the exorcist, not by the psychiatrist or the doctor, then the exorcist will make an appointment for the individual and will administer the Rite of Exorcism to remove either the devil and/or his demon(s).[38]

Those who don't believe in God and/or Satan are not bothered by the devil and his demons because they already are where Satan wants them to be, so there's no point in wasting time with them – there's no real gain for him there. In fact, there's a possibility that a tormented unbeliever may react in a negative way to Satan's involvement and become a believer, which is something Satan does not know might happen (since he does not know the future), but also something he would not want, so he won't chance it. This is why he torments and possesses those who are trying to live a holy life according to God's Will. Out of envy and malice, he does not want them to go to Heaven after death. [39]

Also according to Father Lampert, Satan likes to possess apostates, those who abandoned their faith in Jesus Christ, who got tired of the Good News and said, "No thanks!" Once Satan possesses one of those, according to Father Lampert, he has a greater claim on that person and the exorcism will take longer to succeed as opposed to one who becomes possessed and then hears the Good News for the first time. The exorcism in this latter case does not take as long to drive the demon(s) out. [40] Satan likes to work in the shadows where he is not perceived or seen; he detests the light and truth. In a twisted way, the reason why Satan possesses an individual's body is to mock Christ's incarnation through Mary; it's his way of mocking it and making fun of it. In fact, those who mock Christ's incarnation are being influenced by Satan. This is the reason why Christ told the Pharisees, who did not believe He was God incarnate:

"If God were your Father, you would love me, for I proceeded and came forth from God; I came not of my own accord, but he sent me. Why do you not understand what I say? It is because you cannot bear to hear my word. You are of your father the devil, and your will is to do your father's desires. He was a murderer from the beginning, and has nothing to do with the truth, because there is no truth in him. When he lies, he speaks according to his own nature, for he is a liar and the father of lies. But, because I tell the truth, you do not believe me. Which of you convicts me of sin? If I tell the truth, why do you not believe me? He who is of God hears the words of God; the reason why you do not hear them is that you are not of God" (Jn 8:42-47; see Jn 12:37).

The main reason for Christ's Mission on Earth was "to destroy the works of the devil" (1 Jn 3:8) and restore the broken relationship between man and God that Satan had caused; a restoration that required the sacrificial death of God Himself in the flesh! True freedom can only be experienced and achieved by living according to God's Will and His

Commandments, not by doing the opposite. Satan wants us to follow his twisted will and not God's Will which is precisely what led to his expulsion from Heaven, and because of envy, he tries everything he can to prevent any human from following God's Will and thereby end up in Heaven after death.

Some people think that evil is not someone or something but the *lack* of something, like virtue, friendship, and love; that evil only exists between men and/or women who hate and fight with each other for lack of virtue, friendship or love, but they are wrong (CCC, 2851). Father Lampert states that evil is indeed an entity, an effective agent, a living spiritual being called Satan, and his demons are also evil. In Wisdom 2:24 we find, "…but through the devil's envy, death entered the world," and in Luke 10:18 we find Jesus telling His disciples, "I saw Satan fall like lightning from heaven." Strange as it sounds, the Sadducees (chief priests) in Jesus' time did not believe in the existence of either Satan or his demons, much to their detriment.

In addition to the *extraordinary* activity of the devil: physical possessions, demonic infestations, obsessions, and vexations, on pages 117-18 in his book, "Exorcism. The Battle Against Satan And His Demons," Father Lampert mentions that we should be aware of the devil's *ordinary* activity we are victim to every single day. Most of this is done in very quiet and subtle ways that are difficult to detect, especially by the untrained, secularized, and irreligious person. Father Lampert here says, "The devil's ultimate goal is to fracture our prayer life, faith life, moral life, sacramental life, and our relationships with one another in such a way that we are pulled further and further away from God." If you look around the world today, if you look close enough, the devil's work will become very clear – and there is so much of it. "All of us need to better understand," says Father Lampert, "how the devil tries to ruin us by pulling us away from God [and one another] in the ordinary circumstances of our lives."

One of the conditions a person exhibits that meets the criteria for demonic possession is extraordinary human strength.[41] Before or during an exorcism, Father Lampert says that some people can become violent to the point that several strong men have difficulty holding the person down. Other exhibits of super human strength by possessed persons have also been observed, such as picking up heavy objects and the like. This reminds me, I was reading the other day about Ellen Gould White, the woman credited in large part for establishing the Protestant sect Seventh-Day Adventists. It is a matter of official record, according to reliable sources, that Mrs. White had a history of "visions" going back to her childhood, and during these visions, in her adult life: ".... she would be instantly **filled with superhuman strength**" [my emph]. [...] "She frequently moved hands, arms, and head in gestures that were free and graceful. But to whatever position she moved a hand or arm, **it could not be hindered nor controlled by even the strongest person**" [my emph]. [...] "In 1845, she held her parents' 18.5 pound family Bible in her outstretched left hand for half an hour. She weighed 80 pounds at the time." [42] If all this information is true, and it appears that it is, then according to professional exorcists, it is evident that Ellen White was possessed by a demon or demons, and perhaps even for many years since her "visions" go back to her childhood.

Since it appears Ellen White was possessed by evil spirits, it is plain to see why she hated the Catholic Church so much. One reason why the Seventh-Day Adventists are so anti-Catholic, and this is tied to the name of their sect, is their belief that the Catholic Church impiously changed the Jewish Sabbath from Saturday (seventh week day) to Sunday, the day Catholics are obligated to go to Mass to worship God at their churches. But the Catholic Church did not change the Sabbath. Followers of Rabbinic Judaism still observe the

Sabbath at their synagogues on Saturdays. Catholics do not observe the Sabbath; they celebrate the Eucharist at Mass, especially on Sundays, the first day of the week, because that is the day Christ resurrected from the dead (see Acts 20:7; 1 Cor 16:2). Those who hate the Catholic Church, for whatever reason, are in effect hating the very religion Christ founded.

God the Father said the following words to St. Catherine of Siena: "I've appointed the Devil to tempt and to trouble My creatures in this life. I've done this, not so that My creatures will be overcome, but so that they may overcome, proving their virtue and receiving from Me the glory of victory. And no one should fear any battle or temptation of the Devil that may come to him, because I've made My creatures strong, and I've given them strength of will, fortified in the Blood of My Son. Neither the Devil nor any other creature can control this free will, because it's yours, given to you by Me. By your own choice, then, you hold it or let it go if you please. It's a weapon, and if you place it in the hands of the Devil, it right away becomes a knife that he'll use to stab and kill you. On the other hand, if you don't place this knife that is your will into the hands of the Devil—that is, if you don't consent to his temptations and harassments—you will never be injured by the guilt of sin in any temptation. Instead, you'll actually be strengthened by the temptation, as long as you open the eyes of your mind to see My love, and to understand why I allowed you to be tempted: so you could develop virtue by having it proved. My love permits these temptations, for the Devil is weak. He can do nothing by himself unless I allow him. So I let him tempt you because I love you, not because I hate you. I want you to conquer, not to be conquered, and to come to a perfect knowledge of yourself and of Me."

Jesus told His twelve Apostles at the Last Supper: "If the world hates you, know that it has hated me before it hated you. If you were of the world, the world would love its own; but because you are not of the world, but I chose you out of the world, therefore the world hates you. Remember the word that I said to you, A servant is not greater than his master. If they persecuted me, they will persecute you; if they kept my word, they will keep yours also. But all this they will do to you on my account, because they do not know him who sent me" (Jn 15:18-21). It is wise to remember that anyone who hates and/or persecutes the Catholic Church is also hating and persecuting Christ. When Saul, a Pharisee (see Acts 23:6; 26:5), who later became known as St. Paul, was on his way to Damascus to persecute and stone the followers of Christ (see Acts 11:26), Christ knocked him off his horse and said to him, "Saul, Saul, why do you persecute me?" (Ac 9:4). Notice Jesus did not say persecute them, but "me." Sometimes our Protestant brothers and sisters say things about the Catholic Church, and even about Mary, the mother of Jesus, that are very insulting without realizing the trouble they are making for themselves and are getting themselves into. They would be wise to refrain from insulting both His Church and His Mother.

Since God already knew–before He created the world–that Adam and Eve were going to Sin because of Satan's temptation, why didn't He warn them about Satan? Perhaps their Sin could have been avoided. I believe the answer is, because God respected the free will He gave them and did not want to interfere with their personal choices. Sometimes God doesn't give clear and explicit information, only clues, because He wants us to think for ourselves. He wants us to use the brains He gave us! He did warn them about eating "the fruit" and the consequences thereof, so it wasn't like He didn't try to help them. He did try, and then left the choice up to them. "And above all, be on your guard not to want to get anything done by force, because God has given free will to everyone and wants to force no one, but only proposes, invites and counsels" (St. Angela Merici). It is true that suffering and death for all mankind–and also for Christ–perhaps would've been avoided if God had told Adam and

Eve what Satan was going to do to them beforehand, but since God did not do that, He must have had a reason that is beyond human understanding. There are many unanswered questions in life and we'll never know all the answers to everything because we're not God. God gives the "light of truth" only to those who believe in Him and who seek Him with sincerity, not to everyone. He does this in order not to impose Himself on those who don't believe because He respects their free will so much. Many who have no desire to know the truth are infected by the indifference of erroneous relativism that proclaims, "Truth does not exist!" This statement in itself, of course, cannot be true, for if it is, then truth does in fact exist. These individuals make up their own "truths" since to them the truth does not exist. Devil's work!

Some people think knowing the truth is not important, but God says it is. Christ said, "If you continue in my word, you are truly my disciples, and you will know the truth, and the truth will make you free" (Jn 8:31-21). Free from slavery to sin, is one. Another freedom you will experience is the freedom from ignorance, for ignorance is quite the opposite of knowing. Ignorance can–and will–lead to error, sometimes with devastating results! Recognizing and understanding truth, however, requires wisdom. We should all be on an intellectual journey seeking truth, the answers to the big questions in life; a desire to learn, grow, and develop the intellect in topics outside our own fields of expertise. Being content with life without interest to find the answers to life's big questions is living a very shallow life.

Ignorance of the truth is a type of blindness, spiritual inner blindness, not physical blindness. Those who are blind in spirit cannot see where they are going spiritually. They can get into all kinds of trouble and fall many times from deception to deception acquiring serious spiritual injuries along the way in life. They also will not be able to help others who, like them, need help in this pilgrimage we call life. More often than not, they get insulted when someone tries to help them. When the disciples told Jesus that the Pharisees were hurt by what He said to them, Jesus replied: "Let them alone; they are blind guides. And if a blind man leads a blind man, both will fall into a pit" (Mt 15:14).

If we fail to defend Christ, His teachings, and His Church because we are afraid of offending someone, we won't be doing Christ's will. Jesus quite often offended others with His teachings; the Pharisees, the Elders, the chief priests and teachers of the Law were the ones most offended by Him. So don't be afraid. You are in good company! You can escape people, but not God. So be mindful of what you say and do; comply with your responsibilities. You don't want to end up in Hell. And for those who do not believe there is a Hell, if there is no Hell, then Heaven is forced on everyone and that's not love. God, who is all love, would never force anyone to anything, even to Heaven which would be for their eternal benefit. This is precisely why there is a Hell: for those who don't want to be with God. The fact that God created Hell for those who don't love Him proves just how much He loves everyone. Including those who don't love Him! So, everyone gets what they want in the end, and, what they deserve. "A cynic is a man who knows the price of everything and the value of nothing" (Oscar Wilde).

It always amazes me when someone says they believe in God but they don't like religion, especially "organized religion," as if God, the most "organized" of all, prefers "disorganized religion." True happiness comes only from God. If you don't have religion, you won't have God. If you don't have God, you won't have happiness.[43] "There is no true, no lasting spirit of charity apart from the practice of religion" (Fr. Basil W. Maturin). Some people say they are "spiritual" but not religious, and are proud of it. But there's a BIG difference between being religious and being spiritual. The religious person has a personal relationship with God, but the spiritual person, who is an agnostic heretic, does not.

While it's ok to have views and opinions about things including God, it is more important to know what you are talking about, to know facts and truth and place more importance on these than on feelings, views, and opinions. Facts, like truth, are not optional. There are only two things you can do with either: accept or reject. The former is wisest and best; the latter always leads to ruin. Every saint has a past (for none of them were perfect) and every sinner has a future: a future in Heaven if they follow Christ. "I hold back my feet from every evil way, in order to keep thy word. I do not turn aside from thy ordinances, for thou hast taught me. How sweet are thy words to my taste, sweeter than honey to my mouth! Through thy precepts I get understanding; therefore I hate every false way" (Psalm 119:101-4).

As Professor Peter Kreeft has said more than once, two thousand years after Christ walked this Earth, we still have Pharisees among us. (Modern Rabbinic Judaism is based on Pharisaic teachings.) These people consider themselves to be "nice people." They try their best to obey the laws, to lead a good life, be kind, pay their bills, and they never hurt anybody on purpose. This is what modern psychology has done to modern society. Jesus was not a "nice person," Professor Kreeft reminds us. "Nice people don't get crucified!" The OT Prophets who warned the Jews to mend their sinful ways and did so continuously were not "nice people." In fact, they were stoned to death by their own people in order to stop them from criticizing them and bothering them so much. How's that for gratitude! This is why "...Jesus himself testified that a prophet has no honor in his own country" (Jn 4:44). So, anyone who is *sincere* about wanting to be good must follow the example set by Jesus.

Good is not the same as nice. Although it is harder to hear it than it is to say it, "God is not nice." For example, did God forgive Adam and Eve after they sinned? Did He say to them, "No problem! All is good! Look! I'm a nice guy!" No, He did not. Are parents "nice" when they punish and discipline their children for good reason? No, they are not. Remember that Jesus calls us to imitate God and be *like* Him, "You, therefore, must be perfect, as your heavenly Father is perfect" (Mt 5:48). It's not easy to be good. If God is supposed to be nice, why didn't He accept Adam and Eve's apologies, "let bygones be bygones," and allow them to stay in the Garden and continue to enjoy the way of life they once had before they sinned? And the answer is, first of all, because Adam and Eve did not possess the "qualifications" to redeem themselves, and secondly, because God is not nice. However, since He is Pure Love, He would provide a remedy.

## Effects Of Sin

Sin has many negative effects on us. One is that it makes us detest what is good and make fun of what is good. That is why criminals make fun of those who do good; they actually think they are superior to them. Sin damages our conscience to the point that right becomes wrong and wrong becomes right. Pornography, for example, has the effect of making us see women only as a pleasure device instead of the human persons made in God's image with dignity that they truly are. All of this can only be corrected by following God's Commandments which is why He gave them to us in the first place: to live a life of peace, harmony, and goodness. We have to break the chains of sin and immorality that society places on us in order to become what God intended us to be, and we can do this if we sincerely ask Him to help us. Conquering our daily temptations is not an easy task, and one that will last a lifetime. Since God gave us free will, He does not–and will not–force anyone to obey Him; He simply proposes and we do whatever we want. Although we are free to choose what actions we make, we are not free to choose the consequences thereof. Thus, if we are wise, we will appreciate His Commandments and obey them, even if we suffer in doing so.

It is good to want to go to Heaven and enjoy eternal life in perfect bliss and happiness forever, but many do not know or want to believe that they need to be saved to get there. A lot of people are not aware of Original Sin and their sinfulness. Many think they'll get to Heaven without religion, without help from anyone. Some say: "I am a better person than those religious nuts." This is false pride: "God opposes the proud, but gives grace to the humble" (Jas 4:6). Men don't like humbling themselves, and less, being humbled by anyone. They'd rather enjoy the pleasures this world can give them here and now instead of giving them up for the pleasures God offers in a future life. They are blind to the dire and horrifying consequences of their sins. Jesus said: "He who loves his life [on Earth] loses it [in Hell], and he who hates his life in this world will keep it for eternal life [in Heaven]" (Jn 12:25; my emph.). Very Sobering Facts!

In Luke 15:11-32, Jesus tells the parable of the young Prodigal Son who asked his father for his share of the inheritance and then left home and "squandered his property in loose living" (v. 13). Adam is the prodigal son, and the inheritance he squandered is the free will God had given him. But all of us are Adam. We like to do things our way too. WE want autonomy; freedom from obeying authority and enjoy life "our" way, without rules. Our main interest? Me! Myself! And I! Myself being # 1 above all others. All of us have received from God the inheritance too. We all have free will, and we squander it every time we disobey God by sinning. The result through Adam? Ruin, sickness, death, and destruction. Every time we sin, we tell God, "I don't want to live with you and your rules anymore! Leave me alone! I want to live life MY way; the way *I* want to live it; not the way

YOU want me to live it." How many years has it been now since Adam went to sleep? About 80,000 years or so.... When are we going to listen? When are we going to learn? We look, but do not see; we hear, but do not understand; and we don't want to! Because we like the way we are living and do not want to change. This is the "hardening of the heart" Jesus spoke about. Only His truth can–and will–set us free from the chains of sin. Sin alienates us from God, destroys our conscience, and brings us closer to Satan and his demons.

"Keep your life free from love of money, and be content with what you have; for he has said, I will never fail you nor forsake you. Hence we can confidently say, The Lord is my helper, I will not be afraid; what can man do to me? [...] My son, do not regard lightly the discipline of the Lord, nor lose courage when you are punished by him. For the Lord disciplines him whom he loves, and chastises every son whom he receives" (Heb 13:5-6; 12:5-6).

Another thing about sin, some of the "social norms" and laws (local, state and federal) we are raised with are actually in direct violation of God's laws; e.g., idolatry, fornication, premarital sex, contraception, divorce, abortion, etc. Modern society is full of them! Children whose parents do not teach them these are sinful and wrong will more than likely live an adult life unaware of the sins they and society are committing. Moreover, sinful behavior and activities become bad habits that are harder to quit the longer they are practiced which leads to a dull and impaired conscience. In this state, repentance becomes difficult if not impossible. Sin is evil.

Evidently, Adam and Eve's apologies to God were not enough to atone for their Sin. In the Heavens, high above the Earth, God had been working on this "problem" for quite some time, and the solution: the Savior, was on His way. It would just be a matter of time.

# Chapter 3

"When one has nothing more to lose, the heart is inaccessible to fear." St. Théodore Guérin.

## GOD PREPARES THE WAY FOR THE SAVIOR

At a specific point in time, somewhere between the 20th and 19th century B.C., a baby boy by the name of Abram ben Terah was born in Ur of the Chaldeans, [44] a small town in Babylonia in what is now southern Iraq. Although Abram was born a Chaldean (Babylonian), he is referred to as a Hebrew because he was either a descendant of Eber (a descendant of Noah) or because he came from "the other side" (eber) of the Euphrates River. The name "ben Terah" means "son of Terah," Terah being his father's name. People of that era in that region of the world did not use last names like we use them today. The system they used to name their children is called "patronymic," which means "based on the father." The word "ben" was used to signify "son" and was followed by the name of the father, and the word "bet" was used to signify "daughter" and was followed by the name of the father also.

Terah, Abram's father, was a descendant of Shem, one of Noah's sons. [45] As many of you know, Noah and his wife, together with their three sons, Shem, Ham, and Japheth, and their wives, together with many animals and birds, survived the worldwide flood sent by God by riding on a huge boat that Noah had made according to instructions given to him by God. [46] This worldwide flood that destroyed all mankind and every other living creature on Earth was sent by God because the human race had become very corrupt, evil, and wicked in the eyes of God. After the flood, humans began to populate the Earth once again and all of them were descendants of the sons of Noah (see Gn 9:19; 10:32). Noah was a descendant of Seth, Adam and Eve's third son. [47] Adam died at the age of 930, Seth died at the age of 912, and Noah lived to the ripe old age of 950. [48] Terah, like Noah, also had three sons: Abram, Nahor, and Haran. Haran, who died in Ur in Babylonia while Terah was still alive, was the father of Lot and Sarai. [49] After Haran's death, Terah took his son Abram, his grandson Lot, and Sarai, now Abram's wife, and left Ur to go to the land of Canaan but only went as far as Haran and settled there. Terah died in Haran at the age of 205 (see Gn 11:27-28, 31-32).

Unlike others, Abram believed there was only one God ("Ant." Bk. 1, Ch. 7:1). At one point in time, the Lord told Abram to leave Haran and move to Canaan, which was situated just north of Egypt, because this was the country that God was going to give to his descendants. So, Abram gathered his wife Sarai, who was also his niece ("Ant." Bk. 1, Ch. 6:5; 7:1), his nephew Lot, and all the wealth and slaves they had acquired in Haran and moved to Canaan in obedience to the Lord. [50] But after arriving in Canaan, they discovered that the land was suffering from a severe famine, so they kept moving south and ended up in Egypt, the land whose people were the descendants of Ham, one of Noah's three sons. [51] As they were about to enter Egypt, Abram said to his wife Sarai, "I know that you are a woman beautiful to behold; and when the Egyptians see you, they will say, 'This is his wife'; then they will kill me, but they will let you live. Say you are my sister, that it may go well with me because of you, and that my life may be spared on your account" (Gn 12:11-13). After this came to pass, the king of Egypt became enamored with Sarai because of her great beauty and made her his wife. And just as Abram had predicted, the king did in fact treat Abram very well and gave him herds of cattle, sheep, camels, and even slaves, silver, and gold. [52] But the Lord was not pleased with this arrangement and inflicted terrible diseases on the king and his entire palace. After realizing that God was punishing him because Sarai was

Abram's wife, the king had Abram banished from the land of Egypt together with Sarai, Lot, and all that they owned. [53] So, Abram, Sarai, and Lot ventured north to the land of Canaan where they had come from, but trouble soon arose among them because there was not enough pasture land for Abram's animals and Lot's animals, so they split up and parted ways. Lot moved east to the Jordan valley and Abram stayed in the land of Canaan. Lot ended up setting camp near the city of Sodom [54] (where the name "sodomy" comes from), "….the men of Sodom were wicked, great sinners against the Lord" (Gn 13:13).

## God's Covenant With Abram

God made a total of five (5) Covenants with mankind in OT times: with Adam, Noah, Abram (Abraham), Moses, and David, and a final and New Covenant through Jesus in the NT. The promised Savior, the one who was going to restore the broken relationship between mankind and God, was going to be a descendant of Abraham, and in order to ensure this, God made a Covenant with Abram, a "Sacred Agreement" that created a special family "Bond" between them. There were two main conditions in this Covenant:

1). God promised Abram that the land of Canaan, where he was now living, would belong to his descendants forever, that he would be the ancestor and father of many nations, that He would give Abram through Sarai a son, even in their old age, to inherit his property, and that He would be his God and the God of his descendants.

2). Abram, in turn, was to promise God that he and all his male descendants, including all male slaves, would be circumcised as a **physical sign** to show the everlasting nature of the Covenant between them. From that point on, all male babies would be circumcised at eight days old and also all adult males, including slaves. [55]

"But he [Abram] said, 'O Lord GOD, how am I to know that I shall possess it?' He said to him, 'Bring me a heifer three years old, a she-goat three years old, a ram three years old, a turtledove, and a young pigeon.' And he brought him all these, cut them in two, and laid each half over against the other; but he did not cut the birds in two. And when birds of prey came down upon the carcasses, Abram drove them away. As the sun was going down, a deep sleep fell on Abram; and behold, a dread and great darkness fell upon him. Then the LORD said to Abram, 'Know of a surety that your descendants will be sojourners in a land that is not theirs, and will be slaves there, and they will be oppressed for four hundred years; but I will bring judgment on the nation which they serve, and afterward they shall come out with great possessions. As for yourself, you shall go to your fathers in peace; you shall be buried in a good old age. And they shall come back here in the fourth generation; for the iniquity of the Am'orites is not yet complete.' When the sun had gone down and it was dark, behold, a smoking fire pot and a flaming torch passed between these pieces. On that day the LORD made a covenant with Abram, saying, 'To your descendants I give this land, from the river of Egypt to the great river, the river Euphra'tes, the land of the Kenites, the Ken'izzites, the Kad'monites, the Hittites, the Per'izzites, the Reph'aim, the Am'orites, the Canaanites, the Gir'gashites and the Jeb'usites.' " [56]

Once the covenant was made, God changed Abram's name to Abraham [57] because he was going to be the father of a multitude of nations, including the tribe of Judah from which King David was to come from, and many years later, Joseph, the husband of Mary and mother of Jesus, the Savior of mankind, the "Christ" ("Messiah"). Mary would also come from the tribe of Judah and the line of David: "Rightly they call Him Son of David, because the Virgin Mary was of the line of David" (Catena Aurea, Vol. 1, St. Mt., Part 1, p. 354, Remigius). Abraham was ninety-nine years old when the

Covenant was made and he was circumcised. [58] God also changed the name of his wife Sarai to Sarah because she was going to be the mother of nations (Gn 17:15-16).

From Abraham forward, circumcision was required for all males in order to enter into the Abrahamic Covenant with God; any Gentile who wanted to convert to Judaism had to be circumcised first. On the other hand, Baptism by water in the name of the Holy Trinity was–and still is–the way to enter into the New Covenant with God instituted by Jesus Christ (see Col 2:11-12; Ez 36:25). In the very early Church, about fourteen years after Pentecost, when St. Paul was busy preaching to the Gentiles and St. Peter was preaching to the Jews, some of the Jews (Pharisees) who were converting to Christianity (the "Way"; see Acts 9:2) were insisting that baptized Gentiles should be circumcised and also subject to Mosaic law which caused a very heated debate between Paul and Peter, a debate that Paul won by insisting and proving that converts were not subject to Mosaic Law because the New Covenant did not require it (see Gal 2:11-21). Paul ended his letter to the Galatians with the following words:

"See with what large letters I am writing to you with my own hand. It is those who want to make a good showing in the flesh that would compel you to be circumcised, and only in order that they may not be persecuted for the cross of Christ. For even those who receive circumcision do not themselves keep the law, but they desire to have you circumcised that they may glory in your flesh. But far be it from me to glory except in the cross of our Lord Jesus Christ, by which the world has been crucified to me, and I to the world. For neither circumcision counts for anything, nor uncircumcision, but a new creation [Ed. note: baptism]. Peace and mercy be upon all who walk by this rule, upon the Israel of God. Henceforth let no man trouble me; for I bear on my body the marks of Jesus. The grace of our Lord Jesus Christ be with your spirit, brethren. Amen" (Gal 6:11-18).

Since circumcision joined a man to the Mosaic Law under the Old Covenant, he was therefore obligated to obey all of its tenets to the letter, something even the Judaizers were incapable of doing, but Jesus Christ freed His baptized followers from slavery to this Law through the New Covenant He established at the Last Supper (see Acts 15:1-12). However, the Jews who converted and were baptized into Christ in the early Church were allowed to keep some Jewish traditions for a short while to ease the transition, but then this practice was abolished altogether soon thereafter.

Today there are sects that mix Rabbinic Judaism with Catholicism and call themselves "Messianic Jews" in the attempt to follow both religions at the same time, somewhat like what these early Jewish converts tried and wanted to do 2000 years ago. However, mixing Judaism and Catholicism does not work; it is futile to do that. You either practice Judaism or Catholicism but not both at the same time. The reason is, Judaism and Catholicism are two separate and distinct religions that have conflicting beliefs, so you can't mix religions together if their beliefs conflict with one another. For example, at the top of the list is the fact that in Catholicism, Jesus is both man and God in one divine Person. Judaism teaches that is not true. That's conflict number one. Number two, Judaism teaches that there's no such thing as Original Sin, and Catholicism teaches that there is. Number three, Catholicism teaches that Jesus died to redeem the entire human race, while Judaism teaches that is not true. Number four, Catholicism teaches that Mary, the mother of Jesus, was born without the "stain" of Original Sin, and since Jews don't believe in Original Sin, they don't believe that Catholic tenet either, and so on. So you see, it is very easy to prove that you can't mix both of them together and come up with a logical and coherent religion to practice because they conflict with one another. Many practices in Judaism became obsolete with the coming of Christ. I will explain this in more detail in chapter 8.

## Abraham Intercedes For Lot

After the Covenant was made between God and Abraham and before Sarah gave birth to the son promised by God, God told Abraham He was going to destroy Sodom and Gomorrah, where Lot lived, because the sins and moral corruption of the people there were too great. Abraham pleaded with God not to destroy these cities because Lot and his family lived there, so God agreed not to do it if He found at least ten people there who were righteous. A short while later, God sent two angels, dressed like men, to Lot's house to rescue him and his family from the coming destruction because God did not find ten people who were righteous. Once the angels entered Lot's house, the men of the city surrounded the house:

"But before they lay down [to sleep], the men of the city, the men of Sodom, both young and old, all the people to the last man, surrounded the house; and they called to Lot, 'Where are the men who came to you tonight? Bring them out to us, that we may know [have sex with] them' " (Gn 19:4-5). Lot offered the excited men his two virgin daughters so they would leave the visitors alone, but the men refused his offer and threatened to break down the door. The angels then, "....struck with blindness the men who were at the door of the house, both small and great, so that they wearied themselves groping for the door" (Gn 19:11; my notes in [ ]).

The two angels succeeded in getting Lot and his family out of the house and far away from the city. Then, burning Sulphur rained down on Sodom and Gomorrah and completely destroyed the corrupt cities and inhabitants because of the grave moral sins that were being committed there. [59]

This now reminds me of another story in Scripture. Just like in the story above, the whole city had gathered around somebody's house, but not for a perverted reason like in

Sodom, but for quite a different reason, a holy reason. In the Gospel of Mark we find: "And immediately he left the synagogue, and entered the house of Simon and Andrew, with James and John. Now Simon's mother-in-law lay sick with a fever, and immediately they told him of her. And he came and took her by the hand and lifted her up, and the fever left her; and she served them. That evening, at sundown, they brought to him all who were sick or possessed with demons. **And the whole city was gathered together about the door.** And he healed many who were sick with various diseases, and cast out many demons; and he would not permit the demons to speak, because they knew him" (1:29-34) [my emph.].

As mentioned earlier, there are actually five (5) Covenants God made with mankind that appear in the OT: the first one is with Adam, the second with Noah, the third with Abraham, the fourth one with Israel through Moses at Mt. Sinai after the Exodus from Egypt, and the fifth one with King David. God made the Covenant with Abram (Abraham) to ensure the lineage through which His Son, Jesus, would come in order to redeem the fallen human race. Abram was skeptical at first that he would be the father of many nations, as God promised that he would be, because he and his wife were both very old (Abram was ninety-nine years old and Sarai was ninety years old) and did not have a son to receive his inheritance. In fact, Abram was afraid that one of his slaves was going to be the one to inherit his property. But God, to whom nothing is impossible, kept His promise and Sarai bore a son in her old age.

### The Birth Of Isaac

"The Lord visited Sarah as he had said, and the LORD did to Sarah as he had promised. And Sarah conceived, and bore Abraham a son in his old age at the time of which God had spoken to him. Abraham called the name of his son who was born to him, whom Sarah bore him, Isaac. And Abraham circumcised his son Isaac when he was eight days old, as God had commanded him. Abraham was a hundred years old when his son Isaac was born to him. And Sarah said, 'God has made laughter for me; everyone who hears will laugh over me.' And she said, 'Who would have said to Abraham that Sarah would suckle children? Yet I have borne him a son in his old age' " (Gn 21:1-7).

## Abraham's Test

The name "Isaac," the name God chose for Abraham's first son through his first wife Sarah, means "laughter" or "he who laughs," and God chose this name because when Sarah heard that God was going to give Abraham a son through her, she laughed in disbelief because she was ninety years old (Gn 17:17). The child grew and grew, healthy and strong with God's favor, and when he was weaned, Abraham gave a great feast the same day to celebrate the event (Gn 21:8). According to Josephus, when Isaac was 25 years-old ("Ant." Bk. 1, Ch. 13:2), God spoke to Abraham and told him, "Take your son, your only-begotten son Isaac, whom you love, and go to the land of Moriah, and offer him there as a burnt offering upon one of the mountains of which I shall tell you" (Gn 22:2). Early the next morning, wondering why God had asked him to sacrifice his only son, the only rightful heir he had, Abraham faithfully gathered some wood for the sacrifice, loaded up his donkey for the trip, and left on this heartbreaking and difficult journey with Isaac and two of his servants. As they approached Moriah, Isaac asked his father, "'My father!' And he said, 'Here am I, my son.' He said, 'Behold, the fire and the wood; but where is the lamb for a burnt offering?' Abraham said, 'God will provide himself the lamb for a burnt offering, my son.' So they went both of them together" (Gn 22:7-8).

"When they came to the place of which God had told him, Abraham built an altar there, and laid the wood in order, and bound Isaac his son, and laid him on the altar, upon the wood. Then Abraham put forth his hand, and took the knife to slay his son. But the angel of the LORD called to him from heaven, and said, 'Abraham, Abraham!' And he said, 'Here am I.' He said, 'Do not lay your hand on the lad or do anything to him; for now I know that you fear God, seeing you have not withheld your son, your only-begotten son, from me.' And Abraham lifted up his eyes and looked, and behold, behind him was a ram, caught in a thicket by his horns; and Abraham went and took the ram, and offered it up as a burnt offering instead of his son. So Abraham called the name of that place The LORD will provide; as it is said to this day, 'On the mount of the LORD it shall be provided.' And the angel of the LORD called to Abraham a second time from heaven, and said, 'By myself I have sworn, says the LORD, because you have done this, and have not withheld your son, your only-begotten son, I will indeed bless you, and I will multiply your descendants as the stars of heaven and as the sand which is on the seashore. And your descendants shall possess the gate of their enemies, and by your descendants shall all the nations of the earth bless themselves, because you have obeyed my voice' " (Gn 22:9-18).

"These are the days of the years of Abraham's life, a hundred and seventy-five years. Abraham breathed his last and died in a good old age, an old man and full of years, and was gathered to his people. Isaac and Ish'mael his sons buried him in the cave of Mach-pe'lah, in the field of E'phron the son of Zo'har the Hittite, east of Mamre, the field which Abraham purchased from the Hittites. There Abraham was buried, with Sarah his wife" (Gn 25:7-10). The date of Abraham's death, given that he was born around 2150 B.C., is c. 1975 B.C. Since God knows all things: past, present, and future, He already knew that Abraham was going to carry out

His orders and sacrifice Isaac. Why, then, did He tell him to do it in the first place only to stop him at the end? Was God playing games with this poor old man of a hundred years old? It's a miracle he didn't die of a heart attack! The answer is no, most certainly not. And yes, of course God already knew that Abraham was going to carry out His orders without fail and sacrifice Isaac, but Abraham himself did not know that! That is, not until the last moment. So God did this as a test for Abraham's benefit, [60] and as a result, Abraham became stronger in his faith for the Lord and also a better human being because he passed that difficult test with flying colors. God's "tests" are always for our benefit. This is why *we* are also tested many times during our lives: for our benefit and spiritual growth. Heaven help the person who is never tested! God already knows very well if we will conquer our temptations and "pass our tests" during our times of trial on Earth, but we don't! Not until the test comes. And when we do conquer them, we become stronger and better able to help others. All in time.

Many of the tests we encounter in life can be very humiliating, and this is good in order to keep our egos in check. In these instances, if we fail the test due to pride, we will miss a great opportunity to grow in spirit, to grow in holiness. One example is criticizing the faults of others without taking measures to correct our own so we can be of help to them. Our Lord brought this to the attention of His listeners when He said: "Why do you see the speck that is in your brother's eye, but do not notice the log that is in your own eye? Or how can you say to your brother, 'Let me take the speck out of your eye,' when there is the log in your own eye? You hypocrite, first take the log out of your own eye, and then you will see clearly to take the speck out of your brother's eye" (Mt 7:3-5).

Notice here that this teaching from Jesus mentions "the speck" in our brother's eye and "the log" in our own eye.

Since Jesus, our Creator, knows human nature all too well, He knows that we have a tendency to see our faults as smaller than those of others; that we are not as bad as others; and some even think that they don't have any faults at all, like the Pharisees. Although this teaching is here given by Christ to everyone for all time, of course, it is with more force applicable to those who, like the Pharisees, think they have no faults at all, for such an attitude and mindset is indeed like a "log" in the eyes since it blinds the person from seeing their own faults and sins. First of all, a small sin is a BIG sin in the eyes of God. Second, having a mindset of being sinless is characteristic of either having a damaged conscience or no conscience at all. In either case, it is still a "log" in the eye that must be removed if Heaven is our destination. Even the "speck" has to be removed too. Jesus reminds us in this regard: "You, therefore, must be perfect, as your heavenly Father is perfect" (Mt 5:48). The only way to wipe the conscience and soul clean and remove the "specks" and "logs" is confessing our sins to God through the priest and receiving absolution from God through him. Forgiveness for our sins only comes from God through His priests (Jn 20:23).

"For want of contrition, innumerable Confessions are either sacrilegious or invalid; the penitent so often breaks his promises to God, and falls again so easily into the same faults, and many souls are eternally lost. Contrition is that true and lively sorrow which the soul has for all the sins it has committed, with a firm determination never to commit them any more . . . Many Christians spend a long time in examining their consciences, and in making long and often unnecessary narrations to the confessor, and then bestow little or no time upon considering the malice of their sins, and upon bewailing and detesting them. Christians such as these, says St. Gregory, act like a wounded man who shows his wounds to the doctor with the utmost anxiety and care, and then will not make use of the remedies prescribed. It is not so much thinking, nor so much speaking of your sins that will procure their pardon, but heartfelt sorrow and detestation of them." Fr. Ignatius of the Side of Jesus.

In closing this chapter, the following regarding Abraham and his descendants is taken from the Catechism of the Catholic Church (CCC). It reveals why God called Abram, the role the chosen people (Jews) would play in Salvation history, and His plan for human unity in only one Church.

"In order to gather together scattered humanity, God calls Abram from his country, his kindred, and his father's house (Gn 12:1), and makes him Abraham, that is, 'the father of a multitude of nations.' 'In you all the nations of the earth shall be blessed' (Gn 17:5; 12:3). The people descended from Abraham would be the trustees of the promise made to the patriarchs, the chosen people, called to prepare for that day when God would gather all his children into the unity of the Church (see Rom 11:28; Jn 11:52; 10:16). They would be the root onto which the Gentiles would be grafted, once they came to believe (see Rom 11:17-18, 24). [. . .] After the patriarchs, God formed Israel as his people by freeing them from slavery in Egypt. He established with them the covenant of Mount Sinai and, through Moses, gave them his law so that they would recognize him and serve him as the one living and true God, the provident Father and just judge, and so that they would look for the promised Savior" (see DV3) (CCC. Pgs. 21, 22. ¶s 59, 60, 62).

A word about the human soul. Some people (especially atheists) do not believe in the existence of the human soul and life after death. Today, there are numerous ongoing studies of near-death experiences (NDEs) and out-of-body experiences (OBEs) that prove the existence of the soul. An OBE is when a person's soul leaves his body after clinical death and tells all about the experience after returning to his/her body. Some of these include people who were born blind and have never seen before, yet they come back and describe people, places, and things they have seen out-of-body with uncanny accuracy. Dr. Kenneth Ring has documented many of these occurrences (kenring.org). I highly recommend a review of his work to those interested in this area of study: "Near-death and OBEs in the blind: a study of apparent eyeless vision." Journal of Near-death Studies, Volume 16, Number 2, Winter 1997. Also, please visit https://iands.org/. The following are brief accounts from "The Self Does Not Die," by Rivas, Dirven, and Smit.

1). During an OBE after a heart attack at a Medical Center, Maria saw a blue man's left tennis shoe on a ledge outside a window on the third floor; "the material was worn over the little toe," and "one lace end was tucked under the heel." Sure enough, the shoe was found exactly as described (p. 32).

2). A woman had an OBE during an operation, and after recovery described her operation "as if she had been [watching it] on the ceiling." She also described the operation that had taken place at the same time in the operating room next to hers where a leg had been amputated and placed in a yellow bag. Details of both were confirmed by staff (p. 58-9).

3). A man's heart stopped during an operation and his soul left his body. During the OBE, "He saw his two daughters and his wife below him, 'huddled together.' " However, this family reunion was taking place in the hospital chapel, one floor below him. He had no prior knowledge they were going to meet there to pray for him to live (p. 84).

4). A 73-year old man had a heart attack and was revived five times; "clinically dead six times in a row." On the sixth try, the doctor told his colleague, "We'll try one more time. If the shock doesn't hold this time, let's quit!" When the man recovered, he told the doctor, "What did you mean, 'We'll quit'? That was *me* you were working on." At the moment the doctor said this, the patient was clinically dead (p. 91-2).

# Chapter 4

"The message of the cross is foolishness to those who are perishing, but to us who are being saved, it is the power of God" (1 Corinthians 1:18).

## THE FALSE "EARTHLY" MESSIAHS

### Beginnings

With the birth of Isaac, the beginning of the great nation of Israel, God's Chosen People, was well under way. Isaac's son, Jacob, had twelve sons, and each son formed his own tribe that together became known as the Twelve Tribes of Israel.[61] They received this name because Jacob's name had been changed to "Israel" by an angel that Jacob had wrestled with one long night (Gn 32:28). The name "Israel" means "wrestles with God." The twelve sons were (listed alphabetically): Asher, Benjamin, Dan, Gad, Issachar, Joseph, Judah, Levi, Naphtali, Reuben, Simeon, and Zebulun. Jacob's sons were born in the land of Canaan where Abraham had settled when he and Lot split up years before after Pharaoh banished them from Egypt (not to be confused with the Exodus, p. 70, 127f). Abraham was of Chaldean/Babylonian descent, born in the city of Ur of the Chaldeans. Isaac, his son, a Canaanite by birth, married Rebekah, a Babylonian woman of great beauty who was a grandniece of Abraham from the city of Nahor. And Jacob, the son of Isaac and Rebekah, also a Canaanite by birth, was the father of the twelve sons that fathered the Twelve Tribes of Israel. Thus, this is how the Twelve Tribes of Israel came to be.

Jacob, his sons and their families lived and prospered in the land of Canaan for many years until a terrible famine came upon the land and they moved to Egypt where Joseph, one of Jacob's sons, had become a powerful assistant to the Pharaoh there.[62] The Israelites prospered there, multiplied, and grew strong. Many generations later, the new reigning Pharaoh noticed how great the Israelites had become in number which greatly alarmed him. He feared they would one day join his enemies and turn against him, so he began to oppress them by forcing them into hard labor and killing their newborn sons to reduce their numbers. Many years later, four hundred and thirty years after they entered the land of Egypt, Moses, sent by God, came to their rescue and freed the Israelites from Pharaoh's cruelty and Egyptian domination and brought them–together with Joseph's bones–back to the land of Canaan, the land where Abraham had settled long ago.[63] However, as punishment for disobeying God, Moses did not make it to the Promised Land after this Exodus; he died (c. 1271 B.C.) just before they got there (see Dt 32:48-52).[64]

## The Monarchy Of Israel

After many years of warring with other tribes and going from hardship to hardship, "...the elders of Israel gathered together and came to Samuel, a priest, prophet, and judge at Ra'mah, and said to him, 'Behold, you are old and your sons do not walk in your ways; now appoint for us a king to govern us like all the [other] nations [have]' " (1Sm 8:4-5). Samuel did not like this request because he felt God was their King and they should have no other but Him, but the Lord told Samuel to heed the people's request, so Samuel appointed Saul, from the tribe of Benjamin, as king of Israel.[65] Saul ruled the Twelve Tribes of Israel and formed it into what became known as the United Monarchy, but Saul was not faithful to the will of the Lord, "And the LORD repented that he had made Saul king over Israel" (1 Sm 15:35). David, from the tribe of Judah and son of Jesse, who as a young man killed Goliath, the giant Philistine, by rendering him unconscious with a stone hurled from his sling and then beheaded him with his own sword, [66] became the second king of Israel after king Saul killed himself in despair battling the Philistines.[67] David (c.1040 - c.970) reigned for 40 years and brought the United Monarchy to great heights and riches. This truly was Israel's "Golden Age." And his son Solomon, who inherited the throne after him, continued this success and ruled (also for 40 years) an even bigger and richer kingdom that was respected and admired by kings and queens of foreign lands who came from great distances to pay him homage.[68] Solomon's reign brought Israel to a world power status; it was admired, respected, and secure. As fate would have it, however, Solomon's love for beautiful women led to his ruin and downfall.[69] He took foreign women as his wives and concubines (over 1000 [70] ) and allowed corruption to enter his kingdom since many of these brought their false idols and gods with them and Solomon allowed this idolatry to take place in order to appease them. The United Monarchy lasted from c.1047 B.C. to c.930 B.C. when Solomon's son, Rehoboam, inherited the throne and became king.[71] At this point in Israel's history, the Monarchy was divided into two: the ten Northern tribes and the two Southern tribes.

King David was the best model of what I call an "Earthly messiah." He set the standard for all future Earthly messiahs, a standard that was never met by anyone in the Davidic line except Jesus Christ, the "Heavenly Messiah" who far exceeded David in both nature and mission. David was the most important and respected of all the kings of Israel, and also, greatly favored by the Lord. Jesus quoted from the Psalms of David more than from any other book in the OT. The Catholic Church uses many of the Psalms in its liturgy. Of the 150 Psalms in Scripture, 76 are attributed to David. The word "Christ," from the Greek "christos," a title, not a name, means "anointed," and the Hebrew "mashiah" also means anointed. However, the Hebrew word "meshiah-YHWH" means "messiah of the Lord," an "anointed king," most likely used to describe king David (although Saul was also an anointed king). According to Hebrew Law, priests, kings, and some Prophets were anointed once chosen. Thus, the meanings of the words "Messiah" and "Christ" eventually became one and the same (see Jn 1:41).

## The False "Earthly" Messiahs

The messiah (meshiah) the Jews were waiting for when Jesus came into the world was not a Messiah from Heaven: the Son of God, both divine and human, who was going to redeem the entire human race and restore the broken relationship between man and God due to Adam and Eve's Original Sin (OS). And perhaps the main reason is because OS was not a doctrine or tenet in Judaism. The Jews did not and still do not believe OS caused the Fall of mankind. According to The Jewish Virtual Library: "The doctrine of original sin is totally unacceptable to Jews. [S]in is an act, not a state of being" [72] (contrary to CCC, 404). According to Judaism, the Jews and the rest of the human race did not need a Savior to redeem them from OS; no Original Sin means no Redeemer is needed and therefore no reason for Jesus to have died on the Cross. This is why Jews still believe that Jesus died for no valid reason. Thus, Judaism became obsolete with the coming of Christ; i.e., no longer to be followed by anyone (Heb 8:8-13; Acts 21:21). Had Jews accepted Christ, Judaism would have been the "Catholic" religion for all to follow, but that is not what happened. God does not want us to practice a religion that is still waiting for the Messiah! The belief in an "Earthly messiah" who would free the Jews from servitude and bring them secular peace and prosperity and herald an era of world peace was an official teaching of either the Pharisees or the Essenes. This belief did not come from the scribes: they basically taught the Torah to the people; and not from the Sadducees: they cared not for the Prophets and their messianic prophecies. Although this belief still exists in modern Rabbinic Judaism, which is based on Pharisaic teachings, it may have originated in the Essene community. The Essenes were more devout than the Pharisees.

The Jewish Maccabean (Hasmonean) Revolt that began in 170 B.C., led by a Judean Levite family, was triggered by the imposition of Hellenistic customs, religion, and laws on the Jewish people by Antiochus IV Epiphanes and his successors, sometimes with the assistance of Hellenized Jewish High Priests. Antiochus made Judaism illegal and brutally tortured and executed those who practiced it. [73] The Maccabean family can be considered "Earthly messiahs" by Pharisaic nationalistic standards because they were able to amass and lead a large Jewish army, defeat their enemies, free the Jews from Gentile domination and recapture Jerusalem and its Temple thus enabling the Jews to practice Judaism in peace and enjoy freedom from servitude for a little over a century, i.e., until Roman general Pompey captured Jerusalem in 63 B.C. Since the Hasmonean Dynasty, the fruit of the Maccabean Revolt, failed to remain in power in order to protect the Jewish people from their enemies, perhaps either the Pharisees or the newly established Essenes, (or both), seeing that observance and knowledge of the law was not enough to free themselves – and remain free – from domination by Gentile forces, interpreted the messianic prophecies to mean that an "Earthly messiah," from the line of David, would one day come to their rescue, and this belief came to a head during the time of Christ when the Romans were in full power. The religious sects of the Pharisees, Sadducees, and Essenes were firmly established during the reign of the Hasmonean Dynasty (c. 140-37 B.C.) which ended when Herod the Great became king of Judaea in 37 B.C. Thus, the messiah the Jews were waiting for when Jesus began His public ministry (c. 30 A.D.) was a powerful military warrior from the line of king David, an "Earthly" messiah, a mortal human being sent by God who would rescue them from Roman rule and build them into a free, rich, and sovereign nation like the one ruled by king David and king Solomon.[74] This is the messiah the Jews were waiting for at the time of Christ, and the one some denominations of Rabbinic Judaism are still waiting for today, what we

Catholics and other Christians call a "false messiah." The only part God plays in this messiah's coming is "The Sender" and nothing more. Failure to recognize Jesus as the Heavenly Messiah, promised by the Prophets (see Jn 1:11), turned out to be a very serious misunderstanding and grave mistake made by the Jews, and most serious of all, by the chief priests (Sadducees), the Pharisees, and the teachers of the Law (scribes) who should have known better! But this grave mistake, this serious misunderstanding that led to the actual brutal murder of God Himself, turned out to be – in the end – the most important, the most valuable, the most precious, priceless and invaluable gift that God has given to mankind: the Restoration of the broken relationship with God and the Redemption of the entire human race.

The following question has been asked many times over the centuries, most of all by Catholics, "Why didn't the Jews accept Jesus as the promised Messiah when He came?" And the simple answer is, "Because Jesus was not the type of Messiah they were waiting for. The Jews were waiting for an Earthly messiah instead of a Heavenly Messiah." The next question is "Why? Were the Messianic prophecies of long ago wrong about Jesus?" And the answer is, "No, not exactly." So, why were they confused about something so important as this by the time Jesus came? "What caused this major confusion?" The answer to this unique question is a little complicated, and it is found in the history of the Israelites themselves. The history of the Israelites is riddled with wonderful and spectacular events, grand promises God made them—and kept! But also wars, calamities, catastrophes, enslavements to exile by one enemy or another, and many other disagreeable things they went through, and all this had much to do with creating the mindset over time that the messiah was going to be an "Earthly" one: a powerful military ruler from the line of king David that God was going to send in order to rescue them from enslavement and servitude and build them into a free, wealthy and great nation, and the

Pharisees and/or the Essenes were responsible for this mindset. The Jews longed for freedom from poverty, from enslavements, forced labor, living in exile, domination by Gentiles, high abusive taxes, not being able to practice their own religion the proper way, etc., and by the time Jesus entered human history, freedom from submission to the Romans. By the time Jesus was born, the Jews had had enough of being dominated by the Romans and the time was more than ripe for revolution. The Jews were NOT waiting for a Messiah that would redeem mankind; they were waiting for one that would save only **them**. After all, they were "God's Chosen People!" Yes, they were living in the "Promised Land," but under Roman rule! Surely God, who always kept His promises and had always looked after His people was not going to forget them now! What they really needed was a New David, a powerful "meshiah" who would finally come to their rescue. But that was not to be; that was not what God had planned for them and the world; even though David himself had written about Jesus in his Psalms (e.g., Ps 110). It is important to know that the details of the Heavenly Messiah, who in fact was coming to redeem mankind, were not explicitly revealed by neither the Torah nor the Messianic prophecies—most of which were veiled and not precise, obscure and not very clear (see CCC, 702). In addition to this, the Pharisees and Essenes had added many rules and regulations to the Law of Moses (see CCC, 581-82), including the belief in an Earthly messiah. Thus, having no tenet of Original Sin or the Trinity, the veiled Messianic prophecies, the numerous regulations they created, and the longing for freedom from Gentile rule led to a misdirection, or misinterpretation of the prophecies and to the adoption of the belief that an "Earthly messiah," instead of a "Heavenly Messiah," was coming to their rescue, and this was propagated. Judaic tradition holds that there are not Ten Commandments to follow, but 613 commandments: the "mitzvot" contained in the Mishneh Torah. This large number of regulations had placed a very heavy burden on the

Jewish people for quite some time, which is why Jesus told His followers that following only two Commandments was enough: "You shall love the Lord your God with all your heart, and with all your soul, and with all your mind. This is the great and first commandment. And a second is like it, You shall love your neighbor as yourself. On these two commandments depend all the law and the Prophets" (Mt 22:37-40; see 1 Jn 4:11-12, 20-21).

According to modern Jewish authorities, the Pharisees are "the spiritual fathers of modern Judaism" (see Jewish Virtual Library.org, pharisees-sadducees-and-essenes). As I stated earlier, the Jews believed that a messiah would one day deliver them from Gentile rule and usher in an era of world peace, a belief still held by many who practice Rabbinic Judaism, the "spiritual children" of the Pharisees. The Sadducees (chief priests, also "Herodians") paid no attention to messianic prophecies and did not honor the Oral Tradition of the Torah expounded by the Pharisees who, together with the scribes, had succeeded in usurping their authority within the Jewish community. Personally, I believe the Pharisees are the ones largely responsible for not only the misinterpretations of the Messianic prophecies, but also for the dissemination of the belief in an Earthly messiah before and during the time of Christ. Since the Jews had a long history of bondage and domination by Gentiles, their adoption of the Earthly messiah Pharisaic construct was not only easy to accept, but also welcomed (see Dt 15:6). The coming of Jesus Christ, the Redeemer of the human race, is the most important event in world history; an Event that, sadly enough, was not recognized nor accepted by His own people (see Jn 1:11).

Jesus reprimanded the Pharisees, Sadducees and teachers of the Law for their hypocrisy many times during His public ministry in front of many onlookers which made them very angry. In one instance, the Pharisees told Jesus that God Himself was the only Father they had and that they were His true sons, but Jesus corrected them and told them: "You are of your father the devil, and your will is to do your father's desires. [...] So they took up stones to throw at him; but Jesus hid himself, and went out of the temple" (Jn 8:44, 59). This, of course, *really* made them mad, so they started to look for a way to eliminate Him. Since Jesus knew very well that the Jews were waiting for an Earthly messiah and not for Him, He did everything he could – at all times – from being mistaken for this expected political and military hero/king who was coming to overthrow the Romans and rescue them (see CCC, 439; Jn 6:15). The further Jesus distanced Himself from this personality – even though He knew this mythical person was never going to come – the better off He was, for anyone who claimed to be this messiah would be put to death at once by the Romans, and Jesus, who knew this all too well, was not going to allow this to happen until the Appointed Time had come. Jesus wanted no trouble with the Romans. He was not, and never was, a political enemy of Rome. The Romans, including Pilate, had known for a long time that the Jews were not happy under Roman rule and in fact detested it. The local soldiers who frequently were called to neutralize protests and anti-Roman demonstrations knew this all too well. The Jews had been under Roman rule in Palestine since Roman General Pompey captured Jerusalem in 63 B.C. After Christ ascended into Heaven, there were three (3) Jewish Revolts (wars) against the Roman Empire. The First Jewish-Roman War was from 66 - 70 A.D.; the second one, the Kitos War, from 115 - 117 A.D.; and the third, the Bar Kokhba Revolt, which lasted from 132 - 136 A.D., was led by the Jewish military leader, Simon ben Kosevah, who later became known as Simon Bar Kokhba.

## Judas, Simon, And Athronges Old Earthly messiahs

Herod the Great was appointed king of Judaea by the Roman Senate in 40 B.C. in large part by paying Mark Antony to assist him toward obtaining that position, much the same as he had previously paid Antony to assist him in becoming tetrarch of Galilee. Herod's older brother, Phasael, who became tetrarch of Jerusalem, committed suicide after the Roman-Parthian war ended in 40 B.C., and it was not long thereafter that Herod was proclaimed king of the Jews. Herod was never accepted by the Jews because he was an Idumean on his father's side and an Arab on his mother's side. In those days, a Jew was only considered a Jew if the mother was Jewish. Even though Herod rebuilt the Second Temple for the Jews and turned it into a magnificent, grand and beautiful structure, the Jews continued to hate him till he died. [75]After King Herod died (c.1 B.C.), his two sons, Herod Archelaus and Herod Antipas, who were rivals, hastened by separate routes to Rome in order to be crowned first the new "king of the Jews" by Emperor Augustus (Caesar).[76] However, neither one received that prestigious title. The next and last king of the Jews would be Herod's grandson, Herod Agrippa I. Archelaus was named ethnarch ("national leader") of Judaea, Samaria, and Idumea. Antipas, who later married divorced Herodias, mother of Salome, who was responsible for the death of John the Baptist, was named tetrarch of Galilee and Perea. And Philip, their half-brother, became tetrarch of the Golan Heights. While the two brothers were in Rome, widespread disturbances and riots broke out led by the rebels Judas, son of Ezekias, Simon of Perea, former slave of king Herod, and Athronges, a shepherd, and his four brothers.[77]

Archelaus' soldiers were not able to deal with these riots and their leaders in an effective way, so Publius Quinctilius Varus, the Roman governor of Syria and close friend of Augustus, was called in to take over. Varus embarked on a massive campaign against these rebels which involved three legions (a legion consists of over 5000 soldiers). At the end of this campaign, around two thousand people had been crucified all over the land, the majority of them Jews, but the concerted efforts by the legions of Romans to capture all of the rebel leaders were in vain.[78] About this time, Joseph, Mary, and Jesus were on their way back to Judea from their exile in Egypt after the Massacre of the Innocents, ordered by king Herod, had forced them to go there for safety (Mt 2:13-18). When Joseph and Mary learned that Archelaus was now ruler of Judea, they were afraid to go there and went to the province of Galilee and settled in their hometown of Nazareth instead (Mt 2:22-23) which was ruled by Antipas.

These three leaders of the rioting and insurrection: Judas, Simon, and Athronges, were considered messiahs by many of the people. Although all three aspired to be labeled as such, only Athronges and Simon crowned themselves as kings (messiahs), even wearing diadems on their heads. Judas, the leader of the three, was indeed caught and perished (Acts 5:37). Simon was beheaded by Gratus (who also "subdued" one of Athronges' brothers), and Athronges, the one who aspired the most to this prestigious title, although all four of his brothers were either killed or imprisoned, nothing more is recorded about him. He just....disappeared! [79]

Judas, the leader of the rebels, and Zadok the Pharisee, were the founders of the "Fourth Philosophy," the "Sicarians." The other three philosophic groups were the Pharisees, the Sadducees, and the Essenes. It is interesting to note, the historian Josephus blames the Sicarians for starting the First Jewish-Roman War in 66 A.D. [80] because they believed that God alone was their ruler and therefore they should not be paying taxes to Rome. This, however, although true in part, was perhaps not the sole reason for the war. The combination of the favoritism the Romans gave to the Gentiles living in Palestine, the exorbitant taxes imposed on the Jews by the Romans, and the Roman contempt and disrespect for Judaism appears to have been what stoked the fires that led to this First War. This war ended in 70 A.D. when Roman forces, led by military commander Titus, destroyed and razed Jerusalem and the Second Temple, a

Temple that had been remodeled and rebuilt into a magnificent super structure by King Herod. The date on record for the destruction of the Second Temple is given as August 10th, 70 A.D. (the 9th of Av).[81]

Mention of Judas, son of Ezekias, also appears in the Acts of the Apostles. Here, a Pharisee named Gamaliel, who used to be Saul's (St. Paul) teacher (Acts 22:3), tells the Sanhedrin not to persecute the Apostles anymore who are now preaching after Pentecost, and to leave them alone. He reminds them that Judas, like Jesus, was also killed and his followers were scattered, and that the same may happen to these followers of Jesus if they are left alone. And then Gamaliel warns the Sanhedrin that if what these men are doing truly comes from God, they won't be able to defeat them, and: "You might even be found opposing God!" (Acts 5:37-39).

During the Third Jewish-Roman war that was led by Simon ben Kosevah, which ended in 136 A.D., Simon was proclaimed the promised messiah by Rabbi Akiva ben Yosef (Aqiba) who at the time was the official religious leader of the Jews. Akiva renamed him "Bar Kokhba" which means "Son of the Star" in Aramaic, from the Star Prophecy verse found in Numbers 24:17: "…a star shall come forth out of Jacob." [82] This proclamation, however, was rendered null and void by later rabbis who disagreed with Akiva because the Kingdom of Israel had not been restored as expected on a permanent basis. A Jewish coin from that era shows the Ark of the Covenant with a star above it in reference to Simon's messiahship.[83] In contrast, a Star is what led the Three Magi to the Birth of Christ, the True Messiah, in Bethlehem.

The Jews who had converted to Catholicism at this time (the Church had already been named "Catholic" by St. Ignatius of Antioch) refused to accept Bar Kokhba as the Messiah because they knew and believed that Jesus was the only one who could claim that title. St. Justin Martyr wrote that Simon

Bar Kokhba had these converts taken away to face "terrible punishment" if they refused to deny that Jesus was the Messiah.[84] In an interesting twist, one of Akiva's disciples, Jose ben Halaphta, renamed Simon Bar Kokhba "Simon bar Koziba," which means in Hebrew "son of the lie," a name that stuck from that time forward and was even recorded in the Jewish Talmud that way.[85] I would like to add here that Simon bar Kokhba did succeed in establishing a three-year-long independent Jewish state during which he ruled as supreme "nasi," which means "prince" in Biblical Hebrew. (The closeness between nasi and nazi is indeed disturbing.) The name nasi, which has very strong messianic connotations, was also used to identify the head or High Priest of the Sanhedrin (Mishnaic Hebrew), the religious Council that acted as the tribunal and Supreme Court for the Jewish people of Palestine. In fact, it was the Sanhedrin that condemned Jesus to death. Today, the name nasi means "president" in modern Hebrew.

Years after the Second Jewish-Roman War ended, Emperor Hadrian visited Judea in 130 A.D. and ordered the construction of a new Jerusalem over the site of the old one. He also ordered the construction of a new temple dedicated to the Roman god Jupiter, a disgust to the Jews. Hadrian (who according to Josephus was a pedophile) forbade the Jewish practice of circumcising young boys which caused a lot of turmoil and unrest, and to make matters worse, during the construction to convert the ruins of Jerusalem into a new Roman city, workers disturbed the tomb of Solomon and it collapsed. This was interpreted by many as a messianic omen and sparked the fires that led to the Third war with Bar Kokhba as leader, a war that was without doubt religious in nature. The rebels who joined Bar Kokhba were convinced this war was the one predicted by the prophet Daniel,[86] but this turned out to be another misinterpretation of Scriptural prophecy. During this war, Bethlehem, the birthplace of Jesus, was destroyed by Emperor Hadrian, but some of it was later rebuilt by Empress Helena,[87] the one who found the True Cross of Jesus and mother of Constantine the Great.

In 135 A.D., the Bar Kokhba Revolt ended at Bethar, Bar Kokhba's headquarters and home of the Sanhedrin.[88] The rebels never surrendered to the Romans at the end of this war and most of them died from famine and thirst. Among the dead bodies, the fearless leader and warrior, Simon, the son of Kosiba, was found. His dead body was beheaded and the head was brought to Emperor Hadrian who said, "If his God had not slain him, who could have overcome him?" [89] Bar Kokhba was a ruthless leader who punished with severity any Jew who refused to join him. Affectionately known as "The Father of Church History," Eusebius, Catholic Bishop of Caesarea in Palestine, later wrote in his work "Chronicon" that Bar Kokhba was very cruel to the Christians and tortured them to death for refusing to fight with him against the Romans.[90] After the war ended, the Romans plowed Jerusalem with a yoke of oxen, sold Jews into slavery (for the same price of horses), and changed the name of Jerusalem to "Aelia Capitolina" and Judea to "Palestina." Moreover, Jews were no longer allowed to live in Capitolina for quite some time. All of the Earthly messiahs listed here were considered "enemies of Rome."

## Shabbetai Zvi And Judah ben Sholom New Earthly messiahs

A little more than a century after the heretical Protestant Reformation reared its ugly heretical head in Germany through the corrupt Catholic monk Martin Luther, a promising Jewish student of the Kabbala from Smyrna, Shabbetai Zvi, was proclaimed the long awaited messiah by Nathan of Gaza, a self-proclaimed "man of God" who lived in Jerusalem. Zvi, believing this was indeed the case, began to act the part and even chose 12 apostles as his followers. News of this quickly spread in Palestine, and before long, in

Europe, resulting in public manifestations of both joy and repentance by many Jews in these places. The messianic sentiment among many Jews reached such incredible frenzied proportions that leaders of Jewish communities everywhere were confirming his messianic title of king of the Jews, even in writing. Books and documents published about him were distributed among believers with one that read, "Messiah the son of David has come." This, however, did not last very long, for Zvi found himself one day in front of the Muslim Sultan who gave him only two options: convert or die. The proclaimed messiah quickly chose the former and was rewarded with the title of "Keeper of the Palace Gates" and given a pension to live on. The apostasy shocked the Jewish world to the point that a campaign was launched to erase his name from all records to avoid shame. [91] Then, two hundred years later, another messiah appeared in Yemen by the name of Judah ben Sholom, an accomplished kabbalist known as Shukr Kuhayl. He claimed the messianic title was given to him supposedly by none other than Elijah himself in a vision. Although he succeeded in gaining many followers, he was eventually beheaded for converting Muslims.[92] Three years later, an impostor claiming to be the "resurrected" Shukr fooled the people for a while, but like a shooting star, soon faded away.

Interestingly, the Essenes were actually expecting two messiahs: one priestly and one kingly. They did not know that God's Messiah, Jesus, would be both priest and king as well as prophet all in one Person, and also, God in the flesh as well. Moreover, the Essenes believed God's Messiah was going to destroy their enemies and usher in an age of perpetual peace; modern Rabbinic Pharisaic Judaism still holds this tenet, but that was not the actual Mission of God's Messiah. God's Messiah, Jesus, was not coming to save the Jews from their enemies; he was coming to redeem the entire human race. Since both the Essenes and the Pharisees shared the belief in an "Earthly" messiah, it is not crystal clear who is actually responsible for originating this belief: the Essenes or the Pharisees; maybe both. What is clear however, is that no one knew the Messiah was going to be God in the flesh, and that He was coming to redeem the entire human race. THAT is absolutely crystal clear.

This topic of false messiahs could fill many books, and indeed it has. However, this partial account suffices for our purposes to illustrate the nature of the topic. After the Third Jewish-Roman War, the Jews remained politically dead with no Jewish state for the next eighteen hundred years or so, but their religion survived. Before the Second Temple was destroyed in 70 A.D., Judaism had three major "philosophies": the Pharisees, the Sadducees, and the Essenes. The Essene community (who were awaiting *two* messiahs) was destroyed by the Romans c. 68 A.D., and the Sadducees ceased to exist after the Second Temple was destroyed. But the Pharisees survived and are considered the "spiritual fathers" of Rabbinic Judaism.[93] After the Second Temple was destroyed, the Jews only met in Synagogues. These, instituted by the Pharisees long before the war, are still in use today. The Sanhedrin relocated to Jamnia after the war.

## Jeremiah And The New Covenant

The four major OT Prophets of Israel are (in order of importance): Isaiah, Jeremiah, Ezekiel, and Daniel. Jeremiah lived during one of the worst times in Jerusalem's history when Babylonian king Nebuchadnezzar II destroyed the city, its First Temple, and deported thousands of Jews to Babylonia in 587 B.C. There were three military deportations of Jews to Babylonia under Nebuchadnezzar II: 605 B.C., 597 B.C., and 587 B.C. The Prophet Daniel was taken in the first one, the second was the largest deportation, and the third included the destruction of Jerusalem and the First Temple. According to Jeremiah, who escaped to Egypt after the last one, these were punishments from God for their many sins

(25:8-14; see Dt 28:32, 36, 41, 47-53). However, the Jews were allowed to return to Jerusalem in 538 B.C. Jeremiah was a very unique prophet. While the other Prophets made predictions regarding the sufferings of the Messiah (notably Isaiah), Jeremiah also made such predictions, but not unlike Christ, he suffered a lot at the hands of his own people because of the harsh criticism he directed toward them due to their sinful ways; even his own family wanted him dead (12:6). Some historians claim the ancient Jews endured much undeserved suffering due to wars, exiles and persecutions, but OT passages from Isaiah, Jeremiah, and Ezekiel reveal that these were punishments sent by God for their sinful and idolatrous ways which included child sacrifice (2 Kgs 17:17). God's Chosen People have a very long history of unfaithfulness to God, a fact rarely found in many history books yet present in the Holy Catholic Bible. Jeremiah predicted the destruction of Jerusalem and the First Temple (Jer 6:1-8). Like Christ, he wept for Jerusalem for stoning the Prophets—failing to realize the value of their messages and criticisms. And also like Jesus, he suffered and died because of his own people: the lack of love and gratitude for what he had done for them.

Throughout his life, Jeremiah found it difficult to understand why he had to suffer so much since he was always doing the Lord's work. It seemed the more he worked for the Lord, the more he suffered, and the more he wondered why God was so slow in coming to his rescue (17:14-18; 20:15-18). Perhaps Christ had Jeremiah in mind when He said: "If any man would come after me, let him deny himself and take up his cross and follow me. For whoever would save his life will lose it, and whoever loses his life for my sake will find it" (Mt 16:24-25). Although his Messianic prophecies—some dictated to Baruch, his friend and secretary—were not as frequent as those of Isaiah, his contribution is most important. Some of these are: "The Lord made it known to me and I knew; then you showed me their evil deeds. But I was like a gentle lamb led to the slaughter" (11:18-19), a reference to the "Lamb of God" sacrificed for mankind; "A voice is heard in Ra'mah, lamentation and bitter weeping. Rachel is weeping for her children; she refuses to be comforted for her children, because they are not" (31:15), a reference to the Massacre of the Innocents ordered by king Herod in order to kill the Christ child. But the most important of his Messianic prophecies, found nowhere else in the OT, is the following: "Behold, the days are coming, says the LORD, when I will make a new covenant with the house of Israel and the house of Judah, not like the covenant which I made with their fathers when I took them by the hand to bring them out of the land of Egypt, my covenant which they broke, and I showed myself their Master, says the LORD. But this is the covenant which I will make with the house of Israel after those days, says the LORD: I will put my law within them, and I will write it upon their hearts; and I will be their God, and they shall be my people. And no longer shall each man teach his neighbor and each his brother, saying, 'Know the LORD,' for they shall all know me, from the least of them to the greatest, says the LORD; for I will forgive their iniquity, and I will remember their **sin** no more" (31:31-34) [my emph. re: singular: Original Sin].

This prophecy refers to the New and Eternal Covenant that Christ will establish with the human race at the Last Supper supplanting the Old Covenants. Like many other OT Jewish Prophets, Jeremiah was stoned to death by his own people while they were exiled in Taphnai, Egypt because of his repeated efforts to stop their idolatrous and sinful ways. Jeremiah is the most explicit of all the OT Prophets in regards to the New Covenant Jesus will establish with mankind, but he does not say as much as Isaiah does in regards to the life and times of Christ. Isaiah is the most important OT prophet.

The Messianic prophecies in the Book of Daniel are regarded by some modern Jews to mean the liberation of Israel and the establishment of their nation by an Earthly messiah and not to the coming of a Heavenly Messiah who would "save the world" from the evil consequences of original sin. But once again, they are misinterpreting these Messianic prophecies, and not only in the Book of Daniel, but also in the other prophetic books as well resulting in the adoption of false secular interpretations and rejecting the Holy originals sent to them by God through the Prophets. This is yet another example of how and why the Jews were waiting for an Earthly messiah instead of the Heavenly One promised by God through the Prophets, many of whom were stoned to death by their own people for trying to get them to change their corrupt and sinful behavior. In fact, more accurately than any other OT Book, the Book of Daniel predicts the precise time when Jesus will come into the world. It refers to Jesus as the "anointed one, a prince" (Messiah), and even predicts His death by saying He will be "cut off" (killed). These predictions were given to Daniel by the archangel Gabriel (9:24-26). [94] Daniel also refers to Christ as "one like a son of man" (7:13), an expression Christ adopted and used frequently when referring to Himself, most likely: (1) to show solidarity with His listeners, fellow human beings; (2) to help conceal His divinity (Son of God); (3) to prevent the title "messiah" from being assigned to him by the Jews who were expecting an Earthly messiah (see p. 196); and most importantly (4) to associate and unite Himself with the "son of man" predicted in the Book of Daniel. Perhaps Daniel's description "son of **man**" may have helped the Pharisees and Essenes to believe that the Messiah would indeed be a human person thus justifying their expectation of an Earthly messiah and not the Son of God. There is a passage in Scripture that reveals just how common the belief in waiting for an Earthly messiah was in Jesus' time. It is found in the 24$^{th}$ chapter of Luke's Gospel. Here, two disciples were walking on the road to Emma'us discussing the crucifixion of Christ when Jesus came along, started to walk with them unrecognized, and asked them what they were talking about. One of them, Cle'opas, said: "Are you the only visitor to Jerusalem who does not know the things that have happened there in these days?" And he said to them, 'What things?' And they said to him, 'Concerning Jesus of Nazareth, who was a prophet mighty in deed and word before God and all the people, and how our **chief priests and rulers** delivered him up to be condemned to death, and crucified him. **But we had hoped that he was the one to redeem Israel'** " (Lk 24:18-21) [my emph]. The "redeeming of Israel" was the expected liberation from Roman Rule. Let's take a quick look at what modern Jews have to say regarding their messiah. The following four (4) excerpts, quoted verbatim, are taken from The Jewish Virtual Library.org, an online encyclopedia published by the American foreign policy analyst Mitchell Bard's non-profit organization American–Israeli Cooperative Enterprise (AICE). It is supposed to represent the views of all Jews, both past and present. The actual source is: *Jewish Literacy,* by Joseph Telushkin. 1991. My comments appear afterwards.

## Modern Jewish Messianic Beliefs

[1]. "Most significantly, Jewish tradition affirms at least five things about the Messiah. He will: be a descendant of King David, gain sovereignty over the land of Israel, gather the Jews there from the four corners of the earth, restore them to full observance of Torah law, and, as a grand finale, bring peace to the whole world."

[2]. "The Jewish belief that the Messiah's reign lies in the future has long distinguished Jews from their Christian neighbors who believe, of course, that the Messiah came two thousand years ago in the person of Jesus. The most basic reason for the Jewish denial of the messianic claims made on Jesus' behalf is that he did not usher in world peace, as Isaiah had prophesied: "And nation shall not lift up sword against

nation, neither shall they learn war anymore" (Isaiah 2:4). In addition, Jesus did not help bring about Jewish political sovereignty for the Jews or protection from their enemies."

[3]. "In the modern world, Reform Judaism has long denied that there will be an individual messiah who will carry out the task of perfecting the world. Instead, the movement speaks of a future world in which human efforts, not a divinely sent messenger, will bring about a utopian age. The Reform idea has influenced many nonorthodox Jews: The oft-noted attraction of Jews to liberal and leftwing political causes probably represents a secular attempt to usher in a messianic age."

[4]. "A sober reading of Jewish history, however, indicates that while the messianic idea has long elevated Jewish life, and prompted Jews to work for **tikkun olam** (perfection of the world), whenever Jews have thought the Messiah's arrival to be imminent, the results have been catastrophic. In 1984, a Jewish religious underground was arrested in Israel. Among its other activities, the group had plotted to blow up the Muslim Dome of the Rock in Jerusalem, so that the Temple Mount could be cleared and the Temple rebuilt. Though such an action might well have provoked an international Islamic **jihad** (holy war) against Israel, some members of this underground group apparently welcomed such a possibility, feeling that a worldwide invasion of Israel would force God to bring the Messiah immediately. It is precisely when the belief in the Messiah's coming starts to shape political decisions that the messianic idea ceases to be inspiring and becomes dangerous." [95]

## Commentary

[1]. Jesus was and is a descendant of King David (Is 11:1-10; Mt 1:6; Lk 1:32, 3:31). Regarding gathering the Jews from the four corners of the earth, i.e., the "New Exodus" from Isaiah,

Isaiah 11:10-16 and 12:1-6 does mention this New Exodus, led by the Messiah/Christ "root of Jesse": i.e., Jesus; and 60:1-22 describes how both Gentiles and Jews will come to the restored Zion: the New Jerusalem: the Bride and Church of Christ (Rev 21:2; see Is 62:5), and together will worship and offer sacrifice (Catholic Mass) on God's altar: the Catholic Church, for Christ's Body (Church) IS the New Temple—the Old Second Temple, destroyed by the Romans, is gone forever. Thirdly, bringing peace to the whole world is not a Messianic promise. The peace Jesus, the Messiah, gives to the world is not a **worldly** political/military peace, but a **personal** interior peace: "Peace I leave with you; my peace I give to you; **not as the world gives** do I give [peace] to you" (Jn 14:27) (see CCC, 2305). "I have said this to you, that in me you may have peace. In the world you have tribulation; but be of good cheer, I have overcome the world" (Jn 16:33). Lastly, the Jews failed to understand that the Messiah would be God in the flesh: Jesus, the Son of God the Father (see chs. 6 & 7 for explanation). Moreover, "The [Catholic] Church has rejected even modified forms of this falsification of the kingdom to come under the name of millenarianism, **especially the intrinsically perverse political form of a secular messianism**" (CCC, 676) [my emph.].

[2]. Is 61:1f was wrongly interpreted by first-century Jews, following Pharisaic teaching, to mean that a powerful leader, an "Earthly messiah" was going to liberate them from the Romans, but the "anointed one": the "Christ" or "Messiah" that Isaiah mentions here was Jesus, the "Heavenly Messiah," who would offer not only the Jews, but all mankind liberation from sin and death and Eternal Life through His sacrificial death on the cross. It is worthy to note that Jesus read Is 61:1-2 in the synagogue in His hometown of Nazareth and told His listeners and neighbors that this passage pointed to Him (see Lk 4:16-30). As mentioned before, world peace is not part of any Messianic prophecy. The Good News Christ brought to the world plants a peace in the follower's soul

whereby the individual knows for certain that he will be with God in Heaven after death by following Christ in *this* life. This peace far exceeds any other type of peace. Moreover, Jesus said: "Do not think that I have come to bring peace on earth; I have not come to bring peace, but a sword" (Mt 10:34); i.e., the Sword of Truth. His Mission **was not** to free the Jews from foreign domination and provide protection from their enemies. This is an erroneous and gross misinterpretation of Scriptural Messianic prophecies.

[3]. The Mission of the promised Messiah was not to perfect the world but to redeem it. "Human efforts" cannot and will not redeem the human race from Original Sin (OS). Only God in the flesh can achieve that atonement and this is precisely what God in fact did through the sacrificial death of Jesus Christ 2000 years ago. Since Jews reject the doctrine of OS, a doctrine deeply rooted in Scripture (New and Old Testaments), they therefore reject the necessity to redeem such Sin and the type of Messiah such Sin requires. Moreover, as history has proven over and over again, liberal and leftwing political movements like socialism and communism do not bring peace and prosperity but rather misery, poverty, hunger, unemployment, oppression, loss of liberty, and death. Russian philosopher Nikolai Berdyaev said: "Socialism claims to become the religion of the new humanity.... socialism is a messianism [and] the proletariat is the new Israel.... The chosen class establishes on earth the promised kingdom, it offers the happiness that the Crucified Messiah did not bring. The proletariat is the new Messiah, the founder of an earthly kingdom in the name of which the old Messiah was rejected, who announced a kingdom which 'is not of this world.'" [96] No, humans cannot redeem themselves from OS. Only God can, and did so 2000 years ago in the Person of Jesus Christ.

[4]. Catastrophe resulted when Jews thought the Messiah had arrived because those were Earthly messiahs who resorted to

violence to free the Jews. Jesus' Mission was not to perfect the world but to redeem it: to restore the broken relationship between mankind and God due to Original Sin. **This is the actual Mission of the Promised Messiah: God in the flesh; planned by God, foretold by the OT Prophets and accomplished by Jesus Christ, both God and man in one Divine Person.** After Christ rose from the dead, He established His "Kingdom on Earth," the Holy Catholic Church: a "Universal Church" that offers membership to all who accept that Salvation is only through Him. Those who come to believe that Jesus is the Savior of mankind can then profess with the other members of His Church:

### The Nicene Creed

"**I believe in one God**, the Father almighty, maker of heaven and earth, of all things visible and invisible. I believe in one Lord Jesus Christ, the Only Begotten Son of God, born of the Father before all ages. God from God, Light from Light, true God from true God, begotten, not made, consubstantial with the Father; through him all things were made. For us men and for our salvation he came down from heaven, and by the Holy Spirit was incarnate of the Virgin Mary, and became man. For our sake he was crucified under Pontius Pilate, he suffered death and was buried, and rose again on the third day in accordance with the Scriptures. He ascended into heaven and is seated at the right hand of the Father. He will come again in glory to judge the living and the dead and his kingdom will have no end. I believe in the Holy Spirit, the Lord, the giver of life, who proceeds from the Father and the Son, who with the Father and the Son is adored and glorified, who has spoken through the Prophets. I believe in **One, Holy, Catholic and Apostolic Church.** I confess one Baptism for the forgiveness of sins and I look forward to the resurrection of the dead and the life of the world to come. Amen." [My emph.]

# Chapter 5

"I have told you this so that you might have peace in me. In the world you will have trouble, but take courage, I have conquered the world" (Jn 16:33).

## THE TRUE "HEAVENLY" MESSIAH

"And the angel of the LORD called to Abraham a second time from heaven, and said, "By myself I have sworn, says the LORD, because you have done this, and have not withheld your son, your only-begotten son, I will indeed bless you, and I will multiply your descendants as the stars of heaven and as the sand which is on the seashore. And your descendants shall possess the gate of their enemies, and by your descendants shall all the nations of the earth bless themselves, because you have obeyed my voice" (Gn 22:15-18). Obedience to God leads to life.

"There shall come forth a shoot from the stump of Jesse, and a branch shall grow out of his roots. And the Spirit of the LORD shall rest upon him, the spirit of wisdom and understanding, the spirit of counsel and might, the spirit of knowledge and the fear of the LORD. And his delight shall be in the fear of the LORD" (Is 11:1-3).

"The people who walked in darkness [Gentiles] have seen a great light [Jesus]; those who dwelt in a land of deep darkness, on them has light shined. You have multiplied the nation, you have increased its joy; they rejoice before you as with joy at the harvest, as men rejoice when they divide the spoil. For the yoke of his burden, and the staff for his shoulder, the rod of his oppressor, you have broken as on the day of Mid'ian. For every boot of the tramping warrior in battle tumult and every garment rolled in blood will be burned as fuel for the fire. For to us a child is born, to us a son is given; and the government will be upon his shoulder, and his name will be called 'Wonderful Counselor, Mighty God, Everlasting Father, Prince of Peace' " (Is 9:2-6). "A star shall come forth out of Jacob, and a scepter shall rise out of Israel; [...] But you, O Bethlehem Eph'rathah, who are little to be among the clans of Judah, from you shall come forth for me one who is to be ruler in Israel, whose origin is from of old, from ancient days. [...] And he said, 'Hear then, O house of David! Is it too little for you to weary men, that you weary my God also? Therefore the Lord himself will give you a sign. Behold, a virgin shall conceive and bear a son, and shall call his name Imman'u-el' " (Nm 24:17; Mi 5:2; Is 7:13-14).

The above passages from Scripture are OT prophecies that describe the coming and birth of the promised Messiah. This is not the Earthly messiah most of the Jews were waiting for, but the Heavenly Messiah: the True Messiah: Jesus the Christ: Son of God and Son of man, both divine and human, in one Person. As these prophecies describe, Jesus would be a descendant of Abraham and therefore a descendant of king David (stump of Jesse). He would be born a Jew, a member of God's Chosen People, in Bethlehem, the birthplace of King David. And His mother, named Mary, who while being a virgin will conceive and give birth to Him in Bethlehem will "call his name Imman'u-el," a Hebrew word which means "God is with us," and His name would be Jesus, which means "God saves," pointing to His Mission on Earth. Since Jesus, being both divine and human, is therefore God in the flesh, we can truly say that "God is with us."

### The Immaculate Conception

The Most Blessed Virgin Mary was preserved free from all stain of Original Sin (OS), even from the first instant of her presence in her mother's womb. God did this for her because she was to be the mother of Jesus Christ, the most singular privilege of grace.[97] God did this for her not only as a gift and reward – in advance – for her faithfulness and co-operation in the Redemption of mankind, but also to cleanse, purify, and sanctify the vessel into which the Son of God would enter in order to become human. Like Eve, Mary, the second Eve, was born without OS and never committed a sin (CCC 411). Mary is also the new Ark of the Covenant.

Although Christ could have come as an adult person already, or could have been conceived in a womb stained by Original Sin and then cleansed that Sin upon entering it, for He can do anything anywhere, God chose not to do it that way and preserved His Holy Mother from Original Sin since the very moment of her conception. It was the "clean," "just," and "right" thing to do. This reminds me of something St. Maximilian Kolbe once said about Mary; something our Protestant brothers and sisters should always remember: "Whoever does not wish to have Mary immaculate as his mother, will not have Christ as his brother."

### The Annunciation

"In the sixth month the angel Gabriel was sent from God to a city of Galilee named Nazareth, to a virgin betrothed to a man whose name was Joseph, of the house of David; and the virgin's name was Mary. And he came to her and said, 'Hail, full of grace, the Lord is with you!' But she was greatly troubled at the saying, and considered in her mind what sort of greeting this might be. And the angel said to her, 'Do not be afraid, Mary, for you have found favor with God. And behold, you will conceive in your womb and bear a son, and you shall call his name Jesus. He will be great, and will be called the Son of the Most High; and the Lord God will give to him the throne of his father David, and he will reign over the house of Jacob for ever; and of his kingdom there will be no end.'

"And Mary said to the angel, 'How can this be, since I have no husband?' And the angel said to her, 'The Holy Spirit will come upon you, and the power of the Most High will overshadow you; therefore the child to be born will be called holy, the Son of God. And behold, your kinswoman Elizabeth in her old age has also conceived a son; and this is the sixth month with her who was called barren. For with God nothing will be impossible.' And Mary said, 'Behold, I am the handmaid of the Lord; let it be to me according to your word.' And the angel departed from her" (Lk 1:26-38).

When I was a young boy, I remember my Jewish friends making fun of me at Christmas time. This kind of took me by surprise at first because I thought all Jewish people celebrated Christmas too. Since all the carols we sung seemed Jewish to me, O Little Town of Bethlehem, The First Noel, Away in a Manger, Silent Night, and the others, they were all about baby Jesus being born far away in a small Jewish village. So naturally, I believed all Jews also celebrated Christmas! When they made fun of me, and I realized they were serious, I said, "Don't you believe in your own religion?" And my friend said, "My dad says all of that was made up by the Catholics. It's a fairy tale! It's not true!" Sixty years later, I find myself writing a book about Jesus, the Heavenly Messiah. I sure wish I could find my Jewish friends now.

## The Nativity Of The Lord
## The Birth of Jesus - Savior Of Mankind

"In those days a decree went out from Caesar Augustus that all the world should be enrolled. This was the first enrollment, when Quirin'ius was governor of Syria. And all went to be enrolled, each to his own city. And Joseph also went up from Galilee, from the city of Nazareth, to Judea, to the city of David, which is called Bethlehem, because he was of the house and lineage of David, to be enrolled with Mary his betrothed, who was with child. And while they were there, the time came for her to be delivered. And she gave birth to her first-born son and wrapped him in swaddling cloths, and laid him in a manger, because there was no place for them in the inn" (Lk 2:1-7).

### The Shepherds and the Angels

"And in that region there were shepherds out in the field, keeping watch over their flock by night. And an angel of the Lord appeared to them, and the glory of the Lord shone around them, and they were filled with fear. And the angel said to them, 'Be not afraid; for behold, I bring you good news of a great joy which will come to all the people; for to you is born this day in the city of David a Savior, who is Christ the Lord. And this will be a sign for you: you will find a baby wrapped in swaddling cloths and lying in a manger.' And suddenly there was with the angel a multitude of the heavenly host praising God and saying, 'Glory to God in the highest, and on earth peace among men with whom he is pleased!' " (Lk 2:8-14).

"When the angels went away from them into heaven, the shepherds said to one another, 'Let us go over to Bethlehem and see this thing that has happened, which the Lord has made known to us.' And they went with haste, and found Mary and Joseph, and the baby lying in a manger. And when they saw it they made known the saying which had been told them concerning this child; and all who heard it wondered at what the shepherds told them. But Mary kept all these things, pondering them in her heart. And the shepherds returned, glorifying and praising God for all they had heard and seen, as it had been told them" (Lk 2:15-20).

The shepherd was a second class citizen in Jewish society, yet Jesus identified Himself as the Good Shepherd who "lays down his life for the sheep" (Jn 10:11). In the previous chapter, examples were given of "Earthly messiahs," mortal human beings like you and I, who attempted to liberate the Jews from foreign rule and domination. But the Messiah promised by God, and prophesied in the Hebrew Bible, was not supposed to be a powerful military leader from the line of King David, but quite the opposite! He was to be a humble, meek, gentle, and loving person from the Davidic Line with no political aspirations whatsoever, and also of most importance, the Son of God! Jesus is Prophet, King, and High Priest. Both divine and human: Son of God and Son of Mary, in one Person. According to Jewish law, a male could not enter the priesthood until he was thirty years old. According to the Gospel of Luke, Jesus was about thirty years old when He began "His work": His public ministry. [98]

As of this writing, in all modern denominations of Rabbinic Judaism (even ultra-Orthodox), there is no such person as a Messiah, past or awaited at present, who is both God and man in one person as is the case with Jesus the Christ. The Jews believed then, 2000 years ago, and still believe now, that God has never assumed—and will never assume—a human form, a human body; God would never "lower Himself" to that point. So to them, the belief that Jesus was both human and divine is in the same category as a fairy tale, just like my Jewish friends used to tell me long ago. [99]

As mentioned earlier, since the Jews did not, and still do not have a doctrine of Original Sin, there is no need for a Divine Messiah to come and redeem mankind from it. Therefore, the messiah they were waiting for, and many are still waiting for, is in fact an "Earthly messiah," a mighty military genius who will rescue and restore Israel to its former glory, free from bondage and calamities; and most important, an Israel that is safe, at peace, and is ruled by no one but the Jews. In short, a "heaven on Earth," so to speak, a New Israel, flowing with wealth, milk and honey. This resembles a materialistic and atheistic mindset! Supposedly, eighty-five (85) percent of

Jews in Israel today are atheists. If true, this is truly alarming! God's Chosen People who do not believe in God!

Unbeknownst to them however, the real Messiah, Jesus Christ, that was sent through them and to them, as well as to the whole world, was going to give the Jews, and to everyone else, something much, much better than heaven on Earth. He was coming to give every person who believes in Him unrestricted Entrance into the Real Heaven: a Heaven that had been closed shut by the Lock of Original Sin since the beginning of mankind, and Jesus was the one–the Only One–who possessed the Key to opening that Lock. But the Jews rejected both: Jesus and Heaven. They exchanged a Diamond for a cubic zirconia! Sad enough to say, the Pharisaic tenet of the Earthly messiah is what many Jews still believe to this day, still waiting for the Earthly messiah. And since things have not changed much in the world, since they are still pretty much the same to them, i.e., we still have wars, violence, corruption, hatred, unrest, and no peace in the world, especially for the Jews who were promised a messiah, Jesus was not accepted – and is still not accepted – as the promised Messiah by all who still practice Rabbinic Judaism.

Although peace, true peace, is no doubt a very important and good thing to have and enjoy, we must always remember what Christ said in this regard, "Do not think that I have come to bring peace on earth; I have not come to bring peace, but a sword. For I have come to set a man against his father, and a daughter against her mother, and a daughter-in-law against her mother-in-law; and a man's foes will be those of his own household. He who loves father or mother more than me is not worthy of me; and he who loves son or daughter more than me is not worthy of me; and he who does not take his cross and follow me is not worthy of me" (Mt 10:34-38). We must not misunderstand what Jesus means in this teaching. He is not saying He does not like peace, or He does not want us to live in peace with ourselves and with one another. He is only saying we must *choose* to believe in Him and then follow *only* Him and no one else if we want to go to Heaven after death and live with God for all Eternity. This involves making a "personal choice" to follow and obey only Christ, even if it means being in disagreement with family, with friends, or with whoever is against Him. It may require breaking relationships with these individuals if necessary, and even more challenging, losing our lives for faith in Christ. "He who finds his life will lose it, and he who loses his life for my sake will find it" (Mt 10:39). In short, he who rejects Christ in order to save his life, or his job, or his wealth, or anything else, including in order to be in agreement and good standing with his unbelieving family or others, will not be accepted in Heaven after death (will "lose" his life), but he who loses these things because of not rejecting Jesus, will "find" his life in Heaven as a reward for being **faithful**. "He who loves his life loses it, and he who hates his life in this world will keep it for eternal life" (Jn 12:25; see Phil 3:7-14). No greater honor has God bestowed on the human race than when He took a human nature to Himself, for all eternity, in the Person of Jesus Christ.

It is not surprising, of course, to find that all modern Jews, regardless of denomination, do not believe in the virgin birth of Christ or the Second Coming of Christ, both of which are sound Catholic doctrines based on absolute facts. Moreover, once their Earthly messiah comes, the Jews believe he will complete his mission in his first coming and therefore will not need a second one, something they say Jesus did not do which adds yet another reason for not believing in Him. And since they also do not believe in His Resurrection, they believe Jesus was a total failure because He was crucified and died on a Cross. This is Total Blindness of God's Plan (Mt 15:14). Now, the Jews would be right, of course, if Jesus had been a mortal human being like you and me, but since He was not, for He was – and still is – both God and man in one divine person, this is where this Jewish argument fails and crumbles into dust. Both Scripture and modern science provide plenty of evidence in defense of Christ's divinity, and in regards to the latter, results from incontrovertible analyses of Eucharistic miracles is opening the eyes of even hard core atheists.

One example (of many) is found in the book, "A Cardiologist Examines Jesus," by Dr. Franco Serafini. On pages 49-50 is a detailed account of a scientific analysis of a sample taken from a consecrated Catholic host (which are made from unleavened wheat flour) that had miraculously turned into living flesh in an Argentinian Roman Catholic church in 1996. One analysis of this miraculous host was performed on April 20, 2004 by "Prof. Frederick Zugibe, chief medical examiner and cardiologist in Rockland County in New York. His academic profile, made up of scientific discoveries and numerous publications, together with his thirty-year experience of ten thousand autopsies, is impressive at the very least" (p. 49)

Looking at the sample under a microscope, unaware of what it was (they did not tell him), Dr. Zugibe said: "I am a heart specialist. The heart is *my business.* This is heart muscle tissue, coming from the left ventricle, near a valvular area. This cardiac muscle is inflamed; it has lost its striations and is infiltrated by leukocytes." Since leukocytes can only exist in a living organism, the sample he was looking at was a "living" sample (it was already eight (8) years old!). When Dr. Zugibe was asked, "How long would these leukocytes survive for, if the tissue were set in water." This sample from the miraculous host had been kept in a vial filled with distilled water since 2001, for three years. "They would dissolve within a few minutes and no longer exist," was his reply. When he was finally told what the sample was and how it had been kept until then, Dr. Zugibe exclaimed: "Absolutely incredible! Inexplicable by science!" Unbeknownst to him, the piece of heart muscle he had examined belonged to God

Himself, Jesus the Christ. "Blessed are those who have not seen and yet believe" (Jn 20:29).

In the following pages, we will review some of the OT Messianic prophecies, including the ones most often quoted by scholars, that predicted the coming of a Heavenly Messiah who would come into the world to redeem the fallen human race, restore the broken relationship between God and man due to Adam and Eve's Original Sin, and open wide the Gates of Heaven to all the faithful who love God and want to live with Him in Heaven after death. We will also take a look at some of the OT passages that Jesus quoted, as recorded in Scripture, and explain why He quoted them.

## Old Testament Messianic Prophecies

(Partial List)

The very first reference to a Heavenly Messiah that is found in the OT is in the Book of Genesis. Here, after Eve told God that the snake had tricked her into sinning, God said to Satan, the snake: "I will put enmity between you and the woman, and between your seed and her seed; he shall bruise your head, and you shall bruise his heel" (Gn 3:15).

The "woman" referred to here is not Eve, but Mary, the mother of Jesus, who will be the "New Eve" so to speak. She will say "Yes" to following God's Will and will never disobey Him during her entire lifetime. And her offspring, "her seed," that will crush the head of Satan and defeat him, is the coming Messiah: Jesus the Christ: the son of Mary and the Son of the Living God; both human and Divine in One Person.

Some may ask, "If the Messiah will be the son of Mary, I can see why he will be called the son of man since she is human, but why call him the Son of the Living God?" [100]

There are passages in the Bible where the title "son of God" is given to Israel: the Chosen People, to their kings, and to the Messiah (CCC, 441). In regards to Israel, we find God telling Moses: "And you shall say to Pharaoh, 'Thus says the LORD, **Israel is my first-born son**, and I say to you, "Let my son go that he may serve me"; if you refuse to let him go, behold, I will slay your first-born son' " (Ex 4:22-23) [my emph.]. And in the case of the latter, Jesus the Messiah, after Jesus is baptized by John the Baptist, we find: "...and behold, a voice from heaven, saying, 'This is my beloved Son, with whom I am well pleased' " (Mt 3:17).

Israel is described as God's "first-born son" in this passage from Exodus because God chose them instead of any other tribe or peoples on Earth to: (1) Bring His only Son, Jesus, through them to redeem mankind; (2) Reveal Himself to them and thereby teach not only them, but the rest of the known world that there is only one true God, as opposed to the polytheism that was widely practiced then. The Israelites became God's Chosen People starting with Abraham and his descendants, and then even the more so with their Exodus from Egypt with Moses as their leader.[101] The Exodus from Egypt cemented them firmly as God's Chosen People. Here's another example regarding Israel where an angry Moses tells his people: "Do you thus repay the LORD, you foolish and senseless people? Is not he your father, who created you, who made you and established you?" (Dt 32:6). Although "son of God" is not used here, the word "father" makes them sons by association. Although there are other places in the OT where Israel is referred to as the son of God, there are other passages where a specific person is referred to as the Son of God.

One of the Four Major Prophets of the OT whose name in Hebrew "Yesa yahu" means "Yahweh is salvation," is Isaiah. Isaiah was born in Jerusalem between 765 and 740 B.C., about 300 years after the reigns of King David and his son,

King Solomon. The following verse from Isaiah states that the Messiah will come from the line of Jesse: "There shall come forth a shoot from the stump of Jesse, and a branch shall grow out of his roots. And the Spirit of the LORD shall rest upon him, the spirit of wisdom and understanding, the spirit of counsel and might, the spirit of knowledge and the fear of the LORD" (Is 11:1-2). Moreover, Isaiah wrote one of the most important and clue giving Messianic prophecies in the OT: "Therefore the Lord himself will give you a sign. Behold, a virgin shall conceive and bear a son, and shall call his name Imman'u-el" (Is 7:14).

The name "Immanuel" means "God is with us" and points to the incarnation of the Word of God. It is one of the most important prophecies in the Book of Isaiah and in the entire OT. Isaiah was sawn in two as ordered by his grandson, King Manasseh (see Jewish Encyclopedia, "Hezekiah," "Isaiah").

A startling prophecy from Zechariah, pointing to Christ's entry into Jerusalem, reveals the following: "Rejoice greatly, O daughter of Zion! Shout aloud, O daughter of Jerusalem! Behold, your king comes to you; triumphant and victorious is he, **humble and riding on a donkey**, **on a colt the foal of a donkey**" (Zec 9:9) [my emph.]. Another passage foretells that the Messiah will come from the tribe of Judah: "The scepter shall not depart from Judah, nor the ruler's staff from between his feet, until he comes to whom it belongs; and to him shall be the obedience of the peoples" (Gn 49:10). [102] King David was from the Tribe of Judah, and it was from his lineage that the Messiah, Jesus, would come from. Most surprising, David, Israel's greatest King, was born in Bethlehem of Judea, the little country town where Jesus was also born, the King of kings: "But you, O Bethlehem Eph'rathah, who are little to be among the clans of Judah, from you shall come forth for me one who is to be ruler in Israel, whose origin is from of old, from ancient days" (Micah 5:2). The name "Bethlehem" means "House of Bread," a stark indication that points to the Eucharist: Jesus, the "Bread of Life," who came down from Heaven.

In another passage, we find: "When you die and are buried with your ancestors, I will make one of your sons king and will keep his kingdom strong. He will be the one to build a temple for me, and I will make sure that his dynasty continues forever. I will be his father, and he will be my son. [...] I will put him in charge of my people and my kingdom forever. His dynasty will never end" (1 Chr 17:11-13, 14; NCSB).

In this passage, the Lord tells the prophet Nathan to tell David that one of his sons will be king, namely Solomon, and it will be he, not David, who will build a temple for the Lord. David had wanted to build a temple dedicated to the Lord to be the permanent resting place for the Ark of the Covenant which, among other holy things, contained the original tablets of the Ten Commandments given to Moses on Mt. Sinai after the Exodus from Egypt (c. mid-13th century B.C.). But David himself gives the reason why he was not to be the one to build the temple: "But God said to me, 'You may not build a house for my name, for you are a warrior and have shed blood' " (1 Chr 28:3). Solomon did in fact build a temple dedicated to the Lord on Mt. Moriah in Jerusalem, the capital city of Judah (2 Chr 3:1). Known as the First Jewish Temple, it was started in c. 964 B.C. and completed in c. 957 B.C.

But there's a reference in this passage that points to the Messiah: the passage that says "His dynasty will never end." Solomon's reign lasted 40 years and did not last forever. After he died (c. 926-922 B.C.) and his son Rehoboam became King, the ten northern tribes of Israel refused to submit to him and revolted resulting in the breakup of the United Monarchy into two kingdoms: Ten Tribes in the North, ruled by King Jeroboam (Israel), and Two Tribes in the South, ruled by King Rehoboam (Judah). So who's dynasty is the Lord referring to here that "will never end"?

The use of the word "dynasty" means a succession of rulers from the same family. King Solomon was the second ruler from the Davidic dynasty (David the first). The last King of the Davidic dynasty from the tribe of Judah was Zedekiah whose reign ended in 587 B.C. when Babylonian king Nebuchadnezzar II conquered and destroyed both Jerusalem (the "City of David") and its Temple and deported thousands of Jews to Babylonia where they eventually adopted Aramaic as their new language (Dn 1:4). Zedekiah was the last of the Davidic kings until the coming of Christ, the King of kings, whose "dynasty will never end."

Another reference to the Heavenly Messiah, a very unique one, is in Psalm 110:1, where we find David saying: "The Lord says to my lord: 'Sit at my right hand, till I make your enemies your footstool.' " The first Lord mentioned here must be a reference to either God the Father or God the Holy Spirit (since it is the Spirit Who spoke through the Prophets), and the second Lord mentioned is a reference to Jesus, the Lord of lords, a descendant of David and the Messiah. Jesus mentioned this specific passage from the OT to the Pharisees in order to question them about the Messiah:

"When some Pharisees gathered together, Jesus asked them, 'What do you think about the Messiah? Whose descendant is he?' 'He is David's descendant,' they answered. 'Why, then,' Jesus asked, 'did the Spirit inspire David to call him "Lord"? David said, "The Lord said to my Lord: sit here at my right side until I put your enemies under your feet." 'If, then, David called him "Lord," how can the Messiah be David's descendant?' No one was able to give Jesus any answer, and from that day on, no one dared to ask him any more questions" (Mt 22:41-46; NCSB).

Note that instead of asking the Sadducees or scribes this extremely important question, Jesus asked the Pharisees who *they* thought the Messiah was, and most likely because He knew the Pharisees did not know the correct interpretation of the Messianic prophecies and had been spreading the false "Earthly messiah" teaching to the people for a long time. And yet, Jesus chose a Pharisee, Saul (St. Paul), one of the worst of all the Pharisees, to spread the Gospel to the Gentiles! How fitting! A very profound Messianic prophecy is found in the Book of Ezekiel: "I will make a covenant of peace with them; it shall be an everlasting covenant with them; and I will bless them and multiply them, and will set my sanctuary in the midst of them for evermore" (Ez 37:26).

## Old Testament Passages Quoted By Christ
(Partial List)

Jesus often quoted passages from the OT during His public ministry in order to prove a point or recall a prophecy that was being fulfilled by Him. The following are some examples. The words of Christ appear first with the numbers for that NT passage followed by the OT numbers Jesus is quoting from or referring to. Explanations appear in [ ]:

"Then Jesus was led up by the Spirit into the wilderness to be tempted by the devil. And he fasted forty days and forty nights, and afterward he was hungry. And the tempter came and said to him, 'If you are the Son of God, command these stones to become loaves of bread.' But he answered, 'It is written, "Man shall not live by bread alone, but by every word that proceeds from the mouth of God' " (Mt 4:1-4) (Dt 8:3). "...and [the devil] said to him, 'If you are the Son of God, throw yourself down; for it is written, "He will give his angels charge of you," and "On their hands they will bear you up, lest you strike your foot against a stone." Jesus said to him, 'Again it is written, "You shall not tempt the Lord your God" (Mt 4:6-7) (Dt 6:16). "Then Jesus said to him, 'Begone, Satan! for it is written,' "You shall worship the Lord your God and him only shall you serve" (Mt 4:10) (Dt 6:12-15).

"You have heard that it was said, 'An eye for an eye and a tooth for a tooth.' But I say to you, do not resist one who is evil. But if any one strikes you on the right cheek, turn to him the other also" (Mt 5:38-39) (Lv 24:20).

"So whatever you wish that men would do to you, do so to them; for this is the law and the Prophets" (Mt 7:12) (Lv 19:18). [The Golden Rule.]

"Those who are well have no need of a physician, but those who are sick. Go and learn what this means, 'I desire mercy, and not [animal] sacrifice.' For I came not to call the righteous, but sinners" [i.e., all mankind] (Mt 9:12-13) (Hos 6:6; Ps 40:6-8).

"And Jesus answered them, 'Go and tell John [the Baptist] what you hear and see: the blind receive their sight and the lame walk, lepers are cleansed and the deaf hear, and the dead are raised up, and the poor have good news preached to them. And blessed is he who takes no offense at me' " (Mt 11:4-6) (Is 35:5-6; 61:1).

"He said to them, 'It is written, "My house [Temple] shall be called a house of prayer"; but you make it a den of robbers' " (Mt 21:13) (Is 56:7).

"And the high priest said to him, 'I adjure you by the living God, tell us if you are the Christ, the Son of God.' Jesus said to him, 'You have said so. But I tell you, hereafter you will see the Son of man seated at the right hand of Power, and coming on the clouds of heaven' " (Mt 26:63-64) (Dn 7:13-14).

"My God, my God, why have you forsaken me?" (Mt 27:46) (Ps 22).

* * *

Towards the end of His Public Ministry, Jesus told His Apostles numerous times that His time was drawing near. One of these is the following: "As they were gathering in Galilee, Jesus said to them, 'The Son of man is to be delivered into the hands of men, and they will kill him, and he will be raised on the third day.' And they were greatly distressed" (Mt 17:22-23). Some denominations of modern Rabbinic Judaism maintain that Isaiah's "Suffering Servant" in chapter 53 refers to the Israelites suffering as a nation and not to one specific person.[103] However, the Suffering Servant is both an individual (Jesus) and a people (the Jews), because Jesus, as King of the Jews, represents His people as well, but the title primarily refers to Jesus, who suffered and died for all mankind.

### Isaiah's Suffering Servant

"For he grew up before him like a young plant, and like a root out of dry ground; he had no form or comeliness that we should look at him, and no beauty that we should desire him. **He was despised and rejected by men; a man of sorrows, and acquainted with grief**; and as **one from whom men hide their faces** he was despised, and we esteemed him not. Surely he has **borne our griefs and carried our sorrows**; yet we esteemed him stricken, struck down by God, and afflicted. But **he was wounded for our transgressions**, he was bruised for our iniquities; upon him was the chastisement that made us whole, and **with his stripes we are healed**. All we like sheep have gone astray; we have turned every one to his own way; and **the LORD has laid on him the iniquity of us all**. He was oppressed, and he was afflicted, yet he opened not his mouth; **like a lamb that is led to the slaughter, and like a sheep that before its shearers is silent, so he opened not his mouth**.

"By oppression and judgment he was taken away; and as for his generation, who considered that he was cut off out of the land of the living, stricken for the transgression of my people? And they made his grave with the wicked and with a rich man in his death, although he had done no violence, and there was no deceit in his mouth. **Yet it was the will of the LORD to bruise him; he has put him to grief; when he makes himself an offering for sin**, he shall see his offspring, he shall prolong his days; the will of the LORD shall prosper in his hand; he shall see the fruit of the travail of his soul and be satisfied; by his knowledge shall the righteous one, my servant, make many to be accounted righteous; and he shall bear their iniquities. Therefore I will divide him a portion with the great, and he shall divide the spoil with the strong; because he poured out his soul to death, and was numbered with the transgressors; yet **he bore the sin of many, and made intercession for the transgressors**" (Is 53:2-12) [my emph.].

As is plain to see, this OT Messianic prophecy from Isaiah 53 describes Jesus in various descriptive and remarkable ways, and does so more than any other Messianic OT prophecy. A few examples are: despised and rejected by men (chief priests, Pharisees & the "crowd" before Pilate); a man of sorrows (His Passion); and acquainted with grief (death of Lazarus and others, wept for Jerusalem and the dead Prophets); one from whom men hide their faces (Pharisees, Sadducees, even Peter's denial); borne our griefs and carried our sorrows (to Calvary); he was wounded for our transgressions....with his stripes we are healed (His Passion and death led to our Redemption); the LORD has laid on him the iniquity of us all (died for our sins); like a lamb that is led to the slaughter, and like a sheep that before its shearers is silent, so he opened not his mouth (during His Passion and crucifixion); Yet it was the will of the LORD to bruise him; he has put him to grief; when he makes himself an offering for sin (His sacrifice redeemed the human race); yet he bore the sin of many, and made intercession for the transgressors (represented the human race in His sacrifice to redeem us).

Although a little difficult to see because the OT Messianic prophecies are not explicit and somewhat obscure, all of them proclaim, in one way or another, that the Messiah God promised to the Jews was going to be a Heavenly Messiah and not an Earthly messiah as the Pharisees and Essenes misinterpreted Him to be. Jesus, the promised Messiah, was and is "the Lion of the tribe of Judah, the Root of David." [104] He was going to be the actual Son of God, both divine and human, in one Person: the Son of God who became a man through the power of the Holy Spirit, possessing a Divine Nature, [105] and the Son of man through Mary, possessing a human nature. [106] Two natures in One Divine Person! (See chapter 6.) Son of man, Suffering Servant, and Son of God.

I sometimes wonder what thoughts went through the mind of young Jesus, who must have been between 2 and 3 years old (perhaps more), when He, Mary and Joseph returned from Egypt and saw the crucified people the Romans had placed next to the roads, lined up along the way. Maybe Mary shielded His young eyes from seeing such a terrible sight. But if He did see them, perhaps only for a split second, you would think His Divinity would have let Him know that He too would one day share that same fate for the benefit of mankind: a stark reminder of His Mission on Earth. Our poor, sweet, young Jesus. So young, so innocent, so pure, so Holy. I am so sorry you had to suffer so much for our sins; for my sins. May I never abandon you again.

I also wonder what it must have been like when Jesus told His mother and father about having to leave home and go out into the world on the Mission the Father had given Him, and as the time got closer and closer to this painful day, how their hearts grew heavy and sad at having to see Him go, all alone into the world; a sick world that had been waiting in agony for thousands and thousands of years for His Remedy. A Painful Remedy only He could give. Was the world going to appreciate it?

Do you think Jesus discussed His Mission with His parents, Mary and Joseph, especially on His 30th birthday? Did He tell them He was about to leave home to tell the world the Good News of His coming? And if so, how did they react? Did they understand, through God-given Grace, that the time to say goodbye was coming soon? That He would be gone for long periods of time, perhaps months? That soon He would not be around anymore to help Joseph with his work, with his needs, or mother with her work and needs? That the neighbors would wonder, and ask, "Where is Jesus? Where did he go?" And Mary might say something like, "He went to help some people in trouble," or something like that.

How would they handle the rumors that would reach their ears about their son barely escaping being stoned to death because He seriously offended the religious leaders in front of crowds? Calling them sons of the devil and hypocrites! Their son? The one they so lovingly raised and took such good care of for so long! The son whose tears they wiped and consoled when he fell and hurt himself. A son that was always very obedient, kind, and courteous to everyone? Would He really say such things to the Pharisees? When Jesus returned, did they ask Him about His Mission? Where has He been, and where is He going? How far did He have to go? Would He come back to visit and have supper with them again? How long would He be gone this time? And most important, When and how will the Mission end?

"Jesus, I know the time has come for you to go. Won't you stay just a little while longer?" "I can't, sweet Mother. I must go now. The time has come. It is here. I must drink the Cup my Father has prepared for me. This is why I came into the world. You know this too. Take care of dad, and don't you worry. You are a sweet and understanding Mother. I'll be back soon. You'll see. I love you both very much mom. I am with you always. Shalom."

## The Plot to Kill Lazarus

As Jesus was getting ready to enter Jerusalem for the last time to face the Holy yet terrible Death instigated by the Jewish authorities and destined for the Redemption of mankind, another sinister death was also being plotted by these sons of the devil: "When the great crowd of the Jews learned that he was there, they came, not only on account of Jesus but also to see Laz'arus, whom he had raised from the dead. So the **chief priests** planned to put Laz'arus also to death, because on account of him many of the Jews were going away and believing in Jesus" (Jn 12:9-11).

## Entry Into Jerusalem

King David entered Jebus (Jerusalem/Zion) around 1058 B.C., defeated the Jebusites who controlled it, and moved his entire family from Hebron to Jebus where he remained as King of the Twelve Tribes of Israel until his death in 970 B.C. David changed the name of the city from Jebus to City of David after conquering it, a name that was used by the Jews for many generations. The name Jerusalem, which came into common use after David's reign, comes from the ancient name Yeru'shalem: Yeru meaning "to establish" and shalem being the name of the dusk god of the ancient Canaanites. According to one of the Dead Sea Scrolls, Jerusalem was once Salem, and in Genesis 14:18, Abram was blessed by Melchizedek, king of Salem; Josephus states that Salem was later changed to Jerusalem ("Ant." Bk. 1, Ch. 10:2).

In a somewhat parallel move, Jesus entered Jerusalem in 33 A.D. at the end of His public ministry also with a conquest on His mind, but this conquest would not be a military one with soldiers, swords, clubs, and other weapons. Although the Jews had been waiting a very long time for an Earthly messiah to restore Jerusalem to the glory it once enjoyed under King David and his son, King Solomon, Jesus had made it quite clear–for quite some time–that He was not the messiah they had been waiting for. And He emphasized this point even the more so by entering Jerusalem riding on a donkey (Zec 9:9) instead of on a big war horse. Although perhaps most of the people assembled got the picture, for they shouted: "Hosanna! Blessed is he who comes in the name of the Lord, even the King of Israel!" (Jn 12:13), it is this last part, "King of Israel" that throws a red flag into the picture here, for the King of Israel was precisely the type of individual who fits the description of the Earthly messiah they had been waiting for. It is therefore possible that some (if not many) participants in the crowd erroneously believed that Jesus was indeed their long-awaited messiah in spite of the fact that nothing He ever did was political in nature.

The conquest Jesus had in mind was not to overthrow the Romans, but to overthrow the evil empire Satan had established in the world since the beginning of the human race: free us from our slavery to sin, restore the broken relationship between God and man, and open wide the Gates of Heaven for those who love God. Here, in Jerusalem, Jesus would bring His Paschal Mystery and Earthly Mission of Love to sure completion as the Heavenly Messiah sent by God the Father [107] and foretold by the OT Prophets:

"Now is my soul troubled. And what shall I say? Father, save me from this hour? No, for this purpose I have come to this hour. Father, glorify your name. Then a voice came from heaven, 'I have glorified it, and I will glorify it again.' The crowd standing by heard it and said that it had thundered. Others said, 'An angel has spoken to him.' Jesus answered, 'This voice has come for your sake, not for mine. Now is the judgment of this world, now shall the ruler of this world be cast out; and I, when I am lifted up from the earth, will draw all men to myself.' He said this to show by what death he was to die" (Jn 12:27-33).

The Passover Seder meal includes 4 cups of wine: the first one is to "sanctify" the meal; the second is "for the preacher" present at the meal; the third cup, drank *after* the meal, accompanies the After the Meal blessing and represents Redemption (from slavery in Egypt); and the fourth cup is for "Hallel," representing Salvation and **Restoration** to God.

## The Last Supper

According to Matthew:

"Now as they were eating, Jesus took bread, and blessed, and broke it, and gave it to the disciples and said, 'Take, eat; this is my body.' And he took a chalice, and when he had given thanks he gave it to them, saying, 'Drink of it, all of you; for this is my blood of the covenant, which is poured out for many for the forgiveness of sins' " (Mt 26:26-28).

According to Luke:

"And he took bread, and when he had given thanks he broke it and gave it to them, saying, 'This is my body which is given for you. Do this in remembrance of me.' And likewise the chalice after supper, saying, 'This chalice which is poured out for you is the new covenant in my blood' " (Lk 22:19-20). And so they ate, drank, and sang a [Hallel] hymn. [108]

When Jesus celebrated His last Passover meal (the Last Supper) with His twelve Apostles on Thursday, April 2nd, 33 A.D., He was preparing Himself for His Crucifixion and Death that would take place the following day: a Sacrifice that would bring those who love God from Earth to Heaven after death; a "journey" that all mankind had been prohibited from taking due to the Original Sin committed by our first parents in the Garden of Eden, that Original Heaven on Earth Paradise. The Passover meal they ate and shared included a Special Supplement that made this particular Meal Complete:

the body and blood of Christ Himself. Jesus became the sacrificial Passover Lamb, the "Lamb of God who takes away the **sin** of the world" (Jn 1:29; see Rv 5:6-10) [my emph.].

Notice the singular word "sin" in reference to the one Original Sin Christ's Sacrifice atones for. While it is true that His Sacrifice is "for the forgiveness of sins," which includes all the sins ever committed – and will ever be committed – by the human race, it is specifically to atone for the one Original Sin committed by Adam and Eve which resulted in the broken relationship between man and God and closed the Gates of Heaven to everyone. [109] Jesus willfully laid down His life for the Redemption of the entire human race; the perfect Passover sacrificial Lamb that atoned for the One sin that brought sickness, suffering, and death to the whole human race.

At this very Special Meal, one that Jesus had waited a long time to share with His close friends: "I have earnestly desired to eat this Passover with you **before I suffer**" (Lk 22:15) [my emph.], Jesus instituted the Holy Eucharist by consecrating and changing the bread into His body (the Flesh of the Lamb), and the "third" Passover chalice of wine, representing Redemption, into His blood (the Blood of the Lamb), and gave these to His Apostles for their spiritual nourishment. Just prior to this, Jesus fed a multitude of Five Thousand with only five loaves of bread and two fish, after which: "Jesus said to them, 'Truly, truly, I say to you, unless you eat the flesh of the Son of man and drink his blood, you have no life in you; he who eats my flesh and drinks my blood has eternal life, and I will raise him up at the last day. For my flesh is food indeed, and my blood is drink indeed. He who eats my flesh and drinks my blood abides in me, and I in him. As the living Father sent me, and I live because of the Father, so he who eats me will live because of me' " (Jn 6:53-57).

In the Old Covenant with Abram, God promised Abram that the land of Canaan would belong to his descendants forever, that Abram would be the ancestor and father of many nations, that He would give Abram through Sarai a son, Isaac, to inherit his property, and that He would be his God and the God of his descendants. Since all of this had already come to pass and God had kept His part of the Covenant, the Old Covenant with Abraham had therefore already been fulfilled. Here, God, in the Person of Jesus Christ, established a New and Eternal Covenant with the entire human race, not just with the Jews, and sealed it with His own blood; not the blood of an innocent animal, but the Blood of an innocent Man – and God – in one Person (see Heb 9:11-22).

Christ's Sacrifice on the Cross is "the restoration of the broken relationship between God and man," broken by Adam and Eve in the Garden of Eden thousands of years earlier. The "Apology" to God for their transgression can now be accepted by God the Father through and from Jesus: both man and God in One Person. And just as the Jews were told by Moses (who was told by God) to celebrate Passover every year without fail, so too did Jesus tell His Apostles at the Last Supper, "This is my body which is given for you. Do this in remembrance of me" (Lk 22:19).[110] And not just once a year, but quite often! Especially on "Resurrection Days," on Sundays.

This is what we Catholics celebrate at every Mass: a Eucharistic meal celebrated every day at Masses throughout the world in obedience to Christ's words of exhortation: "Truly, truly, I say to you, unless you eat the flesh of the Son of man and drink his blood, you have no life in you" (Jn 6:53), which is tied with His words of Consecration at the Last Supper, "And he took bread, and when he had given thanks he broke it and gave it to them, saying, 'This is my body which is given for you' " (Lk 22:19). It does not get any clearer than that. If anyone has any doubts that the Eucharist in Catholic Masses is the actual body, blood, soul, and divinity of Christ, read the above passages until it becomes clear (a note to our Protestant brothers and sisters, and all other unbelievers). Then, read the scientific evidence for it. [111]

Jesus chose this specific Passover, Friday, April 3rd, 33 A.D., to offer Himself as a sacrifice for us over the other Passovers celebrated during His public ministry because this one fell on the Sabbath (a "high day", Jn 19:31 ), the seventh day of rest; the day He would "rest" in the grave. Therefore, the Passover and the Sabbath are here, at the Last Supper, combined and fused by Christ into One Eternal Event for all time; an event that will become known as the Roman Catholic Mass: the unbloody re-presentation of Christ's Holy Sacrifice on the Cross when He died for all mankind as the "Lamb of God" and then rested in the grave. Two massive events now made One by God Himself. The partaking of the Lamb of God in the Holy Eucharist at Mass, which mirrors eating the lamb at Passover, is when Christ lives in us and we in Him. Jesus created a "New" Sabbath and a "New" Passover, both made one, under a New Eternal Covenant (restored relationship) with God, and all sinners are made New (the "new man") by following Him: "Behold, I make all things new" (Rv 21:5).

## The Garden Of Gethsemani

After the Last Supper, when they reached the Garden of Gethsemani at the foot of the Mount of Olives, Jesus distanced Himself from the Apostles, "And going a little farther he fell on his face and prayed, 'My Father, if it be possible, let this chalice pass from me; nevertheless, not as I will, but as you will.' [...] And being in an agony he prayed more earnestly; and his sweat became like great drops of blood falling down upon the ground" (Mt 26:39; Lk 22:44). The chalice Jesus is asking the Father to take away is the "fourth" Passover Chalice, representing Consummation and "Restoration": the shedding of blood and death, the very

Mission that He, as the Second Person of the Holy Trinity, had willingly agreed to undertake for the eternal benefit of mankind – even before the creation of the universe: the very Mission of the Heavenly Messiah. But if Jesus is truly God, and He is, why is He asking the Father to remove this cup of suffering from Him? He cast out countless demons, calmed violent storm winds, and stood up to many death threats leveled at Him by His enemies, to name only a few; so why would he be afraid now? Is He changing His mind about going through with the last part of His Mission as Heavenly Messiah, the most important part?

The answer is both yes and no! Jesus has two natures: a human nature and a divine nature, and it was His human nature that pleaded with the Father in Heaven to take away the chalice of suffering and death if it was possible.[112] The logic here is: (1) His divine nature would not feel pain and therefore had nothing to fear; and (2) His divine nature would not abandon such an important Mission. But after seeing a vision of the terrible suffering He was going to go through, His human nature instinctively recoiled and wanted to avoid it, so He pleaded with the Father to save Him from it, which of course, is completely understandable from a human point of view. Yet, the person doing the pleading was both man and God in one Person, not just human. It's as if the divine nature of Christ: the second Person of the Blessed Trinity, cloaked Himself and allowed His human nature to endure the coming Passion and crucifixion without interfering in any way. This is quite mysterious. When Jesus cried out from the Cross: "My God, my God, why have you forsaken me?" (Mk 15:34), perhaps He was echoing the feelings Adam had after he was banned from the Garden of Eden.

"The Passion is described as the mystery of Christ's suffering. It was a mystery at the time because people could not reconcile it with what they had expected. In the sense that we can never fully understand the idea of God suffering, the

Passion is still a mystery. Now if our sufferings are somehow or other to fit into the Passion of Christ—and this is no fiction because this is where they belong—there will surely be an element of mystery about them. They will make demands on our faith." (Fr. Hubert van Zeller, OSB).

### The Arrest, Trial, And Condemnation[113]

"So Judas, procuring a band of soldiers and some officers from the **chief priests and the Pharisees**, went there with lanterns and torches and weapons. Then Jesus, knowing all that was to befall him, came forward and said to them, Whom do you seek? They answered him, Jesus of Nazareth. Jesus said to them, I am he. Judas, who betrayed him, was standing with them. When he said to them, I am he, they drew back and fell to the ground. Again he asked them, Whom do you seek? And they said, Jesus of Nazareth. Jesus answered, I told you that I am he; so, if you seek me, let these men go. This was to fulfil the word which he had spoken, Of those whom you gave me I lost not one. Then Simon Peter, having a sword, drew it and struck the high priest's slave and cut off his right ear. The slave's name was Malchus. Jesus said to Peter, Put your sword into its sheath; shall I not drink the chalice which the Father has given me? So the band of soldiers and their captain and the officers of the Jews seized Jesus and bound him. First they led him to Annas; for he was the father-in-law of Cai'aphas, who was high priest that year. It was Cai'aphas who had given counsel to the Jews that it was expedient that one man should die for the people" (Jn 18:3-14). Unbeknownst to Cai'aphas, Jesus was no ordinary man, and moreover, was not going to die for just the Jewish people, but for all mankind – at the instigation of the Jews.

Jesus was then brought to Cai'aphas, High Priest of the Sanhedrin, for a trial that had already been arranged for Him for quite some time. Some who were present there accused Him of many things, but none of these were serious enough to condemn Him. What is Jesus, the Lamb of God "without blemish," guilty of anyway? Telling the truth? Guilty! Curing the sick? Guilty! Raising the dead? Guilty! Expelling demons? Guilty! Exposing their hypocrisy? Guilty! Guilty! Guilty!!!

Nevertheless, Scripture says: "At last two came forward and said, 'This fellow said, "I am able to destroy the temple of God, and to build it in three days." ' And the high priest stood up and said, 'Have you no answer to make? What is it that these men testify against you?' But Jesus was silent. And the high priest said to him, 'I adjure you by the living God, tell us if you are the Christ, **the Son of God**.' Jesus said to him, 'You have said so. But I tell you, hereafter you will see the Son of man seated at the right hand of Power, and coming on the clouds of heaven.' Then the high priest tore his robes, and said, 'He has uttered blasphemy. Why do we still need witnesses? You have now heard his blasphemy. What is your judgment?' They answered, 'He deserves death.' Then they spat in his face, and struck him; and some slapped him, saying, 'Prophesy to us, you Christ! Who is it that struck you?' " (Mt 26:60-68) [my emph.]. Since the Jews were completely ignorant of the existence of the Trinity, asking Jesus if He was the "Son of God" is very odd and perhaps reveals that Cai'aphas was familiar with that Essenic term (it appears among the Essenic Dead Sea Scrolls, 4Q246 1:9).

Jesus was then taken by these "experts in religion" to Pontius Pilate, Roman governor of Judea, to be put to death because the Jews did not possess the authority to put anyone to death. This "authority" was only possessed by the Romans. But after questioning Him, Pilate found nothing to condemn Him for, so he asked the crowd that had gathered, "Then what shall I do with Jesus who is called Christ? They all said, 'Let him be crucified.' And he said, 'Why, what evil has he done?' But they shouted all the more, 'Let him be crucified.' So when Pilate saw that he was gaining nothing, but rather that a riot was beginning, he took water and washed his hands before the crowd, saying, 'I am innocent of this **righteous man's** blood; see to it yourselves.' And all the people answered, 'His blood be on us and on our children!' [see Ex 24:8.] Then he released for them Barab'bas, and having scourged Jesus, delivered him to be crucified" (Mt 27:22-26) [my emph.]. Once again we see here, in Pilate's own words, that Jesus was not considered an enemy of Rome ("righteous man").

### Crucifixion And Death

According to John:

"So they took Jesus, and he went out, bearing his own cross, to the place called the place of a skull, which is called in Hebrew Gol'gotha. There they crucified him, and with him two others, one on either side, and Jesus between them. Pilate also wrote a title and put it on the cross; it read, Jesus of Nazareth, the King of the Jews. Many of the Jews read this title, for the place where Jesus was crucified was near the city; and it was written in Hebrew, in Latin, and in Greek. The chief priests of the Jews then said to Pilate, Do not write, The King of the Jews, but, This man said, I am King of the Jews. Pilate answered, What I have written I have written.

"When the soldiers had crucified Jesus they took his garments and made four parts, one for each soldier; also his tunic. But the tunic was without seam, woven from top to bottom; so they said to one another, Let us not tear it, but cast lots for it to see whose it shall be. This was to fulfil the Scripture, They parted my garments among them, and for my clothing they cast lots. So the soldiers did this. But standing by the cross of Jesus were his mother, and his mother's sister, Mary the wife of Clopas, and Mary Mag'dalene. When Jesus saw his mother, and the disciple whom he loved standing near, he said to his mother, Woman, behold, your son! Then he said to the disciple, Behold, your mother! And from that hour the disciple took her to his own home.

"After this, Jesus, knowing that all was now finished, said (to fulfill the Scripture), I thirst. A bowl full of vinegar stood there; so they put a sponge full of the vinegar on hyssop and held it to his mouth. When Jesus had received the vinegar, he said, It is finished; and he bowed his head and gave up his spirit. Since it was the day of Preparation, in order to prevent the bodies from remaining on the cross on the sabbath (for that sabbath was a high day), the Jews asked Pilate that their legs might be broken, and that they might be taken away. So the soldiers came and broke the legs of the first, and of the other who had been crucified with him; but when they came to Jesus and saw that he was already dead, they did not break his legs. But one of the soldiers pierced his side with a spear, and at once there came out blood and water. He who saw it has borne witness–his testimony is true, and he knows that he tells the truth–that you also may believe. For these things took place that the Scripture might be fulfilled, Not a bone of him shall be broken. And again another Scripture says, They shall look on him whom they have pieced" (Jn 19:17-37).

When Jesus drank the vinegar (sour wine) just before He died, that was the "fourth" Passover Chalice He had asked His Father to take away: the consummation of the Passover: "It is finished." [114] As Christ's nailed body was being raised on His Cross by the Roman soldiers on Calvary (**Mt. Moriah**), the lambs for the Jewish Passover Feast were being slaughtered in the Temple not far away; a slaughter that ended at 3:00pm, the same time Jesus died. Moses had repeatedly asked God to forgive the sinful Israelites after the Exodus, and so did Jesus ask the Father from the Cross, "Father, forgive them; for they know not what they do" (Lk 23:34); they did not know they had crucified God incarnate (see Acts 3:17).

There are sections of David's Psalm 22 that describe in great detail our crucified Lord:

"My God, my God, why have you forsaken me? [...] All who see me mock at me, they make mouths at me, they wag their heads; [they say] 'He committed his cause to the LORD; let him deliver him, let him rescue him, for he delights in him!' [...] Yes, dogs are round about me; a company of evildoers encircle me; they have pierced my hands and feet—I can count all my bones—they stare and gloat over me; they divide my garments among them, and for my clothing they cast lots" (Ps 22:1, 7-8, 16-18). A remarkable account of what took place that fateful day.

It was Jesus Christ's sacrificial death that redeemed the entire human race over 2000 years ago. If Christ had not died for mankind, the whole human race would have ended up in Hell for all Eternity with no one going to Heaven. Not one single person! Let us make sure to give thanks to our Lord Jesus Christ, every single day, for what He has done and suffered for all of us.

"It is suffering, more than anything else, which clears the way for the grace which transforms human souls. Suffering, more than anything else, makes present in the history of humanity the powers of the Redemption." — Pope St. John Paul II

## Satan's Surprising Role In Redemption

(An Imaginative Rendition)

In an unexpected and complicated twist that not even the devil with his superior intelligence was able to foresee,[115] the tables on Satan and his evil Plans were overturned in a very surprising and Masterful way on April 3rd, 33 A.D. For three long years during Christ's public ministry, the devil had witnessed countless miracles performed by Jesus, heard many of His lofty sermons and parables that captivated large crowds, and, with much hatred, saw Jesus casting out legions of demons liberating the oppressed. This was not sitting too well with this evil monster. In fact, all of this had become extremely irritating to him; a thorn in his side, you might say. The devil did not know what to do to solve this "Jesus problem."

Then one day, toward the end of Christ's ministry, he saw a way to get rid of Jesus once and for all. The devil noticed that the Pharisees had reached a boiling point where their desire to kill Jesus had become enormous because He kept humiliating them in front of others thus undermining their authority and making them look very bad. As mentioned earlier, the Sadducees had plotted to kill Lazarus too after Jesus resurrected him from the dead "because on account of him many of the Jews were going away and believing in Jesus" (Jn 12:9-11). Grasping this evil intent the Pharisees and Sadducees had with all his might, he saw an opportunity to get rid of Christ once and for all by helping them with their plans to kill Jesus (see Jn 11:45-53; Mt 26:1-5; Lk 22:1-2).

Using his superior deductive reasoning, it didn't take Satan too long to put 2 and 2 together: Judas Iscariot was the perfect link between Jesus and the bloodthirsty Pharisees and Sadducees. The devil knew Judas liked money very much for he had seen him stealing money many times from the money box entrusted to his care that contained the donations people had given to Jesus and the Apostles (Jn 12:6; 13:29), so he played on his greed and put the idea into his head to visit the Pharisees and make a deal with them (see Lk 22:3): he would hand Jesus over to them, and in return, they would pay him for this "favor." And sure enough! Judas, the Pharisees and the Sadducees fell for his evil plan: hook, line, and sinker!

What Judas did not know, however, was that the Pharisees were going to have Jesus put to death, but that didn't bother Satan one bit; in fact, that is exactly what he wanted them to do! The devil had had enough of Jesus interfering with his "work," and this time he was going to get rid of Him for good. Little did Satan know however, his "plan" was actually going to *help* Jesus.

As Jesus struggled to raise Himself on the Cross in order to exhale and breathe, I can imagine the crooked smile that must have been on Satan's face watching Jesus dying on the Cross. The onlooking legions of demons that must have accompanied Satan, perhaps surrounding the Cross and laughing, mocking, and insulting the Savior in concert with the Pharisees and Sadducees – who were also doing the same, must have been a disgusting sight to see. This horrible scene of our sweet Lord, disfigured, gasping for breath, in total agony, and slowly dying on His Cross, was precisely what Satan had hoped to see; and here it was! The moment Christ breathed His last, I can imagine the devil's boastful and arrogant roars of laughter, making the demons tremble and reverberating throughout the deepest bowels of Hell. Victory, yes! was his at last!

I can't help but imagine what might have happened next. There's thunder, lightning, rain begins to fall. A loud noise, like a trumpet, cuts through the air. Satan turns to see, and there's Christ, right in front of his face. "Satan!" shouts Christ, with the force of a hurricane, causing a tremendous earthquake; the dead saints come out of their graves and the boulders split in two. The coiled Serpent and his shriveling demons are blown backwards and fall to the ground in complete horror. Then, I imagine Jesus saying, "Behold, Satan! I make all things new!"

Satan turns and watches with horror as millions of righteous souls are being ushered from Limbo into Heaven by "the woman," Mary, the Blessed Mother. She's leading all of them to the Heavenly Kingdom of the Father, aided by legions and legions of powerful beautiful angels. "No!" Satan says with utter disgust. "This can't be! Those are mine…."

The devil now remembers that day, long, long ago, when God had said to him in front of our first parents, "I will put enmity between you and the woman, and between your seed and her seed; he shall bruise your head, and you shall bruise his heel" (Gn 3:15). Satan thought, "So that's what that meant!" realizing that Christ's death turned out to be quite the opposite of what he wanted; what he was expecting. Instead of dying and going to the grave for good, Jesus had turned the tables on him and was rescuing all the souls that he was planning to add to his "collection" in Hell. And right then, I imagine Christ raising His mighty arm, and as a bolt of lightning flashes from the east to the west across the night sky, Satan and his demons were cast to the Bottomless Pit where they belonged… For a time.

## Why Jesus Was Crucified On Passover

From its very beginning, the entire OT is an account of the preparation for the coming of our Lord Jesus Christ, the only Son of God, eternally begotten of the Father, the Messiah. His coming into the world is an event that would be documented in the New Testament (NT) for all Eternity, and an event that had been awaited by all Creation since the beginning of time. The coming of Christ into this world, which God had planned and prepared to take place through His Chosen People, the Israelite Jews, is marked by both tremendous tragedies and glorious triumphs. Around the middle of the 13th century B.C., after living in Egypt for about 430 years (Ex 12:40), God chose Moses to deliver the Israelites from the cruel dictatorship of the Egyptian Pharaoh and lead them into a wonderful and beautiful life in the land of Canaan, the "land flowing with milk and honey" (Ex 3:8), what one may call a "Heaven on Earth."

I should add here that the Exodus of the Israelites from Egypt into the promised land of Canaan was God's way of bringing His people to worship Him instead of the Egyptian idols thus giving birth to Judaism: the only true religion at that time in Earth's history. This cemented them as His Chosen People. The Exodus is also a parallel account of the story of mankind itself: Moses led the Israelites out of bondage from Egypt into a "Heaven on Earth" lifestyle in Canaan, and Jesus leads mankind out of bondage to Satan and sin in this world and into a life of Eternal Bliss and Happiness in Heaven after death. So, In order to get Pharaoh to release the Jews and let them go free with Moses, something Pharaoh did not want to do at first since the Jews formed a very large part of his work force, God sent nine plagues to change his mind, and when that didn't work, he sent a tenth and final plague: "I will go forth in the midst of Egypt; and all the first-born in the land of Egypt shall die, from the first-born of Pharaoh who sits upon his throne, even to the first-born of the maidservant who is behind the mill; and all the first-born of the cattle. And there shall be a great cry throughout all the land of Egypt, such as there has never been, nor ever shall be again" (Ex 11:4-6). In order to preserve the Jews from this terrible calamity, God instructed Moses to tell the people:

"Tell all the congregation of Israel that on the tenth day of this month they shall take every man a lamb according to their fathers' houses [. . .] Your lamb shall be without blemish, a male a year old; [. . .] the whole assembly of the congregation of Israel shall kill their lambs in the evening [. . .] and you shall not break a bone of it [. . .] Then they shall take some of the blood, and put it on the two doorposts and the lintel of the houses in which they eat them [. . .] They shall eat the flesh that night, roasted [. . .] And you shall let none of it remain until the morning [. . .] In this manner you shall eat it: your loins girded, your sandals on your feet, and your staff in your hand; and you shall eat it in haste. It is the LORD's Passover [. . .] For I will pass through the land of Egypt that night, and I will strike all the first-born in the land of Egypt, both man and beast [. . .] The blood shall be a sign for you, upon the houses where you are; and when I see the blood, I will pass over you, and no plague shall fall upon you to destroy you, when I strike the land of Egypt. This day shall be for you a memorial day, and you shall keep it as a feast to the LORD; throughout your generations you shall observe it as an ordinance for ever" (Ex 12:3, 5, 6, 7, 8, 10, 11-12, 13-14, 46).

This Passover Feast, which was repeated once a year without fail from the time of the Exodus from Egypt up to the time that Jesus was arrested, tortured, and crucified on April 3RD, 33 A.D., [116] this Feast was an annual preparation for–and a "preview" of–the day when the Son of Man, the Messiah, the "Lamb of God," would be sacrificed by crucifixion for the Redemption of mankind. So, for 1,300 years or so, the Jews celebrated this mandatory annual Festival/Holiday to remind them that they were saved by Moses from the throes of Egyptian domination and escorted to the "land of milk and honey," the Heaven on Earth that God had promised them for being His "Chosen people." I say mandatory because this Holiday/Festival was so sacred and important to the Jewish people, since it was instituted by God Himself, that anyone caught not celebrating it was expelled from the faith and the community (Nm 9:13). The Sacrifice of Christ, the "Passover Lamb of God," secured for mankind a "Passover" from condemned crawling creatures to upright adopted children of God; from defacement by Satan to the restored image of God; from spiritual darkness to the Light of Truth in Christ; and from Eternal Death in Hell to Everlasting Life in Heaven for all who believe in Him and "obey Him" (see Heb 5:9).

Notice in the above passage that God tells Moses, "Your lamb shall be without blemish" (Ex 12:5), i.e., without any deformities, imperfections, or defects of any kind, and Jesus, the "Lamb of God," since He is God, was sinless and therefore "without blemish." In support of this, when Jesus was arrested and taken to Cai'aphas, High priest of the

Sanhedrin, for His trial, He was found "without blemish": "Now the **chief priests** and the whole council sought false testimony against Jesus that they might put him to death, but they found none, though many false witnesses came forward" (Mt 26:59-60).

Another parallel is the two doorposts and lintels of the houses in Egypt painted with the blood of the lamb. Since a door is the entryway to the inside of a house, this is a presage to Christ crucified who is "painted" with blood on the Cross and is "The Way" through whom one must pass to enter into the Father's House in Heaven (Salvation) after death: "I am the way, and the truth, and the life; no one comes to the Father, but by me" (Jn 14:6). Moreover, the angel of eternal death in Hell (the Second Death) will "Passover" the followers of Christ when he sees that their garments have been cleansed in the blood of the Lamb (see Ez 9:1-11).

Another parallel is the consumption of the sacrificial lamb "without blemish" and the consumption of the Holy flesh of Christ, the "Lamb of God," in the Eucharistic bread at the Last Supper and thereafter at all Catholic Masses throughout the world. Another example, the Passover meal was to be eaten fully dressed with shoes on and staff in hand, ready to go. Likewise, we are pilgrims in this life, in this valley of tears, and must be ready – at all times – to leave it in order to live with God in Heaven after our Exodus from Earth to His Kingdom.

Abraham had taken Isaac, his only beloved son, to this very same place, Mt. Moriah/Calvary, a thousand years before the Crucifixion of Christ, to sacrifice him as God had commanded him to do. Young Isaac, who like Christ, carried his wood for his sacrifice, whose name means "he who laughs," whose father had told him not to worry because "God will provide himself the lamb" (Gn 22:8), was spared from a terrible death by a Loving and Merciful God. And sure enough, a thousand years later, God did in fact provide the "Lamb": Jesus, the "Lamb of God," the only beloved Son of God, with whom the Father is well pleased, who was not spared from death by the Father because His Holy Mission required it: to redeem the entire human race, who was brutally sacrificed for the Redemption of Mankind at the very same place called, "The Lord Will Provide," and then rose Gloriously from the tomb, it is now He, Jesus, the Heavenly Messiah, who is doing the laughing.... right in Satan's face!

"For, Him whom the devil had known as a man, wearied by His forty days' fast, without being able by tempting Him to prove whether He was the Son of God, he now by the power of His miracles understood or rather suspected [Him] to be the Son of God. The reason therefore why he persuaded the Jews to crucify Him, was not because he did not think that He was the Son of God, but because he did not foresee that he himself was to be condemned by Christ's death." (Catena Aurea, Vol II, St. Mark, p. 30. Bede.)

And so, infuriated by the thought that he had assisted Christ in the Redemption of man by tempting Judas and fanning the fires of hatred in the hearts of the Pharisees, the Sadducees, and the scribes, Satan pledged, from that time forward, an all-out war on all mankind, especially on the followers of Christ; a war he would never win. (In any war with God, it is best to surrender!)

## The Resurrection

According To St. Matthew:

"Now after the sabbath, toward the dawn of the first day of the week, Mary Mag'dalene and the other Mary went to see the tomb. And behold, there was a great earthquake; for an angel of the Lord descended from heaven and came and rolled back the stone, and sat upon it. His appearance was like lightning, and his clothing white as snow. And for fear of him the guards trembled and became like dead men. But the angel said to the women, 'Do not be afraid; for I know that you seek Jesus who was crucified. He is not here; for he has risen, as he said. Come, see the place where he lay. Then go quickly and tell his disciples that he has risen from the dead, and behold, he is going before you to Galilee; there you will see him. Behold, I have told you'.... While they were going, behold, some of the guard went into the city and told the chief priests all that had taken place.

"And when they had assembled with the elders and taken counsel, they gave a sum of money to the soldiers and said, 'Tell people, 'His disciples came by night and stole him away while we were asleep.' And if this comes to the governor's ears, we will satisfy him and keep you out of trouble.' So they took the money and did as they were directed; and this story has been spread among the Jews to this day" (Mt 28:1-7; 11-15).

According To St. John:

"Now on the first day of the week, Mary Mag'dalene came to the tomb early, while it was still dark, and saw that the stone had been taken away from the tomb. So she ran, and went to Simon Peter and the other disciple, the one whom Jesus loved, and said to them, They have taken the Lord out of the tomb, and we do not know where they have laid him.

"Peter then came out with the other disciple, and they went toward the tomb. They both ran, but the other disciple outran Peter and reached the tomb first; and stooping to look in, he saw the linen cloths lying there, but he did not go in. Then Simon Peter came, following him, and went into the tomb; he saw the linen cloths lying, and the napkin, which had been on his head, not lying with the linen cloths but rolled up in a place by itself. Then the other disciple, who reached the tomb first, also went in, and he saw and believed; for as yet they did not know the Scripture, that he must rise from the dead. Then the disciples went back to their homes.

"But Mary stood weeping outside the tomb, and as she wept she stooped to look into the tomb; and she saw two angels in white, sitting where the body of Jesus had lain, one at the head and one at the feet. They said to her, Woman, why are you weeping? She said to them, Because they have taken away my Lord, and I do not know where they have laid him. Saying this, she turned round and saw Jesus standing, but she did not know that it was Jesus.

"Jesus said to her, Woman, why are you weeping? Whom do you seek? Supposing him to be the gardener, she said to him, Sir, if you have carried him away, tell me where you have laid him, and I will take him away. Jesus said to her, Mary. She turned and said to him in Hebrew, Rab-bo'ni! (which means Teacher). Jesus said to her, Do not hold me, for I have not yet ascended to the Father; but go to my brethren and say to them, **I am ascending to my Father and your Father, to my God and your God**. Mary Mag'dalene went and said to the disciples, I have seen the Lord; and she told them that he had said these things to her" (Jn 20:1-18) [my emph.].

After making a careful examination of the Gospels, it should become obvious to the reader that the majority of Jews in both Jerusalem and the surrounding country did not think or know that Jesus was the Messiah, both God and man, who was sent by God to redeem the human race and restore the broken relationship between man and God due to Original Sin. Instead, the majority saw Him as a great prophet (Lk 24:19; Mt 21:11, 46; Lk 7:16; Jn 4:19) sent by God to teach them and heal them. Because if the Jews had truly believed that Jesus was the Messiah, the Son of God – and I am including here the Pharisees, Essenes, chief priests, and teachers of the Law, the ones responsible for Jewish religious education – they would have never insisted on or allowed His crucifixion to take place. In fact, not even a hair on His head would've been touched if they knew who He was.

Moreover, it can also be said that the majority–if not all–of His Apostles did not know who Jesus was during most of His public ministry (Mt 8:27; Mk 4:41; Lk 8:25), and this, I suppose, makes sense. Being next to another human person and thinking that he is also God, the Creator of all things, would be very, very strange to say the least. If I had been alive in those days and someone had told me that Jesus was God, or if Jesus Himself had told me, I would have said something like, "Oh come on now! You've got to be kidding, right?"

Doubts about Christ's divinity even existed *after* His Resurrection, even among the twelve! (Mt 28:16; Lk 24:12, 21; Jn 20:25.) However, Andrew, Simon Peter's brother, who was a disciple of John the Baptist, appears to have had some considerable faith in this regard, for we find in John's Gospel: "He [Andrew] first found his brother Simon, and said to him, We have found the Messiah (which means Christ)" (Jn1:41). So it appears that Andrew had an idea of who Jesus was at the beginning of His ministry, but maybe not. Perhaps Andrew's idea of the Messiah was the Earthly messiah that everyone was expecting. Then there's Nathanael's testimony, who declared: "…Rabbi, you are the Son of God! You are the King of Israel!" (Jn 1:49). Even though this bold declaration is close to Peter's declaration found in Mt 16:16, it still may refer to an Earthly messiah. Both Son of God and King of Israel are titles that were commonly used to describe the expected messiah (more on this in Chapter 7). Nevertheless, it is not surprising that Nathanael was chosen as one of the twelve Apostles, but he was known by a different name: Bartholomew.

It is quite interesting to see that anyone who claimed Jesus was the expected Messiah, the Christ, was punished by the

Pharisees (Jn 9:22, 30-34). With this in mind, they must have had their hands full punishing people, on the left and on the right, because many were attracted to Him. In fact, the Gospel of Matthew records that a certain scribe wanted to follow Jesus: "Now when Jesus saw great crowds around him, he gave orders to go over to the other side. And a scribe came up and said to him, 'Teacher, I will follow you wherever you go' " (Mt 8:18-19). We are not sure if he got in trouble for that, but I wouldn't be surprised if he did. No mention of this, or his name, is ever given.

Here's a question you can ask a Jewish person who does not believe that Jesus was the Heavenly Messiah: "Scripture teaches that the Jews were God's Chosen People.[117] What were they chosen for?" I think most educated Jews will say: "The Jews were chosen by God to teach the world what God had taught them: that there is only one True God, creator of all things, and not many gods." And this, of course, would be true and correct. But then ask, "What else were they chosen for?" Although some may give some other reason(s) why they were chosen, most will not give the correct answer to this question, the most important one, namely, that God chose the Jewish people through whom His only Son would be born a man, would suffer, die, and resurrect from the dead in order to redeem not only the sinful Jews, His own people, but also the entire sinful and fallen human race. *That* is the main and primary reason why God chose the Jewish people: the people from the Tribe of Judah. To teach the whole known world that there is only one true God, not many, was secondary. This "oneness" of God, as explained in Chapter 6, does not pertain to only one divine person, but to three: the Father, the Son, and the Holy Spirit (the latter formerly known as the Holy Ghost).

As mentioned on page 72, due to false Pharisaic teaching, the Jews in 30 A.D. did not know the prophesied Messiah was going to be God's Son, redeemer of the human race. This "unknown mission" is related in the following statement: "The concept that the Jewish people are a 'consecrated brotherhood' destined to be purified by suffering toward the carrying out of some yet-unknown mission remains fundamental to Judaism in the 20th century." [118] Yet, in the Book of Acts, after Christ's Ascension, a Jew named Apol'los proved to the Jews that Jesus was the foretold Messiah **using the Holy Scriptures!** (see Acts 18:24-28). Regarding "chosenness," The Jewish Virtual Library states: "During most of Christian history, and even among some adherents to the present day, Christian chosenness meant that only Christians go to heaven while the nonchosen are either placed in limbo or are damned." [119] Although some Protestants agree with this error, this tenet has never been held, is now not held, nor will ever be held by the Holy Catholic Church. [120]

In hindsight, it is not difficult now to see that Judaism was a religion and way of life that God gave to the Israelites in order to preserve them from total corruption (something that the neighboring peoples were falling prey to) which would have made bringing the Heavenly Messiah through them quite difficult! (See Ex 23:32-33.) Keeping the Jews as His Chosen People was not an easy task for God, for they deviated from and abandoned their faith countless of times. From the time of Moses to the birth of Christ, the Jews abandoned God numerous times through the sins of idolatry, adultery, fornication, murder, theft, even child sacrifice to Mo'lech (Ez 22:1-12; 16:20-21). They also stoned to death the very Prophets who tried to get them to change their sinful ways and return to God. In spite of their sinfulness, God always forgave them, helped them, and put them back on track time after time. It seems they always managed to get back on track just in time before God's Wrath put an end to them. God is merciful, God is kind, loving, and patient. Very patient. With the coming of Jesus Christ into the world, and especially after His death and Resurrection from the dead, it became quite clear to the Apostles and disciples that

Judaism was no longer the religion to follow anymore, so they abandoned it and preached to both Jews and Gentiles that salvation is only attainable through Jesus the Christ (see The Need For A New Religion, Ch. 8).

"In many and various ways God spoke of old to our fathers by the Prophets; but in these last days he has spoken to us by a Son, whom he appointed the heir of all things, through whom also he created the ages. He reflects the glory of God and bears the very stamp of his nature, upholding the universe by his word of power. When he had made purification for sins [through His death], he sat down at the right hand of the Majesty on high, having become as much superior to angels as the name he has obtained is more excellent than theirs" (Heb 1:1-4).

"St. Peter and St. Paul were the foremost Apostles of Jesus Christ; St. Peter was the leader of the Twelve, while St. Paul followed Christ after His ascension into heaven. Together the two saints are the founders of the Church in Rome through their apostolic preaching, ministry, and martyrdom in that city. They are the solid rock on which the foundation of the Catholic Church is built, and they will forever remain her protectors and guides. To them Rome owes her true greatness, for it was under God's providential guidance that they transformed the capital of the Roman Empire into the heart of the Church, with the mission to radiate the Gospel of Our Lord Jesus Christ throughout the world. Both saints were martyred in close proximity to one another; Peter first, then Paul, though some traditions claim they were killed on the same day. St. Peter was crucified upside down and buried on the hill of the Vatican where St. Peter's Basilica now stands. St. Paul was beheaded on the via Ostia and buried where the Basilica of St. Paul Outside the Walls now stands. St. Peter and St. Paul are the patron saints of Rome and they share a feast day on June 29, a tradition going back to the earliest centuries of the Church." [121]

Science cannot prove the Resurrection of Christ took place because science demands a repeatable incident in order to be proven "scientifically." Since Jesus is not here to be examined, it can't be proven (according to science). But forensics can prove it, and actually has! Two books come to mind that present this evidence: "Witnesses To Mystery," by Ignatius Press, and: "A Cardiologist Examines Jesus," by Dr. Franco Serafini. The evidence here is incontrovertible.

The First Temple was built by both Israeli and Gentile workers (1 Kgs 5:1-18) on Mt. Moriah in Jerusalem (2 Chr 3:1), the same place where Abraham had taken Isaac to be sacrificed as commanded by God almost 1100 years earlier.[122] Note that it was God, not Abraham, who picked this particular mountain over all the others for this particular sacrifice, and He had a very special reason for doing so. Also note, Abraham named this place, "The Lord Will Provide." [123]

The Second Jewish Temple, which was started in the same location by Zerubbabel in 538 B.C. after the Jews returned to Jerusalem from the Babylonian exile, was completed in 516 B.C. However, this was a modest structure compared to what it ended up being 500 years later. Of all people, it was king Herod, the one responsible for the Massacre of the Innocents in the attempt to kill the Christ child, who rebuilt the Second Temple, from 20 B.C. to about 10 B.C., and turned it into a huge magnificent edifice, a project he undertook with great zeal in large part for the perpetuation of his name. (Herod was not even Jewish!)

Fifty years later, quite unbeknownst to Herod (he was already dead), Jesus, the only Son of God, the one who escaped Herod's death sentence when He was a child, was tortured and put to death by crucifixion for the Redemption of mankind on this very same magnificent site Herod had created to satisfy his enormous ego; the same site God Himself had picked for the sacrifice of Abraham's only son,

Isaac, the grandfather of the Twelve Tribes of Israel; the place Abraham had named, "The Lord Will Provide." Coincidence? I believe not!

Forty years after Christ's Resurrection, this magnificent Second Temple and testament to Herod's infamous "greatness" was destroyed by the Romans after The First Jewish-Roman War ended in 70 A.D., just as Christ had predicted. "And as some spoke of the temple, how it was adorned with noble stones and offerings, he [Jesus] said, 'As for these things which you see, the days will come when there shall not be left here one stone upon another that will not be thrown down' " (Lk 21:5-6).

### Beit HaMikdash - The Old Jewish Temple

The Temple was the most important and central part of Judaic worship. It was only in the Temple, according to "halakha" (Jewish Law), where "karbanot" (sacrifices) to God were allowed to be made, and these were exclusively made only by the "kohanim," the priests. The sacrifices were only performed in the Temple in Jerusalem and nowhere else. No one else could perform them and nowhere else could they be performed. Thus, the practice of karbanot ceased with the destruction of the Second Temple in 70 A.D. Some sacrifices were allowed during the Third Jewish-Roman War but were terminated on a permanent basis when they lost that war because the Torah forbids them anywhere else, a mandate still in force to this day [124] (the Torah is the first five (5) Books of the OT). Not unlike the Gentiles in the Levant, the Israelites engaged in idolatry and even burned their children as a sacrifice to Mo'lech at times (2 Kgs 17:17; Jer 7:31; 19:5; 32:35), leading to severe punishments from God. But when they followed the Decalogue God gave them through Moses at Sinai, they only sacrificed animals, birds, certain plants (harvest items), and even wine. These sacrifices were made not only for the atonement of sins, but also for becoming closer to God, for giving thanks to Him, and for being cleansed from impurities. Animal sacrifices were made on a large scale during the Pilgrim Festivals: Shavuot (Pentecost), Sukkoth (Tabernacles), and Pesah (Passover), and also on the High Holidays: Rosh Hashana (New Year) and Yom Kippur (Day of Atonement). However, the largest number of animals were sacrificed on Passover, with lambs being the greatest in number.

The sacrifice of a red heifer is one of the most mysterious sacrifices in Judaism. A heifer is a young cow, typically one that has not yet given birth to a calf. The main reason for this sacrifice is to purify a person from contact with the dead. Although this sacrifice purifies the impure, it also renders the pure participants impure – who then have to purify themselves through another ritual. Most interesting, it is a tenet in Rabbinic Judaism that this sacrifice will be performed by the messiah when he comes because everyone is impure from contact with the dead. Therefore, the presence of a red heifer may be a sign that the messiah is on his way, but not necessarily.[125]

Worthy of note, while the Jews were captive in Babylonia, they started to assemble for prayer in houses since they had no Temple there. These, which became the prototypes of the synagogues of later use, especially after the destruction of the Second Temple in 70 A.D., are still in use today. The crucial elements necessary for making sacrifices to God in the Temple were: The item to be sacrificed, the Jewish High Priest, the Temple, the reason for the sacrifice, and of course, God, to receive the sacrifice. But the Jews never offered sacrifices for the Original Sin committed by Adam and Eve. This sacrifice would be made by God Himself.

## Jesus The Christ – The New Temple

When Jesus allowed Himself to be crucified in order to atone for mankind's Original Sin and all personal/actual sins, He incorporated all of the crucial elements necessary for making sacrifices to God in the Temple in His *own* Person. Jesus became the Sacrifice, the High Priest, the Temple, the Reason, and God, all in One. Thus, the Jewish practice of sacrificing innocent animals to pay for their sins came to an abrupt end with Christ's Ultimate Sacrifice on the Cross (Heb 7:27; 9:11-14; 10:1-18; 13:11-12; Ps 51:16). As mentioned earlier, although it is still considered a sin in Rabbinic Judaism to sacrifice animals, those who continue this obsolete and offensive practice, as is still the case in occult and satanic sects, are committing a very grave sin: the denial of the Redemption of man through Christ's sacrifice on the Cross. A more serious sin is hard to imagine.

On the one hand, Orthodox Jews say they will resume the practice of animal sacrifices after their Earthly messiah comes, restores Israel, and rebuilds the Temple, while on the other, most Reform Jews say they will not resume animal sacrifices after their Temple is rebuilt. Suppose the Temple is rebuilt (which is doubtful since God Himself does not want it rebuilt, for Christ is the New Temple), who is going to run the Temple? Will it be the Orthodox, the Conservative, or the Reform? Will all three be allowed to worship there in alternating schedules and run it? If so, what will stop the Orthodox from animal sacrifices if the Reform is set against it? Or will three Temples be built, one for each?

This is an example of what happens when people cling to falsehoods and refuse to let go of them.

We must always choose the works of God over the works of the Devil and be in communion with Christ at all times. In the Gospel of Luke we find: "Being asked by the Pharisees when the kingdom of God was coming, he [Jesus] answered them, 'The kingdom of God is not coming with signs to be observed; nor will they say, "Behold, here it is!" or "There!" for behold, the kingdom of God is in your midst' " (Lk 17:20-21). The kingdom of God is being in total communion with Christ and with His followers, His Church. All of us are capable, through our free will, of entering that Kingdom if we choose God over Satan and follow only Him, the Christ, the Heavenly Messiah. From another angle, Jesus Himself is also the kingdom of God, and He is telling them that He, God, was right in front of them, "in your midst"; i.e., right in front of their eyes; teaching them, curing them, casting demons from them, and so on.

Before Christ came to Earth to redeem mankind, direct access to God was only permitted to the "Kohen Gadol," the Temple High Priest, who was considered to be in the presence of God when he entered a certain section of the Temple called the Holy of Holies, and only once a year, on the holiday of Yom Kippur. The Holy of Holies was separated from the rest of the Temple interior by a huge curtain, the Torah Ark curtain (in Hebrew the "parokhet"), which served as a partition between the Ark of the Covenant and the prayer hall. The Ark, which was kept in the Holy of Holies, contained the two broken stone tablets given to Moses by God listing the Ten Commandments, Aaron's rod, and a vessel containing some of the manna God had given the Israelites as food to eat on their journey through the desert after the Exodus from Egypt. When Christ breathed His last on the Cross and died at 3pm (the exact time the priests had finished sacrificing the Passover lambs in the Temple), the Torah Ark curtain was mysteriously torn in two, top to bottom (Mt 27:51), signifying the removal of obstructions separating the people from God. Direct access to God in Heaven was now possible through Christ's death, which opened the Gates of Heaven to those who love God, and restored the broken relationship between man and God due to Original Sin. Christ's death on the Cross, putting into effect the New Covenant established at the Last Supper, also marked the end of the Davidic line of kings with Christ being the King of kings and Lord of lords.

Jesus is not only the New Temple for the Jews who believe in Him to worship God in, but also for the Gentile members of His Church as well. All of these are the "New Stones" of the "New Temple," and they worship God **through** Christ, **with** Christ, and **in** Christ, in the unity of the Holy Spirit. All glory and honor belongs to our almighty Father in Heaven, for ever and ever. It is Jesus Christ, this "New Temple," that was raised on the third day from the dead for the glory of God, just as Christ had predicted: "Destroy this temple, and in three days I will raise it up" (Jn 2:19). This made the Second Jewish Temple – and any other Jewish Temple – no longer needed and literally obsolete in the eyes of God Almighty. Thus, the followers of Jesus also became – and are still now, the "New Chosen People of God": i.e., chosen to spread the Good News throughout the world that the Son of God, the Heavenly Messiah, came to Earth to redeem the entire human race and save us from the eternal punishment we deserve due to our sins. Halleluiah!

Jesus referred more than once to His body as a Temple. One example already given is found in John's Gospel: "Destroy this temple, and in three days I will raise it up. The Jews then said, 'It has taken forty-six years to build this temple, and will you raise it up in three days?' But he spoke of the temple of his body. When therefore he was raised from the dead, his disciples remembered that he had said this; and they believed the Scripture and the word which Jesus had spoken" (2:19-22). Jesus is the New Temple that will last "for evermore" (see Ez 37:26); Jerusalem will never have another stone Temple.

There is no doubt whatsoever that Jesus is the New Temple, replacing all others and making them obsolete, and His followers are the "Stones" that make up that Magnificent New Temple. It is also very important to know that we, our bodies, are also temples of the Holy Spirit. St. Paul reminds us of this truth in 1st Corinthians: "Do you not know that your body is a temple of the Holy Spirit within you, which you have from God? You are not your own; you were bought with a price [Christ's blood]. So glorify God in your body" (1 Cor 6:19-20). So, it is safe to say that our bodies, the Stones that make up the Temple of Christ, the Body of Christ, are mini temples in themselves; mini temples that together form the big Temple of Christ for the Glory of God, and the Book of Revelation confirms this truth: "And I saw no temple in the city, for **its temple is the Lord God the Almighty and the Lamb**" (Rev 21:22) [my emph.] (see Eph 2:19-22).

"We have to accustom ourselves to pray in all places and at all times. The real place to pray in is the soul, for God dwells there. If we wish to obey our Lord's counsel, when we pray we should enter the chamber of our soul, close the door, and speak to the Father, whose loving eyes seek ever our own. This inner chamber of our soul is the true temple, the sacred sanctuary, and we carry it with us and can at any time either remain there or quickly return to it, should we have been obliged to leave it." — Dom Augustin Guillerand.

As the time neared for Jesus to be handed over to the Jewish authorities by the Apostle Judas to be executed, the Apostles themselves did not fully understand or expect this tragedy, "And taking the Twelve, he said to them, 'Behold, we are going up to Jerusalem, and everything that is written of the Son of man by the Prophets will be accomplished. For he will be delivered to the Gentiles, and will be mocked and shamefully treated and spit upon; they will scourge him and kill him, and on the third day he will rise.' But they understood none of these things; this saying was hidden from them, and they did not grasp what was said" (Lk 18:31). "Jesus answered them, 'Do you now believe? The hour is coming, indeed it has come, when you will be scattered, every man to his home, and will leave me alone; yet I am not alone, for the Father is with me. I have said this to you, that in me you may have peace. In the world you have tribulation; but be of good cheer, I have overcome the world' " (Jn 16:31-33).

After my father died in 1969 due to a failed experimental operation on both kidneys, my family stopped going to Mass on Sundays and I was left, at 17years old, without a father; without a father in a strange country: the USA. This was at the height of the "Hippie Movement" and the "Free Love Movement." School didn't interest me anymore so I dropped out of high school after completing my sophomore year, and like many other teenage boys, I started getting into mischief, taking drugs with friends for fun, playing music, and living the carefree life of a musician, an "Artist," with little responsibilities. My years of sacrifice and devoted practice at the drums finally paid off and I became a member of a very popular local band, "Orphan Annie," playing percussion. I was the envy of my friends.

We toured the Pacific Northwest and Canada with much success and had a lot of fun together. I then accepted a position with an even more popular band in the San Francisco area and signed a contract with Warner Brothers to record our first album. I was only 19 years old. After playing to audiences that were so drugged out they did not even know where they were, I became very disillusioned with the music scene and went back home to live with my mother, "Mima"; God Bless her soul. She always supported me, always loved me, always helped me. Rest in peace Mima.

I signed up for college music theory classes to learn how to read and write music (I had played "by ear" until then), got a degree in both music theory and musical instrument repair, left home for my first job repairing instruments, and started a family at 24 years old. I fathered two healthy and wonderful children and truly enjoyed being a father and husband. Ten years later, I found myself in a nasty divorce and turned to alcohol for relief which did not work. Then, one Saturday evening, I said to Tania, my fiancée, "Let's go to Mass tomorrow morning. I'd like to hear the homily. I need peace." So we went to Mass the next day. When the priest started to give his homily, it was like he was talking to me *personally* and only to me. It seemed like the entire homily was directed to me and only to me, that's how it felt; that's how *I* felt. This made quite an impression on me, so I called the priest the next day and made an appointment to see him.

His name was Father Michael Tabit. He was about 80 years old and was from Lebanon. I remember I said to him, "Father, it seems like God has abandoned the human race! We don't hear about great miracles anymore, like parting the sea, raising the dead to life, stuff like that." He chuckled then told me about the apparitions of the Virgin Mary. I remembered the ones at Guadalupe and Fatima, but I said, "That was a long time ago Father; nothing is happening now to make people believe in God. He's abandoned us, and I don't blame Him! No one wants to have anything to do with Him anymore!" And then I asked him, "How come God punished Adam and Eve with so much severity? Isn't He supposed to be a loving God? Why didn't God just forgive them which would have prevented Jesus from having to die such a horrible death? Why didn't God accept their apology? I am sure they repented and said they were sorry!" The following was his answer.

### Why Jesus Had To Die For Our Sins

Adam and Eve did not possess the necessary "qualifications" to redeem themselves. Even if they had spent the rest of their lives prostrated on the ground as proof of being sorry for their sin, it would not have been enough. Let me explain. For example, let's suppose that two army privates get into a fist fight and a visiting Captain from another city gets punched in the mouth by one of the privates while trying to break up the fight. Although the punching private will be put on "kp duty" for sure as punishment after he apologizes to the Captain, the Captain in charge of the punching private – who represents the private's unit – will also have to apologize to the visiting Captain with the sore jaw – rank for rank – because the private's apology by itself is not good enough.

Another example, say the Queen of England is visiting America and is riding down the street during a parade with the president in a convertible limousine. A heckler in the crowd throws a tomato and hits the queen squarely in the face. Even though the captured heckler has to apologize to the queen for his transgression, the president himself – who represents the American people – will also have to apologize to the queen with the red face – rank for rank – because the heckler's apology by itself is not good enough.

When Adam and Eve, representing the human race, offended God through their Original Sin of disobedience, their own personal apologies to God were not good enough to atone for their offense. They did not possess the qualifications, the "Rank", to give an adequate "apology" to God. Even if they had apologized for all Eternity, prostrated on the ground, it still would not have been good enough. The "Apology to God" had to be done by someone who possessed the proper qualifications: the capability and "credentials." Since it was Jesus that "through Him, with Him, and in Him" all things were made, only He – after assuming a human body through Mary – would possess the Proper Qualifications to "Apologize" to God for the sins of mankind by being and representing both God (the "Rank") and man (Adam's representative) in one Person.

It is important to know that it was Christ's sacrificial death that redeemed the fallen human race and not His Resurrection. Although His Resurrection closely followed His death, it was the shedding of His precious blood and death that brought redemption to mankind. The Resurrection was mainly twofold: for the greater glory of God, and to show us how the righteous will be after the Resurrection of the Dead at the End of Time. I believe it was also a "Fatherly Reward."

Even though sin and death were not His fault but of our first parents, Jesus, Our Lord, the One Who gave us the entire universe as our playground to enjoy, willingly endured the humiliations, rejections, terrible sufferings, torture, and death on a Cross because of His Tremendous and Great Love for us. Jesus chose the same consequences of Original Sin: pain, suffering, and death, as the means He would use to redeem the human race; this shows the pure and divine empathy He had for us; i.e., Jesus wanted to suffer and die too (Jn 15:13).

### Analysis Of The Redemption

The Redemption of the human race required the sacrificial death of God incarnate. Why such a high price? Nothing else was capable of restoring the broken relationship between God and man due to Adam and Eve's Original Sin of disobedience. That's how serious the sin of disobedience to God was – and is! Father Rumble noted: "God willed that the scales of justice should be balanced, and for that a man had to die for the sin of man" (Radio Replies, # 439, p. 228). Thus, God's Son, through Mary, became man, and through His death atoned for the sin of man. (For more on this see "Why Jesus Had To Die For Our Sins," p. 146.) But why did Jesus have to die to atone for man? Was there no other way? St. Paul said: "Indeed, under the law almost everything is purified with blood, and **without the shedding of blood there is no forgiveness of sins**" (Heb 9:22) [my emph.]. The fact Jesus willingly died for us proves the immensity of God's

Supreme Love for us: "Greater love has no man than this, that a man lay down his life for his friends" (Jn 15:13). Since God the Father created all things through, with, and in His Son, it was therefore fitting and proper that the work of the Redemption of mankind would be performed by Him.

For the sake of argument, if Jesus had chosen suicide to redeem mankind, that would have rendered Redemption null and void for at least two (2) reasons: (1) the person who takes his or her own life is usually not of sound mind and mainly does so for a selfish reason; i.e., not wanting to live anymore regardless of anything or anyone else. This, of course, would not redeem anyone including the person committing the act; (2) the taking away of sin in Judaism was only effective if an innocent victim (lamb, goat, bull) was slaughtered and then offered as a sacrifice by the priest in behalf of the sinner. The innocent victim, normally an animal, could not be offered as a sacrifice in behalf of a sinner if it had somehow killed itself (accidental or otherwise). So, the taking of His own life to redeem mankind would not have been efficacious or "legal" according to Jewish Law.

Therefore, since Jesus had consented (from all Eternity) to willingly die for the Redemption of the human race, He must be accused of a crime terrible enough to justify being put to death. This would not be an easy thing for a Man like Jesus, who is also God, since God does not commit crimes. God is not a criminal. The answer, then, would seem to be the **absence** of a crime; i.e., convicted of something very serious He would (or could) not do. To come "dressed" as a human being and then claim to be God would either classify Him as a lunatic, or in the mind of the Jewish religious authorities, a person deserving the death penalty for blasphemy.

Thus, the die was cast (before the creation of the world), and "In the fullness of time" (Gal 4:4-5), Jesus came to Earth, was born of a woman, lived a life of seclusion until He was 30 years old, and then embarked on a public ministry designed and orchestrated to last just long enough to: (1) proclaim the Good News; (2) train followers to administrate the New Religion and Church He would have to establish (see The Need For A New Religion); (3) be found guilty of a serious crime He was innocent of in order to be executed and thereby redeem the human race.

The above brief description of the Redemption is not intended to trivialize Christ's Mission or make it sound routine in some way, or Heaven forbid, label it an unremarkable event. I am only showing here, for the sake of brevity, the main points of His Sacred Mission on Earth. In regards to number (3), since the Jews were waiting for an Earthly messiah to free them from Roman rule, Jesus could have come as this expected messiah, organize a revolution, and arrange His arrest by the Romans which, no doubt, would have led to His speedy crucifixion as an enemy of Rome.

But freeing the Jews from Roman rule was not the objective of His Mission; the Mission of the promised Messiah was to redeem and "free" the entire human race, not just the Jews! So, for the sake of argument, the question then becomes, if Christ had been crucified by the Romans for sedition and insurrection, would that have redeemed the human race? And the answer has to be no, because that would have been just punishment for such a crime. Certainly not the inhumane cruelty of crucifixion, but death for such a crime would have been justified; that's the reason why Jesus did not assume the Earthly messiah role. No, it would have to be a crime He was not guilty of; a crime He was innocent of, like the innocent lambs that were sacrificed for the atonement of the sins of the Jews. A crime He would be found guilty of by the Jews, not by the Romans. Why the Jews and not the Romans? Because the Romans were not God's Chosen People.

This brings to mind the first Passover in Egypt, instituted by God Himself, when the angel of death "passed over" the houses of the Israelites that had the blood of the lamb on the doorposts. During this first Passover, the first-born Egyptian males were put to death by the Hand of God and the first-born male Israelites were spared death, followed the next day by the Exodus, a momentous event that solidified the Jews as God's Chosen People through whom the Messiah was to come to redeem mankind. The Israelites were freed by God from continued slavery in Egypt through Moses, and mankind was freed from slavery to sin and death through Jesus Christ. But let's return to the crime Jesus would be found guilty of by the Jews that would justify the death penalty.

The first and original reason why the Pharisees and Sadducees decided to put Jesus to death was because His popularity was growing so much due to the miracles He was performing, especially the raising of Lazarus, they feared the number of His followers would reach such a high number that the Romans – out of fear – would destroy the Temple and all of them as well. So, putting Jesus to death would eliminate that growing possible threat (Jn 11:45-53). But what serious crime could they accuse Him of? Well, Jesus would solve that problem for them. The most serious offense Jesus could make that would justify being condemned to death by the Jewish authorities would be to make Himself equal to God. That not only would justify being executed, but it would be the easiest "crime" for Him to commit since He **was** indeed God in the flesh. But there was a problem: the Jews did not have the authority to execute anyone because it had been taken away by Roman rule. In the Gospel of John we find: "The Jews said to him [Pilate], It is not lawful for us to put any man to death. This was to fulfil the word which Jesus had spoken to show by what death he was to die" (Jn 18:31-32). This passage tells a lot.

1. Under Roman law, the Jews could not legally execute Jesus themselves.

2. If permitted, they would have stoned Him to death since that was the usual method of execution used by the Jews. (Several attempts to stone Him had already been made to no avail.) But Jesus, according to destiny, was not supposed to be stoned to death; He was supposed to be crucified, which means He would have to be put to death by the Romans ("…to show by what [type of] death he was to die." Jn 18:32).

3. Therefore, the Jews had to find a way to get the Romans to execute Jesus for them.

4. Pilate asked Jesus, "Are you the King of the Jews?" (Jn 18:33). He asked this question to find out if He was the expected King/messiah that would attempt to overthrow Roman rule and therefore justify execution.

5. Jesus answered, "My kingship is not of this world" (Jn 18:36).

6. Satisfied He was not their King/messiah and posed no threat to Rome, Pilate told the Jews, "**I find no crime in him**" (Jn 18:38). This is the first time he said this; no enemy of Rome.

7. After having Jesus scourged, perhaps thinking this would be enough punishment to satisfy the Jews, Pilate said, "Behold, I am bringing him out to you, that you may know that **I find no crime in him**" (Jn 19:4). This is the second time he said this. Again, no threat to Rome and no enemy of Rome.

8. "When the **chief priests** and the officers saw him, they cried out, Crucify him, crucify him! Pilate said to them, Take him yourselves and crucify him, for **I find no crime in him**"

(Jn 19:6). The third time he found Christ innocent. No threat to Rome and no enemy of Rome.

9. "The Jews answered him, We have a law, and by that law he ought to die, because he has made himself the Son of God" (Jn 19:7). Pilate became afraid and asked Jesus where He was from, but no answer was given. ("He was oppressed, and he was afflicted, yet he opened not his mouth" (Is 53:7).

10. When Pilate again tried to release Jesus, the Jews changed their charge against Him this time and said, "If you release this man, you are not Caesar's friend; everyone who makes himself a king sets himself against Caesar.... Away with him, away with him, crucify him! Pilate said to them, Shall I crucify your King? **The chief priests answered, We have no king but Caesar.** Then he handed him over to them to be crucified" (Jn 19:12, 15-16) [my emph.].

11. Pilate authorized the execution/crucifixion (Mk 15:15; Lk 23:24), but it was DEMANDED by the Jews (Mt 27:22,23; Mk 15:13,14; Lk 23:21,23; Jn 18:31, 19:6, 15). By changing the charge from blasphemy against God to treason/sedition, a crime against Rome, Pilate now had justification – although without solid evidence – to have Him crucified. Much to their content, the chief priests quickly noticed that changing the charge from a religious one to a political one was all they needed to do, because their religious views and beliefs did not interest the Romans one bit. "Christ lived and died in a remote corner of the Roman world **and had caused no political disturbance**. Again, the Romans had supreme contempt for the Jews, and reports connected with Jewish religious happenings held very little interest for them" (Radio Replies, # 443, p. 230) [my emph.]. Although Pilate did indeed authorize the execution and ordered his soldiers to crucify Jesus to satisfy the demand of the Jews, the Jews were the ones with the greater guilt, and Jesus reminded Pilate of this: "You would have no power over me unless it had been

given you from above; therefore **he who delivered me to you has the greater sin**" (Jn 19:11) [my emph.]. Jesus wanted no trouble with the Romans and was not a political enemy of Rome during His entire life, and certainly was not the Earthly messiah the Jews were waiting for either. As already mentioned, excellent proof of this is found in the Gospel of John when Pilate asked Him, "Are you the King of the Jews?" and Jesus answered, "My kingship is not of this world." [126] This, of course, must have put Pilate at ease since this made him realize that Jesus was not a competitor who was going to help the Jews overthrow the Romans, for rumors to that effect had been circulating for quite some time all over the land. That is why Pilate said to the crowd, "**I find no crime in him**" (Jn 18:38) [my emph.].

It appears the sign, "Jesus of Nazareth, the King of the Jews," that Pilate had ordered be placed on the Cross (Roman soldiers customarily placed these signs on crosses to denote the charge against the victim) was placed there to: (1) justify the crucifixion charge to onlookers as a formality; and (2) to irk the chief priests (Sadducees, see Jn 19:21). Since Scripture makes clear, more than once, that Pilate believed Jesus was innocent of any crime, he therefore also believed he had indeed crucified an innocent man; an execution that was carried out at the furious instigation of the Jews, **led by the chief priests and the Pharisees** (see Mt 27:20; Mk 15:11). According to the historian Eusebius, Pontius Pilate committed suicide in 37A.D.,[127] though it is difficult to say if condemning Jesus played any part in it.

In "Antiquities of the Jews," Book 13, Chapter 10, § 5, Josephus mentions the great power and influence the Pharisees had over the Jewish people: "These have so great a power over the multitude, that when they say anything against the King, or against the High Priest, they are presently believed." And in Ch. 15, § 5, we find: "For he [king Alexander Jannaeus] told her [Salome Alexandra], they [the

Pharisees] had great authority among the Jews, both to do hurt to such as they hated, and to bring advantages to those to whom they were friendly disposed." (Josephus himself, by the way, was a Pharisee.) From this information, it is certainly easy to deduce that the ones most responsible for inciting the crowd to condemn Jesus were the Pharisees. When the Jews in the crowd saw that Jesus had been scourged and in terrible physical condition, they realized this was not the strong and powerful Earthly messiah they were expecting, and furious at this lost opportunity to free themselves from the Romans, they shouted all the more with rage – egged on by the **Pharisees** and **Sadducees:** "Crucify him! Crucify him!"

## SUMMARY

Q: "Why did the Jews fail to recognize Jesus as the promised Messiah? And why do they continue to reject Him to this day?"

A: Most of the Jews, following a teaching of the Pharisees and Essenes, were expecting an "Earthly messiah" to rescue them from Roman rule and restore the Davidic kingdom. They were not expecting the Son of God in the flesh, the "Heavenly Messiah" foretold by the Prophets who was coming to redeem the entire human race. Many modern Jews are still following this Pharisaic teaching and believe that God is going to send them an Earthly messiah, and so they continue to wait in vain.

Q: Why were they expecting an Earthly messiah instead of the Heavenly one foretold by the Prophets?

A: As recorded in the OT, the Hebrews, later known as the Israelites, and still later as the Jews, had been conquered and enslaved many times by their enemies. In Egypt alone, prior to the Exodus in c 1250 B.C., they had been captive there for about 430 years by the time Moses succeeded in rescuing them from Pharaoh's rule and led them to the promised land of Canaan. They were also conquered by the Assyrians in c. 723 B.C. (Northern tribes) and later by the Babylonians in 605, 597 and again in 587 B.C. (Southern tribes). In the latter four instances, they were taken captive and deported to the lands of their conquerors where they remained for quite some time. Then in 63 B.C., the Roman general Pompey conquered Jerusalem and the Jews remained under Roman rule through the time of Christ until the early part of the 4$^{th}$ century A.D., about 400 years or so – about the same amount of time they spent in Egypt before the Exodus. The ability of the Jews, particularly the Pharisees, to comprehend the Messianic prophecies as delivered by the Prophets – the majority of which were not explicit to begin with – was hampered by their deep longing and desire for freedom, sovereignty, security, stability, and wealth, to the point where they reduced the Messianic prophecies to nationalistic aspirations, namely, that an Earthly messiah would be sent to their rescue when in all actuality a Heavenly Messiah – God Himself – would come to Earth through their people to redeem the entire human race, which by the way, included them, of course.

In addition to this, the Jews did not have a very good relationship with their Prophets. In fact, they stoned them to death because they kept bothering them with repeated warnings to abandon their sinful ways and turn to the Lord before severe punishments were sent by God, which is something the people were hesitant to do since they were enjoying their sinful way of life (thus punishments came in being conquered by their enemies and being sent into exile), so their remedy was to kill the Prophets and be bothered by them no more. This resulted in the people not taking the Prophets too seriously which somewhat affected the credibility of their prophecies when they reached the ears of the people, leading only to more misdirection and more misinterpretation of the prophecies; in particular, the Messianic ones.

In short, it was a combination of the Essenes and Pharisees misinterpreting Scripture, deep seated desires to finally be free from foreign domination ("becoming a kingdom like other nations" [128] ), and disgust of being exiled to foreign lands to be used for the benefit of their conquerors which led to the erroneous belief that God was going to send them an Earthly messiah, another Moses, to rescue them from all this and forge them into a great and powerful nation. Moreover, since the doctrine of Original Sin was absent in Judaism, they therefore lacked the belief in a Savior to redeem them and the entire human race from it, which was precisely the actual Mission and objective of the foretold Heavenly Messiah: Jesus the Christ. The Jews wanted a mighty military ruler to come and free them forever from forced servitude and establish a powerful kingdom that would protect them–on a permanent basis–from being conquered and enslaved by anyone else. Sad enough to say, that was not the actual Mission of the real Messiah that God had promised the world from the very beginning of time.

Using very colorful and cryptic language, the Book of Revelation calls Jerusalem the Whore of Babylon (harlot), and Rome, the "scarlet beast" she is sitting on (Rev 17). When Pilate asked the Jews: "Shall I crucify your King? **The chief priests answered, We have no king but Caesar**" (Jn 19:15) [my emph.]. The OT Prophets had repeatedly referred to Jerusalem as a harlot because of the repeated violations of Her Covenant with God through sinful and idolatrous ways. Ezekiel 16:15-43, 23:1-35 are examples. In this passage above, she is "in bed" with the Romans ("no king but Caesar") even though she had been waiting–for a long time–for the Earthly messiah to rescue Her from them. And in fact, Jerusalem did enter into a "relationship" with Rome, for both of them together persecuted and killed many of the early Christians with Rome continuing this brutal and barbaric practice for almost 300 years until the early part of the fourth century when Constantine I became the first Christian Emperor of

Rome in 306 A.D. and issued the Edict of Milan in 313 A.D. which ended the persecution of Christians in the Roman Empire; with the exception of Emperor Julian the Apostate, a nephew of Constantine, who reigned from 361 to 363 A.D. He was the last non-Christian ruler of the Roman Empire. Julian strongly supported the Jews, opposed Christianity (the "Way"; see Acts 9:2), persecuted and put Christians to death (St. Bibiana was one), restored Hellenistic polytheism in Rome, and allowed and urged the Jews to rebuild their Temple in Jerusalem in 363 A.D., a project that was terminated that same year due to the Galilee Earthquake.

It is interesting how God at times acts **after** His Church on Earth acts (Mt 16:19) as shown in the Book of Revelation. Example: the scroll held by the Father in Heaven is opened by the Lamb only **after** John (symbolizing the Church) writes the letters to the Seven Churches. Thus, Eternity is connected to Time on Earth. God's actions – in Eternity – follow the ones made by the Church – in Time – here on Earth. This is fascinating! Moreover, God speaks to the members of His One Church on Earth through His Word (Jesus). This is how we remain united to His Will in order to merit Salvation. But to the rest of mankind outside the Church, He "communicates" through natural disasters, through Nature, to induce them to repentance and conversion and bring them to their senses, for their sake, not His. The Book of Revelation summarizes what is in the entire Bible and shows the Conclusion thereof. We are now living in the "Millennium of Christ's Reign on Earth," for He "reigns" through the Holy Catholic Church He established here. The "thousand years" is not to be taken literally, like much in Revelation. It is only 10 (totality) X 10 X 10 (the Jewish superlative) which equals 1,000; i.e., never ending. His Catholic Church is the "dynasty" that will never end (p. 101).

The following describes just how special one human person is in the eyes of God, our Creator.

"That which our Lord and Savior Jesus Christ did and suffered for all men, He did and suffered for each one in particular; and He would not have thought it too much to do if it had been a question of saving only a single soul. The salvation of a soul is, then, the price of the blood of God, the price of the death of God, the price of the greatest sacrifice that God, clothed in our human nature, could possibly make! This is incomprehensible! … It proves that the dignity of a soul is beyond understanding—for God to abase Himself, for God to annihilate Himself, for God to sacrifice Himself, only to save that soul and make it happy forever! … As for us, who believe humbly and firmly all that God has revealed to us, let us learn, by the contemplation of God upon a Cross, what is the value of our souls. Let us not lose our soul; let us not prostitute it to creatures; and to make sure of our eternal salvation, which cost so much to the Son of God, let us beg of Jesus Christ Himself to take charge of it, to lead us in the right way and guide us always. Such an inestimable treasure runs too great a risk in our own hands. Let us trust it to God and our Savior. Let us make Him the Master of our liberty, which we may so easily abuse, and the abuse of which may bring about such terrible consequences. Once abandoned to the safe and infallible guidance of His grace, we have no more to fear. He loves us too much, He takes too much interest in our salvation, ever to lose the price of His blood and His sufferings" (Fr. Jean Nicholas Grou).

I came across some very interesting information regarding the Nativity of Jesus while doing research for this book. When Christmas comes and we celebrate one of the most important events in world history (the other one being Easter), we give presents to one another in imitation of the gifts of gold, frankincense, and myrrh the Three Kings brought to the infant Jesus (Mt 2:11). However, according to Father Mitch Pacwa, these were not actual "gifts" but rather the "tools of the trade" they used in their work of astrology. Thus, when they arrived at the stable, "they saw the child with Mary his mother, and they fell down and worshiped him. Then, opening their treasures [of the trade], they offered him gifts, gold and frankincense and Myrrh" (Mt 2:11). The actual occurrence here is that the Magi **abandoned** the items they treasured and ceased practicing the false work of astrology thereafter! [129] Here is another example of correct interpretation of Scripture that leads to the revelation of truth.

I'd like to close this Chapter with one of my favorite Scripture passages.

### Jesus And The Woman of Samaria

"Now when the Lord knew that the Pharisees had heard that Jesus was making and baptizing more disciples than John (although Jesus himself did not baptize, but only his disciples), he left Judea and departed again to Galilee. He had to pass through Samar'ia. So he came to a city of Samar'ia, called Sy'char, near the field that Jacob gave to his son Joseph. Jacob's well was there, and so Jesus, wearied as he was with his journey, sat down beside the well. It was about the sixth hour. There came a woman of Samar'ia to draw water. Jesus said to her, 'Give me a drink.' For his disciples had gone away into the city to buy food. The Samaritan woman said to him, 'How is it that you, a Jew, ask a drink of me, a woman of Samar'ia?' For Jews have no dealings with Samaritans. Jesus answered her, 'If you knew the gift of God, and who it is that is saying to you, Give me a drink, you would have asked him and he would have given you living water.' The woman said to him, 'Sir, you have nothing to draw with, and the well is deep; where do you get that living water? Are you greater than our father Jacob, who gave us the well, and drank from it himself, and his sons, and his cattle?' Jesus said to her, 'Everyone who drinks of this water will thirst again, but whoever drinks of the water that I shall give him will never thirst; the water that I shall give him will become in him a spring of water welling up to eternal life.' The woman said to him, 'Sir, give me this water, that I may not thirst, nor come here to draw.' Jesus said to her, 'Go, call your husband, and come here.' The woman answered him, 'I have no husband.' Jesus said to her, 'You are right in saying, I have no husband; for you have had five husbands, and he whom you now have is not your husband; this you said truly.' The woman said to him, 'Sir, I perceive that you are a prophet. Our fathers worshiped on this mountain; and you say that in Jerusalem is the place where men ought to worship.' Jesus said to her, 'Woman, believe me, the hour is coming when neither on this mountain nor in Jerusalem will you worship the Father. You worship what you do not know; we worship what we know, for salvation is from the Jews. But the hour is coming, and now is, when the true worshipers will worship the Father in spirit and truth, for such the Father seeks to worship him. God is spirit, and those who worship him must worship in spirit and truth.' The woman said to him, 'I know that Messiah is coming (he who is called Christ); when he comes, he will show us all things.' **Jesus said to her, 'I who speak to you am he.'** Just then his disciples came. They marveled that he was talking with a woman, but none said, What do you wish? or, Why are you talking with her? So the woman left her water jar, and went away into the city, and said to the people, 'Come, see a man who told me all that I ever did. Can this be the Christ?' They went out of the city and were coming to him" (Jn 4:1-30) [my emph.].

# Chapter 6

"Faith is to believe what you do not see; the reward of this faith is to see what you believe." St. Augustine.

## THE "MORE THAN ONE GOD" JEWISH PROBLEM

The MAIN problem the Jews had in believing that Jesus was the Son of God, in particular the Sadducees, Pharisees, Essenes and scribes, is that since childhood, they, and all Jewish children, were explicitly taught that there was only one God: one Almighty Person who was God, the Creator of all things. The prayer that all Jewish children learn to memorize (and therefore internalize) regarding the monotheistic oneness of God is the *Shema Yisrael*, and the very first verse of this prayer is:

**"Hear, O Israel: The Lord our God, the Lord is ONE."** (Mk 12:29; see Dt 6:4.)

Thus, to all Jews, "the Lord is ONE" meant (and means) "There is only ONE God," not two, or three, or a hundred. This monotheistic oneness of God was extremely important to the Jewish people because other surrounding ethnic cultures, including the Romans who ruled them during Christ's time, were polytheistic believing in and worshipping many gods, pagan gods made of stone, clay, gold, and other things, who obviously had nothing to do with the creation of the universe. As a matter of fact, the first of the Ten Commandments given to the Jews through Moses at Mt. Sinai is:

"I am the Lord thy god, who brought thee out of the land of Egypt, out of the house of bondage."

Therefore, for someone to come along and say that *he* is the Son of God, meaning he too is God, which is precisely what Jesus eventually did, was the greatest and worse form of blasphemy that could have entered the ear of any Jew, especially the ear of a Pharisee, chief priest, or Essene, for that would mean that there is more than just one God. This would be diametrically opposed to what they had been taught all their lives, and taught to them by God Himself! Such a statement, coming from another human being, which is what Jesus was to the Pharisees, Essenes, scribes, and Sadducees, was the greatest and worse form of blasphemy possible, punishable only by death. Since this is what Jesus in fact did after He was arrested and taken to the house of Cai'aphas, the High Priest of the Jews, the capital punishment of crucifixion was the only and proper way to punish this terrible crime. And since the Jews under Roman rule were not allowed to execute anyone, for that "authority" was reserved only to the Romans, the Pharisees, Sadducees, and teachers of the Law (scribes) demanded that Jesus be crucified, and after much debate back and forth, the cruel and unjust act was carried out.

A very important clarification needs to be made here. The concept and reality of the Holy Trinity: the Father, the Son, and the Holy Spirit, was not known to the Jews prior to the arrival of Christ. No one on Earth knew about this sacred mystery. It was Jesus Himself who taught His Apostles this mysterious and profound reality, and He started by introducing the Father to them, talking about Him; how He and the Father were one, for example (Jn 10:30); and that His Father's house (Temple) was not a marketplace (Jn 2:16); and when the Jews persecuted Him for healing on the Sabbath, He replied: "My Father is working still, and I am working" (Jn 5:17). The Gospels reveal that Jesus went off by Himself to pray to the Father many times during His public ministry, and I am sure many times even before that. Sometimes Jesus would pray to the Father early in the morning when no one else was up yet (Mk 1:35), and at other times during the entire night (Lk 6:12). And then there's the time when Jesus taught His disciples how to pray to *our* Father, now known as the Lord's Prayer and the Our Father Prayer (Mt 6:9).

The Jews had never heard that there was a "Holy Spirit" (see Acts 19:2). [130] It was toward the end of His ministry, as His Passion drew near, that Jesus spoke to His Apostles at length about the Holy Spirit, third Person of the Trinity, calling Him the "Helper," the "Counselor": "I have yet many things to say to you, but you cannot bear them now. When the Spirit of truth comes, **he** will guide you into all the truth; for **he** will not speak on **his** own authority, but whatever **he** hears **he** will speak, and **he** will declare to you the things that are to come. **He** will glorify me, for **he** will take what is mine and declare it to you. All that the Father has is mine; therefore I said that **he** will take what is mine and declare it to you" (Jn 16:12-15) [my emph.]. The words "holy spirit" appears many times in the Dead Sea Scrolls, but they don't refer to the Holy Spirit, third Person of the Holy Trinity. The devout Essenes, mystics who wrote the Scrolls, also had no knowledge of the Holy Spirit. Theophilus of Antioch is credited with being the first to use the word "Trinity" in describing the Triune God. (In Acts 13:2, the Holy Spirit speaks.)

I'll never forget, one time I was out doing yard work and some Jehovah's Witnesses came up to me and started talking about the Bible. I used to tell them I was Catholic, was very happy to be so, and they would walk away, but this time I continued the conversation which led to them mentioning the Holy Spirit not being a person but only a force or power that one can get by being close to God. This was too much of a temptation for me, so I told them to wait and went and got my Bible. At that point in my life, I did not know where to look in the Bible for evidence on this topic, so I just opened it, and miraculously, it opened to John's Gospel, Chapter 14. I read verses 15-17, 25-26, and then skipped to 16:12-15 (quoted above), where the Spirit is repeatedly referred to as "he" and "his." I then said to them, "So you see, if the Spirit is only a force or power, why does the Bible call the Spirit 'he' and 'his'?" The two elders looked at each other and didn't say anything, but the two younger ones were really excited and interested in what I said, but before I could say anything else, the two elders took the young ones by the arms and led them away saying their farewells. I waved back and said, "Have a nice day! Come back anytime. I have some very good videos on Jehovah's Witnesses that you'll like!" I never saw them again, but I prayed for them!

### Nature And Person

In order to get some understanding of the doctrine of the Holy Trinity, we must first understand the difference and relationship between nature and person. In his outstanding book, "Theology and Sanity," Frank Sheed explains this topic very well. I will try my best to synthesize it here. God the Father is not God the Son, and God the Son is not God the Holy Spirit, and God the Holy Spirit is not God the Father. Yet, the Father is God, the Son is God, and the Holy Spirit is also God, but there are not three Gods, only One. The key to understanding here is in the words "person" and "nature." There is no arithmetical miracle here where three equals one somehow; or that three persons are stuffed into one person; none of that. To say, for example, that I possess a human nature automatically means that I am a person. I would certainly not be a human person if I did not possess a human nature, but it is me, the person, who possesses that human nature, not the other way around! Therefore, the word "nature" describes "what" I am, and the word "person" describes "who" I am. Every living being has a nature but not all beings are persons. If you are startled by something moving in the bushes at night, you'll probably say, "What is that?" And if a cat walks out, you'll say, "Oh, it's just a cat!" But if you suddenly see instead a profile of a man, you wouldn't say "What is that?" but rather "Who is that?" What refers to the nature of the being and who refers to the person. On Earth, only rational human beings are persons; nothing else is. If you called a rock or a potato a person, people would look at you funny!

Nature says what we are and also what we can and can't do. Human nature allows us to walk, run, jump, think, laugh, love, cry, sleep, and many other wonderful things, but a snake can only do one of these – sleep; and a rock can do none of them. Bird nature allows it to walk, swim, and fly, yet we humans can do the first two but not the last one (although we can now fly in a plane). And fish nature allows a fish to naturally live underwater which we naturally can't do (see 1 Cor. 15:39). Although it is the nature that determines what operations are possible for us to do, it is we, the persons, who do them. So, although one might be tempted to think that there are two distinct realities co-existing in every human: the what (nature) and the who (person), or perhaps two levels of only one reality, we cannot see clearly enough into our souls to be totally sure.

It is truly baffling to ponder the actual mystery of our existence. The only person who truly knows us very well is ourselves; i.e., no one knows you better than you do, right? Yet, if you look into your soul, your "self," and try to see what is the distinction between the what and the who in you, it is not a clear picture at all, but rather a veiled one. If someone asked you, "Tell me about yourself," for example, "but leave out all of the qualities you have, your name, where you were born and raised, and all the things you have ever done in life, only tell me about the self that possesses those qualities and has done all those things," you would not be able to tell that person anything about your "self." You know, of course, that there is something, someone there, but as Frank Sheed said, it is out of focus, you can't get a good glimpse of it; it's as if the soul does not want to be looked at!

## Three Divine Persons – One Nature

Although we can't see that deep into our selves enough to make out the distinction between our human nature and our personhood, we can at least see that only one nature can be possessed and operated by only one person. But the concept that one nature can be totally possessed and operated – at one and the same time – by three distinct Persons is difficult to see and understand. It isn't difficult to accept it as true, but it is difficult in seeing what it means. It is very important to note that the three distinct Persons of the Trinity are not three separate Persons, only three distinct Persons because they can't be separated since each one totally possesses the one same divine nature. And they don't "share" this nature; each one totally possesses it in its entirety. As I mentioned earlier, since the nature says what we are and what we can and can't do, each Person is God, wholly and equally with the other two, and each one can do everything that the divine nature allows them to do: to be God. The one unique quality of the Oneness of God, the oneness of divine nature, is that all three Persons have only one Will and only one Intellect because there is only one nature. Unlike three humans who possess three separate human natures with three separate wills and intellects, which means all three think differently, know differently, love differently, and act differently, all three Divine Persons totally possess only one Will and only one Intellect. Thus, all three Know all things with only One Intellect and all three Love with only One Will. Three Persons, One will, One Intellect, not three Gods. Only One God: Jesus said, "I and the Father are one" (Jn 10:30). The "Oneness" of the Trinity is a profound Mystery.

It is equally important to know that the word "God" is not the Father's name, nor is it Jesus' name, nor is it the name of the Holy Spirit. The word "God" simply refers to the nature, the divine nature, and some of the characteristics or attributes of this utterly perfect divine nature are: Unity, Immutability,

Simplicity, Omnipotence, Omniscience, and Omnipresence. We humans, on the other hand, only possess a human nature which does not have any of those qualities. But the Father possesses the divine nature, Jesus, the Son, possesses both the divine nature and also a human nature, and the Holy Spirit possesses the divine nature. They don't share the divine nature. They each possess it entirely. Although all three Persons possess the divine nature, there are not three Gods but only one God: one nature. Thus, there *is* only ONE God! [131]

When we Catholics say there is only one God, much the same as when the Jews say there is only one God, both of us, in actuality, are right, because there is in fact only one divine nature, which is what the word "God" refers to. But that divine nature, unbeknownst to the Jews, which included the Pharisees, Essenes, Sadducees, Elders, and scribes (teachers of the Law) is totally and completely possessed by three distinct Persons: the Holy Trinity: a deep and profound mystery that has been taught and handed down from generation to generation by the Holy Roman Catholic Church: the One, Holy, Catholic, and Apostolic Church founded by Jesus Christ (God) over 2000 years ago. The doctrine of the Trinity is something the Jews were not taught and therefore were ignorant of. It does not appear anywhere in the OT, nor in the Hebrew Bible, the Talmud, or in any other Jewish publication or written record to date, but Jesus taught it to His Jewish disciples. The doctrine of the Holy Trinity is a very profound mystery. We humans will never totally come to understand it fully, but that's ok! We don't need to. But we should look forward to one day being able to enjoy the utter bliss of gazing upon Them in Person for all Eternity. Without Time.

"Now surely I do see what an immense effect such a doctrine [of the Holy Trinity] must have upon life. It is no mere question for theologians, but one that concerns every living soul. Whatever is allowed by God's power must be guided by His wisdom and urged on by His love. All that happens to me in life, the little worries and the great anxieties, the crises and the daily annoyances, the sorrows and the joys, the harms that reach me through the sins of others, the great crimes of history, the huge and devastating wars, the partings and loves and the whole cycle of human experience are permitted by Power, which is itself wise and loving. These three Persons determine my life, and, since I walk by faith, I must surely grow very patient in my attitude toward life. For how can I complain or criticize God's Providence, since it all comes under that triple influence of Power, Wisdom, and Love? Under the guidance, then, of this mystery, I can walk through the valley of death or the more perilous borders of sin without loss of courage or hopefulness. Nothing can make me afraid. How these are separate, yet one, I do not know, nor can I reconcile in my concrete experience the claims of each. It is always a mystery, but a mystery in which I believe. Whatever Power allows on earth is designed in Wisdom and attuned by Love." (Fr. Bede Jarrett.)

Only faith will bring a person to believe in the Trinity. Reason alone will not suffice. [132]

One of the most profound and difficult mysteries to understand about God is that God has never had a beginning. That is, God has always existed and will always exist – forever and ever! The Three Persons of the Holy Trinity: Father, Son, and Holy Spirit, are omnipotent, are pure spirit (except Jesus, who now also has a human body), and have always existed. And moreover, they live "outside" our physical universe in a place called "Heaven." Our imagination, with some effort, can picture God living outside our universe, but an omnipotent God that has always existed ? Ponder that for a while.

# Chapter 7

"And as they were coming down the mountain, Jesus commanded them, 'Tell no one the vision, until the Son of man is raised from the dead' " (Mt 17:9).

## WHO DO *YOU* SAY I AM ?
## The Messianic Secret

For some strange reason, the above passage from Matthew's Gospel took me completely by surprise one fine day while reading Scripture. Even though I had read and heard that same passage countless times, this time it struck me totally different. The words acted like a spark thrown into a pile of dry kindling and my curiosity was set on fire. "Tell no one the vision? Why the secrecy?" I asked myself. I began to search through all four Gospels to see how many similar passages I could find and was surprised at what I found. Further research led to the discovery that the term "Messianic Secret" had been created to identify the NT passages where Jesus forbids the disclosure of His healings, exorcisms, miracles, and supernatural incidents, and eventually, His true identity. This was truly fascinating! I had never heard of this before! And I again wondered, "Why the secrecy?"

The parallel to Matthew's passage quoted above in Mark's Gospel is: "And as they were coming down the mountain, he charged them to tell no one what they had seen, until the Son of man should have risen from the dead. So they kept the matter to themselves, questioning what the rising from the dead meant" (Mk 9:9-10). Even more mystery! After reading this, the thought occurred to me, "What or who was responsible for making sure that nothing and no one would interfere with and/or prevent the death of Christ in order to make Redemption a successful reality?" I agree this may sound like a silly question, but it really isn't. For surely, if the Pharisees, Sadducees, and the crowd yelling at Pilate to crucify Jesus actually knew and believed that Jesus was the foretold Messiah, and moreover, the Son of God, God in the flesh, they certainly, of course, would not have demanded His execution, and consequently, the Redemption of mankind would not have taken place.[133] Would I even be here, writing this today? Therefore, and it is a very interesting question, "What and/or who kept the Pharisees, Essenes, scribes and chief priests from realizing and believing that Jesus was indeed the prophesied Messiah, the Son of the Living God?"

This brought me back to the initial question, "Why did Jesus want to keep His divinity a secret?" That question kept running through my mind, over and over again. I thought, "There must be a very good reason for this. Jesus always had – and has – a very good reason and purpose for everything He says and does." As I mentioned earlier, the word "Christ" is not a name at all but a title. It is derived from the Greek word "christos" which is a translation of the Hebrew word "meshiah" (Messiah), "the Anointed One." This explains why we find the expression in the NT "Jesus the Christ," which means "Jesus the Messiah." And as I described in Chapter 5, there are prophecies in the OT that describe the expected Messiah or Christ, the "Anointed One," as the Son of God.

As I continued my research, I discovered, much to my surprise, that the Jews never had a doctrine of Original Sin, and still don't to this day! I was literally shocked by this surprising fact. So naturally, from the Jewish point of view, there was no need for a Heavenly Messiah to come and redeem the human race from it. This, I thought, must have contributed, perhaps to a great degree, to their misinterpretation of the Messianic prophecies, making them think that these pointed to an Earthly messiah who would one day come to save only them from servitude and not to redeem the entire human race. Logic dictates that this would account, and perhaps mainly, for why the Jews were not—and still are not—expecting a Heavenly Messiah. This, the root cause. Add to this the fact that since the Jews were ignorant of the Holy Trinity, that there existed more than one Divine Person, it was truly and completely inconceivable to them that God the Father would send His only begotten Son to Earth one day, assume a human body, and walk side by side with them like an ordinary person. So, adding these together, it is not surprising to see why Jesus was found guilty of blasphemy when He told the High Priest after His arrest the truth, that He indeed was God. To the Sadducees, Pharisees, Essenes and scribes, the "experts" in religion, this was the most serious crime of all, a crime punishable only by death, but this death, interestingly enough, would ensure the Redemption of the entire human race! What a mystery!

Evidenced by the above passages from Matthew and Mark (and also Luke), since Jesus kept telling his followers and also those He cured not to tell anyone who He was and who had cured them, did this "cloak of secrecy" contribute to or further the ignorance of His divinity on the part of the Pharisees, Essenes, the chief priests and teachers of the Law? The answer would seem to be "Yes." Even though Jesus performed supernatural miracles impossible for a human to perform: curing the born blind and mute, raising the dead, instantly curing leprosy and physical deformities, casting out demons, etc., the "conditioned" minds of the Pharisees, Sadducees, and others were not able to realize this was God in the flesh. In fact, they attributed His power to perform these miracles to Satan and not to God (Mt 12:24).

As mentioned earlier, this very unique "phenomenon" became known after the Resurrection as the Messianic Secret (MS), and it is important to know that the MS, together with the Three Contributing Factors (TCF) shown below, were and still are largely responsible for the ignorance the Jews had – and still have – about Jesus Christ being the foretold Heavenly Messiah: the Son of the Living God in the flesh.

**The Three Contributing Factors**

**1. No Doctrine of Original Sin** (see p. 72).
**2. Due to 1, no reason for - or expectancy of - a Redeemer.** (Led to the misinterpretation of Messianic prophecies).
**3. No Doctrine of the Holy Trinity** (see p. 163).

The fact that the Jews did not have a doctrine of Original Sin and were therefore not expecting a Heavenly Messiah to redeem the human race from this Sin, and much less, that the Messiah was going to be God in the flesh, facilitated the concealment of Christ's divine identity which was aided by implementing the "policy of secrecy" (MS) in order to secure and bring the redemptive Sacrifice on the Cross for the eternal benefit of mankind to certain completion.

In short, the TCF combined with the MS explains fully why the Jews did not accept Christ as the Heavenly Messiah that He was then and still is now. Some may say, "But what about Peter, Nathanael, and Simeon? They called Jesus the Christ, the Son of God, and King of Israel. What about them?" One must remember that in the case of Peter, his declaration was a revelation given to him by God the Father (Mt 16:17); he did not come to that conclusion on his own.

With Simeon, the NT says he was "a good, God-fearing man….**waiting for Israel to be saved.** The Holy Spirit was with him and had assured him that he would not die before he had seen the Lord's promised Messiah" (Lk 2:25-26 [my emph.] NCSB). It isn't fully and explicitly clear here that Simeon clearly understood that the baby he was holding was the Heavenly Messiah, the Son of God, who came to redeem the entire human race, because keep in mind, this was not the Messiah the Jews were waiting for. Nevertheless, the Church teaches that Simeon knew who the baby really was through the Holy Spirit. However, Nathanael perhaps saw Jesus as the expected Earthly messiah who like King David was 'son of God' and 'King of Israel' (cf. Psalm 89:26-27) now sent by God to liberate the Jews from Roman rule. Only my opinion.

It is important to always keep in mind when reading the NT that the Messiah Jesus was (and is) is not the messiah the Jews were (and are still) waiting for. WE now know that is who He was, but THEY did not know that then. None of them did! And in the case of the prophetess Anna, we find: "That very same hour she arrived and gave thanks to God and spoke about the child **to all who were waiting for God to set Jerusalem free**" (Lk 2:38 [my emph.]; NCSB). Although this clearly refers to the Earthly messiah the Jews were waiting for that would "**set Jerusalem free**" from the Romans, it can also mean that she told those who were expecting an Earthly messiah that the child was in fact the Heavenly Messiah instead, the One they were *not* expecting. God only knows for sure, but the Church teaches that Anna, like Simeon, was inspired by the Holy Spirit. Nevertheless, these examples are very isolated cases, for the majority of the Jews, including the Pharisees, Essenes, Sadducees, Elders, and the teachers of the Law, were eagerly expecting an Earthly messiah, of that there is no doubt whatsoever, and the official Jewish record is very clear on this.[134]

On many occasions (not all are recorded in Scripture), Jesus told His followers, as well as those He cured, not to tell anyone who He was or who cured them. And moreover, He also told them not to mention to anyone certain miracles He had performed, including supernatural events they had witnessed in His presence (Mk 1:44, 5:43, 7:36, 8:30, 9:9; Mt 16:20; 17:9). Jesus even commanded the demons – more than once – not to say who He was! (Mk 1:34; 3:12.) One excellent explanation of this is found in the "Catena Aurea" by St. Thomas Aquinas: "Furthermore, the reason that He forbade the devils to speak, was to teach us not to believe them, even if they say true. For if once they find persons to believe them, they mingle truth with falsehood." [135] This technique of mingling truth with lies (half-truths) was fathered by Satan himself and was first used on Eve in the Garden of Eden with Catastrophic results.

Although Jesus told many of those He cured not to say anything to anyone about the cures, many of these did not listen to Him and spread the news everywhere. Here are some examples:

### Evidence Of Secrecy

**MATTHEW**: "When he entered the house, the blind men came to him; and Jesus said to them, 'Do you believe that I am able to do this?' They said to him, 'Yes, Lord.' Then he touched their eyes, saying, 'According to your faith let it be done to you.' And their eyes were opened. And Jesus sternly charged them, 'See that no one knows it.' But they went away and spread his fame through all that district" (9:28-31).

"He said to them, 'But who do you say that I am?' Simon Peter replied, 'You are the Christ, the Son of the living God'.... Then he strictly charged the disciples to tell no one that he was the Christ" (16:15-16, 20; see 12:16).

After Jesus' Transfiguration up on a high mountain, where Moses and Elijah talked with Jesus, "And as they were coming down the mountain, Jesus commanded them, 'Tell no one the vision, until the Son of man is raised from the dead' " (17:9).

**MARK**: "And immediately there was in their synagogue a man with an unclean spirit; and he cried out, 'What have you to do with us, Jesus of Nazareth? Have you come to destroy us? I know who you are, the Holy One of God.' But Jesus rebuked him, saying, 'Be silent, and come out of him!' And the unclean spirit, convulsing him and crying with a loud voice, came out of him. And they were all amazed, so that they questioned among themselves, saying, 'What is this? A new teaching! With authority he commands even the unclean spirits, and they obey him.' And at once his fame spread everywhere throughout all the surrounding region of Galilee" (1:23-28).

"That evening, at sundown, they brought to him all who were sick or possessed with demons. And the whole city was gathered together about the door. And he healed many who were sick with various diseases, and cast out many demons; and he would not permit the demons to speak, because they knew him" (1:32-34).

"And a leper came to him begging him, and kneeling said to him, 'If you will, you can make me clean.' Moved with pity, he stretched out his hand and touched him, and said to him, 'I will; be clean.' And immediately the leprosy left him, and he was made clean. And he sternly charged him, and sent him away at once, and said to him, 'See that you say nothing to any one; but go, show yourself to the priest, and offer for your cleansing what Moses commanded, for a proof to the people.' But he went out and began to talk freely about it, and to spread the news, so that Jesus could no longer openly enter a town, but was out in the country; and people came to him from every quarter" (1:40-45).

"And they brought to him a man who was deaf and had an impediment in his speech; and they begged him to lay his hand upon him. And taking him aside from the multitude privately, he put his fingers into his ears, and he spat and touched his tongue; and looking up to heaven, he sighed, and said to him, 'Eph'phatha,' that is, 'Be opened.' And his ears were opened, his tongue was released, and he spoke plainly. And he charged them to tell no one; but the more he charged them, the more zealously they proclaimed it. And they were astonished beyond measure, saying, 'He has done all things well; he even makes the deaf hear and the mute speak' " (7:32-37).

"And Jesus went on with his disciples, to the villages of Caesare'a Philip'pi; and on the way he asked his disciples, 'Who do men say that I am?' And they told him, 'John the Baptist; and others say, Eli'jah; and others one of the Prophets.' And he asked them, 'But who do you say that I am?' Peter answered him, 'You are the Christ.' And he charged them to tell no one about him" (8:27-30).

Similar to the passage in Matthew's Gospel, after Jesus' Transfiguration we find: "And as they were coming down the mountain, he charged them to tell no one what they had seen, until the Son of man should have risen from the dead. So they kept the matter to themselves, questioning what the rising from the dead meant" (9:9-10).

**LUKE**: "Now when the sun was setting, all those who had any that were sick with various diseases brought them to him; and he laid his hands on every one of them and healed them. And demons also came out of many, crying, 'You are the Son of God!' But he rebuked them, and would not allow them to speak, because they knew that he was the Christ" (4:40-41).

"While he was in one of the cities, there came a man full of leprosy; and when he saw Jesus, he fell on his face and begged him, 'Lord, if you will, you can make me clean.' And he stretched out his hand, and touched him, saying, 'I will; be clean.' And immediately the leprosy left him. And he charged him to tell no one; but 'go and show yourself to the priest, and make an offering for your cleansing, as Moses commanded, for a proof to the people.' But so much the more the report went abroad concerning him; and great multitudes gathered to hear and to be healed of their infirmities. But he withdrew to the wilderness and prayed" (5:12-16).

"And when he came to the house, he permitted no one to enter with him, except Peter and John and James, and the father and mother of the child. And all were weeping and bewailing her; but he said, 'Do not weep; for she is not dead but sleeping.' And they laughed at him, knowing that she was dead. But taking her by the hand he called, saying, 'Child, arise.' And her spirit returned, and she got up at once; and he directed that something should be given her to eat. And her parents were amazed; but he charged them to tell no one what had happened" (8:51-56).

**JOHN**: Interestingly enough, I did not find a single example of the Messianic Secret in John's Gospel, only in the Synoptics.

* * *

So again, the question is, "Why the secrecy?" Why did Jesus command His followers and even the demons not to tell anyone who He really was? In fact, you would think that the opposite would have been the case; i.e., that Christ would have wanted everyone to know who He was, that the True promised Messiah had finally come, and moreover, that He was also God's Son: God in the flesh. This would have corrected the false "Earthly messiah" notions that most of them had and adhered to. But that is not what happened; that was not what Jesus wanted. Why not?

Some of the early Church Fathers believed that Jesus told some of those He cured not to say anything about the incidents because He wanted to teach His followers the value of humility, to avoid vainglory, showiness, and not to profit from the Good News they were going to preach and the miracles they would perform themselves, and yet other Church Fathers believed that Jesus was indeed trying to keep His divinity a secret in order to eliminate obstructions and impediments to the Redemption of mankind through His sacrificial death on the Cross.

Let's take a look at the Patristic evidence on this and see what the early Church Fathers had to say in this regard. The following excerpts are taken from St. Thomas Aquinas' "Catena Aurea" (CA).

### Examples Against Vainglory/Profit

On Mt 8:1-4: The curing of a leper: "Jesus when healing his body bids him tell no man; *Jesus saith unto him, See thou tell no man.* Some say that He gave this command that they might not through malice distrust his cure. But this is said foolishly, for He did not so cure him as that his purity should be called in question; but He bids him tell no man, to teach that He does not love ostentation and glory. How is it then that to another to whom He had healed He gives command to go and tell it? [Mk 5:19] What He taught in that was only that we should have a thankful heart; for He does not command that it should be published abroad, but that glory should be given to God. He teaches us then through this leper **not to be desirous of empty honour;** by the other, not to be ungrateful, but to refer all things to the praise of God." (CA, Vol. I, St. Mt., Part 1, p. 300. Chrys.) [My emph.]

On Mk 1:40-45: The curing of a leper: "As if He said, It is not yet time that My works should be preached, I require not thy preaching. By which He teaches us **not to seek worldly honour** as a reward for our works." (CA, Vol. 1I, St. Mark, p. 34. Chrys..) [My emph.]

On Lk 5:12-14: The curing of a leper: "*And he commanded him that he should tell it to no one*, that in truth he might teach us that our good deeds are not to be made public, but to be rather concealed, that **we should abstain not only from gaining**

**money, but even favour**" (CA, Luke, p. 182. Ambrose.) [My emph.]

On Lk 5:12-14: The curing of a leper: "And although the Lord in giving out remedies advised telling them to no one, **instructing us to avoid pride**." (CA, Luke, p.183. Chrys.) [My emph.]

### Examples On Secrecy Of Divinity

On Lk 4:41: The declaration of demons: "The devils confess the Son of God, and as it is afterwards said, *they knew him to be Christ*; for when the devil saw Him distressed by fasting [in the desert], he perceived Him to be truly man, but when he prevailed not in his trial [with Pilate] he doubted whether or not He were the Son of God, but now by the power of Christ's miracles he either perceived or suspected Him to be the Son of God. He [Satan] did not then persuade the Jews to crucify Him because he thought Him not to be Christ or the Son of God, but because he did not foresee that by this death he himself would be condemned. Of this mystery hidden from the world the Apostle says, that none of the princes of this world knew, **for if they had known** [His divinity] **they would never have crucified the Lord of Glory.**" (CA, Luke, p. 169. Bede; see 1 Cor 7-8.) [My emph.]

On Lk 4:41: "But the Apostles themselves are commanded to be silent concerning Him, lest by proclaiming His divine Majesty, **the dispensation of His Passion should be delayed.**" (CA, Luke, p. 170. Bede; see 1 Cor 2:6-9.) [My emph.]

On Mk 1:32-34: The declaration of demons: "For the devils knew that He was the Christ, who had been promised by the Law: for they saw in Him all the signs, which had been foretold by the Prophets; **but they** [the Jews] **were ignorant of His divinity**, as also were *their princes,* **for if they had**

**known it, they would not have crucified the Lord of glory.**" (CA, Vol II, St. Mark, p. 29-30. Pseudo-Aug.) [My emph.]

On Mt 17:9: After the Transfiguration: "**Or, because if His majesty should be published among the people, they should hinder the dispensation of His passion, by resistance to the chief Priests; and thus the redemption of the human race should suffer impediment**" (CA, Vol I, St. Mt., Part 1, p. 607. Remigius.) [My emph.]

* * *

In this last passage, St. Remigius believes that if Christ's divinity had been regularly divulged, disseminated and spread widely throughout the land, the people would have learned that Jesus was indeed God in the flesh, the True and Heavenly Messiah, and therefore would have prevented the Pharisees and Sadducees from demanding His execution before Pilate and the Redemption of the human race would not have taken place.

An email reply I received from Father George W. Rutler in this regard contained the following:

"The explanation of Saint Remigius became the standard way of dealing with the so-called Messianic secret although it was considered more often in recent times than traditionally by the fathers."

Although St. Remigius, who lived from 437-533 A.D., is not considered a Father of the Church (even though the middle of the eighth century is generally regarded as the close of the age of the Fathers), St. Gregory of Tours refers to Remigius as "a man of great learning, fond of rhetorical studies, and equal in his holiness to St. Silvester." [136] Moreover, St.

Thomas Aquinas considered his beliefs important enough to include them throughout his Catena Aurea.

The above four examples have considerable weight in showing that Jesus most likely wanted to keep His real identity a secret, at least for as long as possible, so that the Pharisees and Sadducees (chief priests) would not come to realize He was indeed the Son of God and therefore see Him as a blasphemer that needed to be put to death when He claimed that title. This perspective cannot be ignored or dismissed in light of the evidence thus presented.

In light of the above, I believe the MS had at least two (if not more) objectives and purposes:

1. Teach His followers the virtues of humility against vainglory, pride, and worldly profit;

2. Conceal His divine identity.

This "Policy of Secrecy" (MS) surely contributed to making His Redemptive Sacrificial Mission a guaranteed success. To what degree? It is hard to say. St. Mark's account stated earlier of the Transfiguration (9:9) strongly supports this point of view: "And as they were coming down the mountain, he charged them to tell no one what they had seen, until the Son of man should have risen from the dead."

QUESTION: Why were they ordered not to reveal His identity until **after** the Resurrection?

ANSWER: To ensure the arrest, condemnation and crucifixion in order to redeem mankind.

There doesn't seem to be a more logical answer. It was not Christ's Resurrection that redeemed mankind, but His Crucifixion and Death. This is why Catholics have Crucifixes with the Corpus of Christ on it in churches, rosaries, holy cards, hanging on walls, etc. : to remind us of our Redemption. Protestants do not have this. I remember at work one day, a Protestant lady said to me, "You Catholics still have Jesus on the cross!" My reply: "A Reminder of our Redemption."

If the Pharisees and chief priests had come to believe that Christ was the Son of God, they certainly would never have harmed a single hair on His head! But as we all know, that's not what actually happened, and we have God to thank for that Blessed Sacrifice He endured for our sake.

Here's another thing to think about. If the Prophets had been completely explicit and included in their prophecies that the promised Messiah was going to be God Himself in the flesh, would come in a human body, and their instructions were to execute Him in order to redeem the human race, do you really think they would have done such a thing? Arrest a person who they knew for sure was God Himself, and then consent to have Him tortured and have huge nails driven through His hands and feet to a tree? And then mock Him, strike Him, make fun of Him, and watch Him die a horrible death? Are you mad? Kill God? And be responsible and guilty for such a heinous and abominable crime, and then be sent to Hell for all Eternity for doing so? Personally, I really don't think so. In fact, if the Prophets had given them explicit instructions to kill the Son of God, the Jews certainly would have had good reason for stoning them to death!

It therefore appears that the reality of the Trinity: three divine Persons in one Godhead, was not revealed to the Jews in OT times perhaps for a very intentional and specific reason: to put it simply, so that the Jews would believe that there ***is*** only one God, only one Divine Person, and this would be very helpful in aiding Jesus to conceal His real identity when He embarked on His public ministry – miracles included. The solitary "oneness" of God was hammered into the Jewish mind so often and so effectively that no one suspected there could have been more than one Divine Person, and much less, that He would send His Son as Messiah to redeem humanity.

**"Hear, O Israel: The Lord our God, the Lord is ONE."**

This crucial point cannot be overemphasized in regards to its role in the Messianic Secret.

Even though Jesus performed many miracles: brought to life many from the dead, expelled countless demons from tormented people, cured instantly many illnesses and deformities, and many others, this still did not make the Pharisees and chief priests realize that He was God in person, and in fact, they believed quite the opposite: that the devil was giving Him this power: "But when the Pharisees heard it, they said, 'It is only by Be-el'zebul, the prince of demons, that this man casts out demons' " (Mt 12:24).

As I mentioned before, since God is "outside of time" and therefore transcends time, this means God knows every single thing that has taken place in human history from its beginning to its end, and this, of course, includes the necessity of Christ's Crucifixion in order to redeem the entire human race. With this in mind, in order to guarantee that the Crucifixion of our Lord would take place at the proper time at the end of His Public Ministry without interruptions of any kind, it seems that God would have had to take certain measures – in advance – to ensure the success of a Mission as important as this one; a success that, needless to say, is extremely important for the eternal benefit of mankind. In this regard, some important measures that God perhaps took that come to mind are:

## Important Measures

1. God did not reveal the doctrine of Original Sin and the explicitness of the need for its Redemption to the Hebrews, the Israelites, or the Jews.

2. God did not give explicit descriptions and detailed information about Jesus as the Messiah to the Hebrews, the Israelites, or the Jews through their Prophets. Isaiah is the only Prophet who gives the most details and clues about Christ in his prophecies. The other prophecies only give vague and cryptic descriptions and obscure information about Him so that it wouldn't be obvious to the Jewish authorities and the people that Jesus would be God in the flesh and therefore refuse to have Him executed thereby preventing the redemptive Crucifixion to the detriment of mankind. Although there were enough combined prophetic clues that pointed to a Heavenly Messiah, the scribes, Pharisees and others did not "assemble the pieces" to realize it.

3. God did reveal the oneness of God to them, but withheld the reality of the Holy Trinity which led to the daily repetition of the Shema "Oneness of God" prayer and a rock-hard monotheistic mentality. Thus, by not revealing the mystery of the Trinity in OT times, the possibility of God the Father sending to Earth His only Son, one of the Divine Persons, on a redemptive Mission that would include assuming a human body would never enter the Jewish mind; it would be totally impossible and inconceivable to them.

4. God's Divine Providence directed and ordered the lives of the Jews in a certain way, from inception of adoption as Chosen People to the coming of the Messiah, that allowed them to undergo severe hardships and suffering from time to time during their history (as punishment for their sins) in order to set their minds firmly on the hopes for an "Earthly messiah" (facilitating the concealment of Christ's divinity)

that would come and free them from Gentile domination; a mindset I believe the Pharisees were largely responsible for.

5. Last but not least, God had the Messiah expose the hypocrisy, sinfulness, lack of Scripture understanding, and unjust behavior of the Pharisees, chief priests, and teachers of the Law – for all to see – to make them "mad as Hell" at the Christ and give them a good reason for wanting to kill Him thereby securing the Redemptive Sacrifice of "the Lamb of God, who takes away the sin of the world" (Jn 1:29).

There is no doubt that numbers 1 and 2 were certainly put in place by God since Judaism did not have – and still does not have – neither the doctrine of Original Sin nor the doctrine of a Heavenly Messiah: God in the flesh, both of which are still absent from Rabbinic Judaism to this day. Number 3 was also put in place by God for the reason stated therein (also missing from Rabbinic Judaism to this day). Number 4 does not mean that God Himself inflicted hardships and sufferings on the Chosen People, but rather allowed these things to take place at certain times and of certain severities, and not only for their own good (as punishment for sins), but for that of mankind as well, for Scripture says that a Loving God punishes those He loves (Prv 3:12; Heb 12:5-11), and the Gardener prunes his Vine in order for it to produce more fruit (Jn 15:1-2). These, however, appear to be secondary while the primary objective was the consequential effect of these: to expect an Earthly messiah to rescue them. And number 5 seems pretty clear-cut as found in Scripture, for the religious Elite: the Pharisees and chief priests, had indeed fallen into a hypocritical mindset (Mt 23:13); they believed they were exempt from sinning (Jn 8:7), did not understand some of the Scriptures properly (Mt 22:46), especially the Messianic prophecies, and treated their people unjustly (Mt 23:1-4; 13-15).

At this point it is important to point out that God is the most Tender and Loving Father, with a Love, Mercy and Compassion way beyond our imaginations and understandings. Concrete proof of this was given to us, beyond the shadow of a doubt, by sending His only Beloved Son to suffer a cruel and horrible death for our Eternal benefit, not His. So don't misunderstand me when I said that He allowed terrible things to happen to His Chosen People, because this was not only as punishment for their sinfulness, but also to insure the success of His Son's Mission on Earth for the benefit of all mankind. It really does not take much to realize that God does indeed work in very mysterious ways, but always, always does so from pure Love for us.

This brings to mind an interesting question: "Why did Jesus embark on a life of public ministry that included performing supernatural miracles – for three long years – if He did not want anyone to know who He really was? Wouldn't the continued performance of miracles over a span of three long years lead others to think He was divine, something He did not want anyone to know? This, at first, does not make sense, for you would think that the last thing He should have done was to perform miracles since it would eventually become obvious that He was not just an ordinary man. But ironically, Jesus had to – and wanted to – perform miracles for several reasons so that His Sacrificial Redemptive Mission **would** be a success. I believe some of the reasons are:

### Reasons For Christ's Miracles
(Partial List)

1. The primary reason Jesus exorcised demons from people and healed their diseases is that, now being normal, they could go and worship God in the Temple; they couldn't do that before. Jesus truly loved His people, created in His Image. He wanted to teach them the importance and beauty of Life, the importance and beauty of truth, and wanted to

tell them the Good News about the Kingdom of God. He also wanted to cure them because He loved them so much: "As he went ashore he saw a great throng; and he had compassion on them, and healed their sick" (Mt 14:14). "When the crowds learned it, they followed him; and he welcomed them and spoke to them of the kingdom of God, and cured those who had need of healing" (Lk 9:11).

2. Jesus needed His Apostles to believe in Him in order to follow Him and later establish His Church on Earth for the dissemination of the Good News, and this required performing miracles.

"This, the first of his signs, Jesus did at [the wedding in] Cana in Galilee, and manifested his glory; and his disciples believed in him. After this he went down to Caper'na-um, with his mother and his brethren and his disciples; and there they stayed for a few days" (Jn 2:11-12).

3. Jesus conducted Himself in such a way that those who heard Him preach and witnessed the miracles He performed would have no doubt that He was a gifted man of God, a prophet perhaps, who was sent by God to teach them and help them with their problems and sufferings: "When the chief priests and the Pharisees heard his parables, they perceived that he was speaking about them. But when they tried to arrest him, they feared the multitudes, because they held him to be a prophet" (Mt 21:45-46). Only His Apostles were eventually given the understanding of who He really was, the Son of God, but this became apparent **after** the Resurrection.

4. By performing supernatural miracles, apart from wanting to help His people out of love for them, Jesus would ensure that masses of people would follow Him and believe in Him in order to create a large following; without a large following, He would not have been able to attract attention to Himself,

and Jesus needed to attract attention to Himself in order to attract the Pharisees and chief priests who would eventually bring His Sacrificial Mission to sure completion by having Him condemned to death for blasphemy; a Mission that would remain a mystery and a secret until the Last Supper.

The Apostles did not understand – until after the Resurrection, that His Mission was to die for the sins of mankind. Although Jesus told perhaps many of those He cured not to say who cured them, He knew very well that some were going to do just that – it is hard to hold back such good news! Moreover, it is also hard for most people to keep a secret. Jesus knew that too. In some instances, telling secrets results in widespread dissemination, a technique widely used by modern sensational tabloids. Although the miracles themselves would eventually bring large crowds to Him, perhaps Jesus employed this technique selectively to ensure attraction. On the other hand, large crowds would inhibit his ability to move about from town to town, and moreover, too much attention would also attract the authorities – Jewish and/or Roman – and possibly cause a confrontation before the time was right. Nevertheless, Jesus handled everything masterfully. It doesn't appear to be far-fetched to imagine that perhaps during the time Jesus spent in the desert after His Baptism, preparing for His public ministry (Scripture says it was forty days), Jesus began to either formulate a plan, or go over a plan He had already formulated that would ensure the success of His main objective: His Redemptive Death for mankind. It would seem that part of this plan would have to include not revealing to anyone who He was, not until His Mission was coming to an end, for at least a couple of reasons:

**Reasons For Secrecy**
(Partial List)

1. Revealing His divinity would more than likely frighten

people and drive them away instead of attracting them, and as I mentioned earlier, Jesus needed to form a following in order for His Mission to be a success. Fear of God is perhaps a trait in human nature that goes way back – to Adam and Eve!

2. Jesus told some of those He cured (perhaps the majority) not to say anything about the incidents because He wanted to teach His followers the value of humility, to avoid vainglory, showiness, and not to seek profit from the Good News they were going to preach and the miracles they would perform themselves.

3. As I mentioned earlier, His divine nature had to remain a secret to ensure being condemned to death by the Pharisees, chief priests, Elders, and scribes when He revealed this truth to them. St. Paul wrote: "But we impart a secret and hidden wisdom of God [the Messiah would be God incarnate], which God decreed before the ages for our glorification. None of the rulers of this age understood this; for if they had, they would not have crucified the Lord of glory" (1 Cor 2:7-8).

At the very beginning of His ministry, Jesus told Simon and his brother Andrew: "Follow me, and I will make you fishers of men" (Mt 4:18-19), for He was going to teach them, as well as His other Apostles and disciples, how to convert sinners into Christians. However, on the other side of the coin, Jesus was also going to teach his Apostles and disciples how to expose the hypocrisy, the ignorance of Scripture, and the hardness of heart of the Pharisees, chief priests and the scribes so that His followers would not imitate them.

If the Pharisees, Essenes and Sadducees had learned at the start of Jesus' three-year ministry that the long awaited Messiah was God in the flesh and had finally arrived, things would have turned out quite different: surely He would not have been condemned to death by the Jews. On the other hand, if His crucifixion had taken place at the start of His public ministry, Jesus would not have been able to announce the Good News, heal the sick, and expel demons from the possessed as He did during those three years of His ministry, but more important, He would not have had the time to gather and train His Apostles, not only for their missionary work, but also to establish His Church after His Ascension.

If Christ had said to Simon Peter, at the beginning: "Good morning Simon. How are you today?" And Peter had replied: "Very well, thank you sir. And who may I ask are you?" And Christ had said: "I am your Lord and your God." I don't think Peter would have taken this too well. And if Peter had stayed there with his mouth wide open in disbelief after Jesus said this, and Christ had waved His hands to produce thunder and lightning to prove that He indeed was God, I don't think Peter would have stayed around too much longer after that. Do you? It therefore seems logical that a very important part of Jesus' plan was to gradually reveal who He was to His Apostles so as not to scare them away. This, of course, makes perfect sense. Since Jesus had acquired a human body, thanks in no small part to His Holy Mother, Mary (our Mother too), this human body would certainly help to keep His divine identity a secret, for no one would ever suspect that the man called Jesus from Nazareth, the son of Joseph the carpenter, was God. How could Jesus be God since it was obvious He was a human person, like they were? In the Gospel of Matthew, we find a relevant statement that was made by a resident of Nazareth, the town where Jesus was from:

"And when Jesus had finished these parables, he went away from there, and coming to his own country he taught them in their synagogue, so that they were astonished, and said, 'Where did this man get this wisdom and these mighty works? Is not this the carpenter's son? Is not his mother called Mary? And are not his brethren James and Joseph and Simon and Judas? And are not all his sisters with us? Where then did this man get all this?' And they took offense at him. But Jesus said to them, 'A prophet is not without honor except in his own country and in his own house.' And he did not do many mighty works there, because of their unbelief' (Mt 13:53-58; see Jn 6:42). It is interesting to note here that faith in Jesus almost always resulted in the performance of a miracle for the benefit of the believer, while lack of faith almost always stifled it. The following in this regard is found in the Catena Aurea: "Or he says *many*, because there were some persons, who could not at all be cured on account of their unfaithfulness. Therefore He healed many of those who were brought, that is, all who had faith." [137]

Jesus knew that he was going to be crucified by the Romans at the instigation of the Pharisees and chief priests way in advance; in fact, before the Creation of the Universe. That was the main objective of His mission: willingly sacrifice Himself and lay down His life to redeem mankind. How was He going to make sure they would execute Him? Was He going to commit robbery? Or commit adultery with someone's wife? How about bear false witness against an innocent person? Or perhaps kill someone? No, none of these. God does not commit crimes, and He also does not lie.

So, how was He going to bring about His condemnation so as to be put to death? By telling the truth: that He was the Son of God, the promised Messiah. Even though this was the truth, in the eyes of the Pharisees, Sadducees, and the Elders, this was indeed a crime: a crime punishable by death. Why? Because they thought He was only a human being. They did not–and could not–believe He was God in the flesh, for in their minds, God would never lower Himself and assume a human body. This was inconceivable to them. Moreover, the Pharisees were so busy trying to get everyone to comply with the 613 commandments (mitzvot) and being faithful to the Torah and the many Kosher regulations they had so that Messiah would come and free them from the Romans that they were not following the "Spirit of the Law": the principles behind the Ten Commandments and the more important precepts of the Law (see 2 Cor 3:6; Mt 23:23-28); nor were they in tune with them, especially the prophecies regarding the promised Heavenly Messiah. If they had been fully aware of their true meaning, they would have known that Jesus was indeed the promised Messiah.

The chief priests—and especially the Pharisees—succeeded in getting the crowd present at Christ's arrest to side with them and condemn Jesus when Pilate presented Him to them: "Now the chief priests and the elders persuaded the people to ask for Barab'bas and destroy Jesus" (Mt 27:20). After Pilate had Jesus scourged, he asked the crowd what they wanted him to do with Jesus, and the crowd answered, "We have a law, and by that law he ought to die, because he has made himself the Son of God" (Jn 19:7). Who in the crowd do you suppose was yelling this? Sounds like the Pharisees and Sadducees to me! From another angle, the crowd asked for the release of the rebel Barab'bas—instead of Jesus—because Barab'bas represented the "Earthly messiah" to them, the type of messiah they were waiting for, the one who might free them from Roman rule. Nevertheless, the core of the Messianic Secret had obviously worked and Jesus was on His way to complete the Mission His Father had given to Him: a Mission of Love that would take Him to Calvary for OUR sake.

Only the Pharisees, Sadducees, scribes and the Elders had problems with Jesus. BIG problems. The Romans did not have a problem with Jesus; Jesus was not an enemy of the Romans. Pilate even said as much: "After he [Pilate] had said this, he went out to the Jews again, and told them, **'I find no crime in him'** " (Jn 18:38) [my emph.]. Scripture tells us Jesus never apologized to the Pharisees, Sadducees and scribes when He offended them, and rightly so for they deserved it. In today's politically correct American society, Jesus would be "thrown under the bus" many times over and surely silenced by the social media giants for everything He said to them. One example: "Then the disciples came and said to him, 'Do you know that the Pharisees were offended when they heard this saying?' He answered, 'Every plant which my heavenly Father has not planted will be rooted up. Let them alone; they are blind guides. And if a blind man leads a blind man, both will fall into a pit' " (Mt 15:12-14).

## CONCLUSION

On page 957 of "A New Catholic Commentary On Holy Scripture" by Thomas Nelson Publishers, 1984, it is noted that two German Lutheran theologians, Georg William Wrede (1859-1906) and Rudolf Bultmann (1884-1976) believed the Apostle Mark invented the messianic secret (that Jesus never said any of this) and added it to his Gospel to serve as the only reason why Jesus had not been recognized as the Messiah, the Son of God, by the Jews. Wrede published this view in 1901.[138] This same Commentary also notes that the English Methodist theologian, Vincent Taylor (1887–1968) disagreed with this view and believed that Jesus' true identity was not revealed to the public until after the completion of His Mission (Death and Resurrection) because this was His "Destiny" (see Mk 9:9); i.e., in order to ensure the completion of His Mission, which accords with St. Bede, St. Paul (1 Cor 2:6-9), and St. Remigius as noted earlier (see pgs. 180-181). In my humble opinion, it is highly doubtful if not quite impossible that the Apostle Mark intentionally inserted such lies - regardless of good intentions - about his Lord in his Gospel considering the consequences thereof, and moreover, that both Matthew and Luke copied Mark in this untruth (Mark's Gospel was written first). Nevertheless, it does not surprise me that the two Protestant theologians in mention allowed their imaginations to run wild in this regard; it certainly was neither the first nor the last time wild Scriptural speculation has appeared from that side of the tracks. (Bultmann claimed the Gospels were "mythology.")

Since Jesus knew of the plot to kill Him (Jn 7:1), timing was of the utmost importance to Him, to the Master of Time, so He avoided getting caught by the Pharisees and be executed before the Appointed Time. Jesus wanted things to go His way; be arrested when He was ready to be arrested; be condemned when He was ready to be condemned; and be executed when He was ready to be executed, and not before; namely, on the Passover Festival of April 3rd, 33 A.D., which would coincide with the Sabbath that particular year (Jn 19:31). Like everything else He does so well, Jesus willingly and skillfully directed His own destiny and only admitted His divinity and Messiahship after Peter's declaration (Mt 16.16) because His execution was imminent. The Lord, Master, and Creator of the Universe, directed all events around Him as a Conductor directs a Symphony, with the exception that the players did not know what notes they were going to play next.

The combination of the Three Contributing Factors and the Messianic Secret reveals why the Jewish people did not believe and thereby accept Jesus Christ as the foretold Heavenly Messiah that He was then and still is now, a chronic lack of faith that continues to this day in all forms of Rabbinic Judaism with the exception of the movement "Messianic Jews" (or other similar groups): a religious belief system that fatally contradicts itself and therefore cannot be taken seriously (see p. 60).

The very fact that Christ came back from the dead and the Pharisees, Sadducees and scribes continued their unbelief and even persecuted the followers of Christ is quite remarkable but not surprising. Jesus gave His disciples and followers a parable in this regard that reveals how stubborn people can be in believing, even when faced with an absolute truth:

"There was a rich man, who was clothed in purple and fine linen and who feasted sumptuously every day. And at his gate lay a poor man named Laz'arus, full of sores, who desired to be fed with what fell from the rich man's table; moreover the dogs came and licked his sores. The poor man died and was carried by the angels to Abraham's bosom. The rich man also died and was buried; and in Hades, being in torment, he lifted up his eyes, and saw Abraham far off and Laz'arus in his bosom. And he called out, 'Father Abraham, have mercy upon me, and send Laz'arus to dip the end of his finger in water and cool my tongue; for I am in anguish in this flame.' But Abraham said, 'Son, remember that you in your lifetime received your good things, and Laz'arus in like manner evil things; but now he is comforted here, and you are in anguish. And besides all this, between us and you a great chasm has been fixed, in order that those who would pass from here to you may not be able, and none may cross from there to us.' And he said, 'Then I beg you, father, to send him to my father's house, for I have five brothers, so that he may warn them, lest they also come into this place of torment.' But Abraham said, 'They have Moses and the Prophets; let them hear them.' And he said, 'No, father Abraham; but if someone goes to them from the dead, they will repent.' He said to him, 'If they do not hear Moses and the Prophets, **neither will they be convinced if someone should rise from the dead**' " [namely Jesus] (Lk 16:19-31) [my emph.].

I personally believe Jesus referred to Himself as "Son of man" for two main reasons: (1) to conceal His divinity (vs. Son of God); (2) to prevent the titles "messiah" and "king" from being assigned to him by the Jews who were expecting an Earthly messiah/king to free them from Roman rule (see Jn 6:15). The Catholic Encyclopedia (under "Son of man") states that in the time of Christ, the term Son of man was not widely known as a Messianic title, and since Jesus wanted to keep His divine identity a secret, this may be one reason why He frequently used this term when referring to Himself: to keep the focus on His humanity. In the Gospel of Mark alone, "Son of man" appears 14 times. The Messianic Secret, together with the Three Contributing Factors, ensured the success of God's Holy Will: Jesus Christ's Sacrifice on the Cross to redeem mankind.

Another thought on the Book of Revelation. Among other things, the Book of Revelation clearly shows how Christ calls mankind to repentance and conversion in order to save us from Eternal Hell after death, for He came to Earth and died on the Cross 2000 years ago to restore the broken relationship between man and God and open the closed Gates of Heaven for everyone because of the Supreme Love He has for every single one of us. And the easiest and surest way to get to Heaven is to remain united to Him: to obey Him and follow His teachings through the Church He established. God the Father ordains the world through the New Covenant established by His Son, Jesus Christ, who "paid the price" with His own blood and "bought" us back from the devil's possession, but the devil, the world, and the weakness of our own flesh can be—and are—obstacles on our way to Heaven that we have to overcome until we finally leave this world through death's door and enter Heaven.

In spite of the clear evidence for secrecy shown in this chapter, there is a passage in St John's Gospel that proves three things: (1) the Jews did not know that the Messiah, the Christ, would be the Son of God, God incarnate; (2) Jesus told them that He was the Christ; and (3) why they wanted to kill Him: "So the Jews gathered round him and said to him, How long will you keep us in suspense? If you are the Christ, tell us plainly. Jesus answered them, I told you, and you do not believe. The works that I do in my Father's name, they bear witness to me; but you do not believe, because you do not belong to my sheep.... I and the Father are one. The Jews took up stones again to stone him. Jesus answered them, I have shown you many good works from the Father; for which of these do you stone me? The Jews answered him, We stone you for no good work but for blasphemy; because you, being a man, make yourself God" (Jn 10:24-26; 31-33).

# Chapter 8

"He said to them, 'But who do you say that I am?' Simon Peter replied, 'You are the Christ, the Son of the living God.' And Jesus answered him, 'Blessed are you, Simon Bar-Jona! For flesh and blood has not revealed this to you, but my Father who is in heaven. And I tell you, you are Peter, and on this rock I will build my Church, and the gates of Hades shall not prevail against it' " (Mt 16:15-18).

## THE ROMAN CATHOLIC CHURCH
### The Religion That Jesus Founded

Today, 2000 years after God came to Earth in the Person of Jesus Christ to sacrifice Himself and die a horrible death on a cross in order to redeem us from the eternal punishment we justly deserve for our sins, and by willingly doing this, restored the broken relationship between the human race and God due to the Original Sin of disobedience committed by Adam and Eve so that repentant believers can go to Heaven after death and live happily forever with their loving Creator, today, twenty (20) centuries later, after Christ went to all this trouble, and then established His one and only Church to teach us all this – and much more, there are tens of thousands of different religions all over the world? Why? One would think that by now, 2000 years later, the actual and absolute truth that there is only One True God and therefore only One True religion/Church would have been understood and adopted by all peoples worldwide, or at least, by the majority of humans on this planet, but that is evidently not the case. Why is this so? Short answer: that's the work of the devil.

Since unlike other creatures, God created humans with free will, humans like to instinctively do things their own way. Frank Sinatra's big hit song "My Way" typifies this egocentric mentality. Generally speaking, people don't like being told what to do. Just ask your adult son or daughter to do this or that, like go to Mass on Sundays, or follow the Ten Commandments daily, or other such good things, and see what happens. If we obey someone else's will and not our own when these two conflict, it makes us feel like our free will is being taken away from us, and that is something we naturally do not want to give up. No one likes it when others impose their will on us, especially without our consent. But a problem arises when obedience to God is rejected and we choose to do our own will instead of His because it suits us better; because we get some enjoyment or some other benefit from it. This is called "sin." Not a popular word these days.

When this happens, when we choose do to our own will in violation of God's Will, even when we think and feel that it is to our own benefit, it never is! This is why there are so many religions in the world today: people simply do not want to accept and then follow what God is telling them to do through His Church, the Holy Catholic Church; i.e., how to live their lives in order to be in harmony with Him and with one another. And so, many will continue – until the End of Time – to do their own will and follow what they *think* is best instead of following God's Will and what He *knows* is best for them. Ignoring God is not a very smart thing to do, by the way; it always ends in disaster and ruin! Doing our own will when it conflicts with God's Will is exactly what our first parents did in the Garden of Eden thousands of years ago that got us into this big mess in the first place!

So, as is plain to see, we really haven't changed very much, have we! Oh, we have great technological advances to be proud of that make our lives so much more comfortable. We've moved out from the grass and stick huts and into fantastic solid structures we call "homes"; instead of wells and outhouses – or holes in the ground – we now have hot and cold running water in these structures and toilets that flush away our bodily wastes; instead of washing our clothes in the river, or scrub them (till our hands turn blue) with soap and well water, we can just throw them into a machine that will do that for us; and instead of campfires and firepits, we now have ovens and stoves we can cook our food on; and refrigerators, to store all our goodies and food in a safe place so they won't spoil; and if we're too tired or lazy, we can either order take out, go buy food already cooked at the store, or go to a restaurant; we have grocery stores where we can buy just about anything one can think of without having to go out and pick it, gather it, or kill it ourselves; we have air conditioning, to keep us cool and comfortable, and electricity that runs all these things for us; and instead of going to the library, or sitting in a classroom in school, we now have the internet and have access to all kinds of information to educate ourselves with (unfortunately often false information); we can communicate all the way around the world in only seconds with our computers and phones; we even have "smart" cell phones that are mini computers; also "smart cars" (some even drive themselves); we have many medical advances to keep us healthy and extend our lives for years; and many other things. And don't forget the old time favorite: we can even go to the moon and back! Technology is now a god for many people who look to it for happiness.

But to make a concerted effort *and take the time* to properly educate ourselves in the topic of religion, to seriously research this subject in order to realize that there really is only one God who created all things, who for our sake and benefit established only one "religion," one Church, so we can learn about Him through it and find out all that He has done for us through it, and then naturally thank Him, and love Him, and then serve Him as we should, so that after this life we can live with Him Eternally in Heaven in total and complete happiness through it, this we can't do? And worse yet, this we won't do? evidenced by so many religions out there now! This may be one of the reasons why some people continue searching for intelligent life on other planets! Truly alarming.

## The Early Church

When did the Catholic Church begin? "When Jesus called the apostles to follow him. They were taught by him, given various necessary powers to act in his name, and finally sent to all the world on Pentecost Sunday, after having received a special communication of the Holy Spirit." [139] When Simon told Jesus: "You are the Christ, the Son of the living God" (Mt 16:16), and Jesus replied, "And I tell you, you are Peter [Petros in Greek for "rock"], and on this rock I will build my Church, and the gates of Hades shall not prevail against it" (Mt 16:18), Jesus here chose Peter as the Church's first leader and Pope. (Peter was later crucified upside down in Rome.)

After Christ's Resurrection, Ascension, and the Descent of the Holy Spirit on Pentecost Sunday, the Church entered its missionary phase. The Apostles and disciples preached the Good News of Jesus Christ in the Temple,[140] the synagogues, the streets, the surrounding countryside, and traveling to faraway places to bring the Good News of Christ to the Gentiles as Christ commanded them to do (Mt 28:19). They were representative priests of the New Covenant and Church, ambassadors for Christ, preaching the Good News to all; baptizing the believers with water in the name of the Father, and of the Son, and of the Holy Spirit and distributing the Holy Eucharist to all believers for their spiritual nourishment. This was the Mission and activity of the early Catholic Church. "And so it was that the church throughout Judea, Galilee, and Samaria had a time of peace. Through the help of the Holy Spirit it was strengthened and grew in numbers, as it lived in reverence for the Lord" (Acts 9:31; NCSB).

Some Protestants believe that Peter was not chosen by Christ to be the head (first Pope) of His Church when He said, "And I tell you, you are Peter, and on this rock I will build my Church, and the gates of Hades shall not prevail against it" (Mt 16:18). They claim that "the rock" Jesus was going to build His Church on was the "faith" Peter had that Jesus was the Christ and Son of God and not Peter himself. First of all, it was not his "faith" that prompted Peter to make that proclamation, for if one reads the passage just before that one, you will find that Jesus told Peter, "flesh and blood has not revealed this to you, **but my Father who is in heaven**" (Mt 16:17) [my emph.], which had nothing to do with Peter's "faith," but rather with the Father conveying that information directly to Peter as pointed out by Christ Himself. Thus, (1) the Father informed the Apostles through Peter that Jesus was the prophesied Messiah and Son of God; and (2) Peter was thereby selected as the leader of the twelve and head of Christ's Church; a Church that would in fact need a leader after His Ascension into Heaven (see CCC 552, 881). And Peter did become the first Pope of the Church Jesus Christ established: the One, Holy, Catholic, and Apostolic Church.

Christ (God) changed Simon's name to Peter (Petros in Greek for "rock") because he was the "solid" **person** Christ wanted to lead His Church on Earth. " 'Everyone then who hears these words of mine and does them will be like a wise man who built his house upon the **rock**; and the rain fell, and the floods came, and the winds blew and beat upon that house, but it did not fall, because it had been founded on the **rock**. And every one who hears these words of mine and does not do them will be like a foolish man who built his house upon the sand; and the rain fell, and the floods came, and the winds blew and beat against that house, and it fell; and great was the fall of it.' And when Jesus finished these sayings, the crowds were astonished at his teaching, for he taught them as one who had authority, and not as their scribes" (Mt 7:24-29) [my emph.]. Trusting and accepting the priceless wisdom of Christ's teachings given to us through Peter and His Catholic Church is the core message here.

It is equally important to understand that Christ said "Church" and not "churches." This means Jesus was indeed going to build and establish only **One** Church, **One** "Religion" on Earth, not many, and with Peter, the "Rock", as its head, leader, and first "Pope." "I will give you [Peter] the keys of the kingdom of heaven, and whatever you bind on earth shall be bound in heaven, and whatever you loose on earth shall be loosed in heaven" (Mt 16:19). These symbolic "keys" Jesus gave to Peter, the head of His Church on Earth, represent the authority given to Peter by Christ to govern His Church. This authority also extends to the forgiveness of our sins (Jn 20:23) and to enact doctrinal teachings and disciplinary actions in the Church when needed as time passes. So, is the Church *really* necessary? Christ says: " Yes!" It is the final doctrinal authority regarding Christianity.

Most important, Peter's declaration that Jesus was the "Christ," the "Heavenly Messiah" and "the Son of the living God," and not just a mere mortal human being like the Earthly messiah the Jews had been waiting for, this stark and sobering truth would be key in separating all other past, present, and future man-made religions from the One and True Church that would eventually be known as the Roman Catholic Church, founded by God Himself, in the Person of Jesus Christ, with His own blood (Acts 20:28), in the year 33 A.D. This is a historically proven and incontrovertible fact.[141]

The first written record of the term "Catholic Church," which literally means "universal church" is attributed to the Church Father Saint Ignatius of Antioch, who in his Letter to the church at Smyrna (circa 110 A.D.), on his way to Rome to be martyred wrote: "Wherever the bishop shall appear, there let the multitude also be; even as, wherever Jesus Christ is, there is the Catholic Church." (Epistle to the Smyrnaeans 8:2.) Although this is the first written record that exists, some scholars believe the term was in use before that to distinguish and separate the Church from other heretical and schismatic sects who were also claiming to be "Christian." (Sound familiar?) [142]

Nevertheless, the truthful and life giving teachings of this One True Faith would be passed from generation to generation by the Apostles and their successors – through the One True Church – to all the ends of the Earth, proclaiming: "God Himself has come to Earth! To die for us! To save us! And to take us to Heaven!" These truthful "Good News," my dear friends, are the most important truths a person can learn in a lifetime. Nothing else compares to it. The fundamental and basic Mission of His One, Holy, Catholic, and Apostolic Church, is to:

## Mission Of The Church

1. Preach the Gospel to all nations. The Good News of Salvation only through Jesus Christ, God's only-begotten Son.
2. Make disciples of all nations, baptizing them in the name of the Father, and of the Son, and of the Holy Spirit, and teaching them to observe all that Christ has commanded.
3. Provide to the members of His only Church the Sacraments instituted by Christ for their Spiritual benefit, and most important of these, the Eucharist, in order to have Real Life in us. [143]

In addition – and also with the Assistance of the Holy Spirit:

1. Educate the faithful using Christ's teachings, the Catholic Bible, Tradition, and the Catholic Catechism.
2. Teach the faithful how to live according to God's Will in order to merit Heaven.
3. Keep the Institution of the Church Holy, faithful, and free from error.

Catholicism will not – and is not supposed to – rid the world of suffering, trouble, and death, but will certainly save believing and repentant souls from all of that in the next life. Happiness is not promised us in this life, only in the next.

These bold and new teachings, preached by the Apostles and disciples to the world, that there is only one God yet three Divine Persons: the Holy Trinity, only one True Christ and one Salvation only through Him, one Baptism, one Heaven and one Hell, only one True Faith, and of course, only one True Church, would send reverberations throughout the world that would shake it to its very foundations. Notice how simple the Good News truly is: everything is One, but we humans tend to complicate things. We say things like, "There has to be more than just one way to get to Heaven!" And we say this because we are so used to doing things in more than just one way, or going somewhere by different routes, but this does not apply to Heaven after death, [144] for Jesus said: "I am the *way*, and the truth, and the life; **no one comes to the Father, but by me**" (Jn 14:6) [my emph.]. This means Jesus is the *only* way to the Father in Heaven; Jesus *is* the truth, no one else is; and Jesus is the *life*, the life we all must imitate, day in and day out, in order to merit Heaven, because: (1) Heaven is not guaranteed to everyone; and (2) everyone will not go to Heaven after death. Some will ask, "Why not? Didn't Jesus die for all mankind?"

### Salvation Is Not "Automatic" Or By Faith Alone

Some of my Protestant friends believe that accepting Jesus as our Lord and Savior is enough to get to Heaven no matter what we do after that, guaranteed! [145] But that is not the actual case. Hell is full of people who believed that Jesus was God and Savior but continued living a life of unrepentant sin much to their detriment. (Note: the Devil and his demons know all too well that Jesus is God and Savior, but that "faith" does not help them one bit!) Jesus Himself warned of this self-deception when He said: "Not everyone who says to me, 'Lord, Lord,' shall enter the kingdom of heaven, **but he who does the will of my Father who is in heaven**. On that day many will say to me, 'Lord, Lord, did we not prophesy in your name, and cast out demons in your name, and do many mighty works in your name?' And then will I declare to them, 'I never knew you; depart from me, you **evildoers**' " (Mt 7:21-23) [my emph.]. Note "evil**doers**."

After reading the above passage, it should become quite clear that calling Jesus Lord and accepting Him as our personal Lord and Savior will not be enough to enter Heaven (Salvation) after death. [146] And note that this even includes those who "prophesy in His name, and cast out demons in His name, and do many mighty works in His name." All of this won't matter either. So what *does* matter? Jesus said it there Himself! "…he who does the will of my Father who is in heaven." And just what is the Will of the Father when it comes to us humans? We find the answer to this critically important question here, at the Transfiguration of our Lord: [147]

"He was still speaking, when behold, a bright cloud overshadowed them, and a voice from the cloud said, 'This is my beloved Son, with whom I am well pleased; **listen to him**' " (Mt 17:5) [my emph]. Another version of this is, "And a cloud overshadowed them, and a voice came out of the cloud, 'This is my beloved Son; **listen to him**' " (Mk 9:7) [my emph]. And in Luke we find: "As he said this, a cloud came and overshadowed them; and they were afraid as they entered the cloud. And a voice came out of the cloud, saying, 'This is my Son, my Chosen; **listen to him**!' " (Lk 9:34-35) [my emph].

So, according to Christ, now that we know that only those who do the Will of God the Father will be the only ones who enter Heaven, and we just learned that the Will of the Father is for us to "listen" to Jesus, His only Son, what exactly did Jesus tell them, and also tells us now, in this regard? "For I have not spoken on my own authority; the Father who sent me has himself given me commandment what to say and what to speak. And I know that his commandment is eternal life. What I say, therefore, I say as the Father has bidden me" (Jn 12:49-50).

### Listening To The Father Through The Son

Let's take a closer look at all this. The Father says: "Listen to my Son," and Jesus, the Son, says, "I only say what the Father tells me to say". So, if we again go to the Father, most likely He will repeat to us, "Listen to my Son," and if we turn to Jesus He again will say, "I only say what the Father tells me to say." At this point, we should get the message and stop. This is obviously a closed circle, which means that whatever Jesus says, the Father is also saying; there will never be conflicting words between the Father and the Son: whenever you hear the Son, you will also be hearing the Father – in total agreement with the Son. Therefore, when we hear Jesus speaking, we are also – at one and the same time – hearing the Father speaking. A passage in Deuteronomy confirms this: "I will raise up for them a prophet like you from among their brethren; and I will put my words in his mouth, and he shall speak to them all that I command him" (Dt 18:18).
Jesus is therefore "the Word" of the Father, and St. John mentions this at the beginning of his Gospel:

"In the beginning was the Word [Jesus], and the Word was with God [Trinity], **and the Word was God** [Jesus]. He was in the beginning with God [Trinity]; all things were made through him, and without him was not anything made that was made. In him was life, and the life was the light of men. The light shines in the darkness, and the darkness has not overcome it" (Jn 1:1-5) [my emph.].

There's only one Savior of the world: Jesus Christ, and only One True Faith on planet Earth: Catholicism. (see 1 Jn 4:14; Eph 4:4-6, 12-13.) Let's take a closer look at these absolute truths.

## Oneness Of Faith
## One Faith - One Church - One Body of Believers [148]

Now that we have learned that only those who do the Will of the Father will enter Heaven, and that the Will of the Father is for us to listen to Jesus, His only Son, and of course, obey Him, we also learned that what Jesus says comes from the Father Himself. Therefore, since Jesus is in fact the Word of God the Father, what does the Word of God the Father together with Jesus the Christ tell us human beings about "religion"? About the Church Christ founded, with Peter the first Pope, and about all the other churches on Earth, even those claiming to be "Christian"?

Does God approve of thousands of different "Christian" Protestant denominations preaching in the name of Christ, but not agreeing with one another on what Salvation is and how to attain it? [149] And disagreeing on what His teachings really mean because they tampered with them? [150] Does God say it is ok for all of these Protestant denominations to have so many different names to identify themselves, confusing many people to the point where they don't want to have anything to do with "religion" anymore? [151] Does God say it is ok that after His Holy Catholic Church put together His Holy Bible, His written Word, in 397 A.D., and then 1200 years later, the Protestants took seven (7) sacred books out of it saying they were not worth keeping because Christ's Church, guided by His Spirit, made a mistake putting them in – in essence blaming the Holy Spirit? [152] Is it ok with God for thousands of nominal "Christian" pastors of thousands of nominal "Christian" denominations to teach errors in Christ's name? [153] Is it ok with God for these "pastors" to establish these denominations, mostly for tax-free money, and using Christ's Holy name to draw people away from Christ's Holy Church? [154] Is it ok with God that these "pastors" are spreading lies about Christ's Holy Church so that people will go to their churches instead? [155]

The answer to the above questions is NO! God does not say any of that is ok. Let's take a look at what Jesus, the Word of God the Father, has to say about all this:

"… whoever causes one of these little ones who believe in me to sin, it would be better for him to have a great millstone fastened round his neck and to be drowned in the depth of the sea" (Mt 18:6).

"**If you love me, you will keep my commandments**. […] He who has my commandments and keeps them, he it is who loves me; and he who loves me will be loved by my Father […] If a man loves me, he will keep my word, and my Father will love him, and we will come to him and make our home with him. He who does not love me does not keep my words; and **the word which you hear is not mine but the Father's who sent me**. […] I am the true vine, and my Father is the vinedresser. […] Abide in me, and I in you. **As the branch cannot bear fruit by itself, unless it abides in the vine, neither can you, unless you abide in me**. I am the vine, you are the branches. He who abides in me, and I in him, he it is that bears much fruit, for **apart from me you can do nothing**. If a man does not abide in me, he is cast forth as a branch and withers; and the branches are gathered, thrown into the fire and burned. […] By this my Father is glorified, that you bear much fruit, and so **prove to be my disciples**. As the Father has loved me, so have I loved you; abide in my love. […] **If you keep my commandments, you will abide in my love**, just as I have kept my Fathers commandments and abide in his love. […] **You are my friends if you do what I command you**. […] When Jesus had spoken these words, he lifted up his eyes to heaven and said, […]

"Father […] I have manifested your name to the men whom you gave me out of the world; they were yours, and you gave them to me, and they have kept your word. **Now they know that everything that you have given me is from you**; for I have given them the words which you gave me, and they have received them and know in truth that I came from you; **and they have believed that you sent me**. [...] Holy Father, keep them in your name, which you have given me, **that they may be one, even as we are one**. [...] As you sent me into the world, so I have sent them into the world. And for their sake I consecrate myself, that they also may be consecrated in truth. [...] **that they may all be one**; even as you, Father, are in me, and I in you, that they also may be in us, so that the world may believe that you have sent me. The glory which you have given me I have given to them, **that they may be one even as we are one**, I in them and you in me, **that they may become perfectly one**, so that the world may know that you have sent me and have loved them even as you have loved me" (Jn 14:15, 21, 23-24; 15:1, 4-6, 8-9, 10, 14; 17:1, 6-8, 11, 18-19, 21-23) [my emph.].

In the selected passages shown above, St. John reveals what Jesus said to His Apostles at the Last Supper after washing their feet just before He was arrested. In the first half of this, Jesus is giving instructions to His Apostles, and in the second half, Jesus is praying to His Father for the unity of His Apostles so that the Church they build will be one, just as He and the Father are one; of this there is no doubt whatsoever. In the first half, Jesus tells His Apostles at the Last Supper:

1. If you love me you will obey me; a crucial link between love and obedience.

2. If you love me (proven by obedience), my Father, together with me, will also love you.

3. Remember that these words of mine are coming from the Father.

4. I am the vine and you are the branches. If you remain united to me, you will bear fruit, but if you separate yourself

from me, you as a branch will be cast out, will wither, and be burned (rejected). This teaching underscores the importance of the Apostles remaining united to Christ so they can succeed in building His Church; **separation from Church is separation from Christ**; no Christ = no salvation.

5. If you are truly my disciples, you will prove your love for me by obeying my command to remain united to me, for the sake of my Church, so you can bear much fruit and thereby glorify my Father in Heaven.

6. As the Father has loved me, so have I loved you; remain in my love by obeying my commands: remain united as One: one body of believers = only one Church. (See Eph 1:22-23.)

7. You are my friends if you do what I command you. No obedience = no friendship; no friendship, no salvation!

It is very clear what Jesus is doing here: telling His Apostles, over, and over, and over again - to solidly imprint the teaching into their minds, that if they truly love Him, the only way to **prove** it is to **obey** His command to remain **united** to Him. If they don't, the Church will not survive. By remaining united to Him, His **One and only Church will be established**. Christ is the Head, the "Vine," and His one and only Church is His Body, the "branches" united to Him. (Christ only has one Body, not many.) Those not united to the Church are like branches separated from the vine, and not receiving Spiritual Life from the Vine will wither and die **spiritually**. Spiritual Life can only be obtained by remaining attached to Christ through His only Church. The Vine gives life to the branches, not vice versa. Christ is also telling His Apostles (and all of us), if they remain united to Him, they will also remain united to the Father for He and the Father are one. If we do not remain united to Christ through His only Catholic Church, we will not be united to God. Without God, there is no Spiritual Life in us. And no Life = Death.

## Actual Proof

What absolute proof exists that the Catholic Church is the only true religion on Earth? Father Leslie Rumble, Catholic priest, gives us the following incontrovertible evidence:

"The proof lies in the fact that the Catholic Church alone corresponds exactly to the exact religion established by Christ [God]. Now, the Christian religion is that religion that:

a. was founded by Christ **personally**;
b. has existed **continuously** since the time of Christ;
c. is Catholic, or universal, in accordance with Christ's command to go to all the world and teach all nations;
d. demands that all her members admit the same doctrine;
e. exercises divine authority over her subjects, since Christ said that if a man would not hear the Church he would be as the heathen.

Now, the Catholic Church alone can claim:

a. to have been founded by Christ **personally**. All other churches disappear as you go back through history. Christ said: 'You are Peter, and on this rock I will build my Church.' There are many claimants to the honor of being Christ's Church. But among all non-Catholic churches, we find one built on a John Wesley, another on a Martin Luther, another on a Mrs. Eddy, etc. But the Catholic Church alone can possibly claim to have been built on Peter, the chief of the apostles, and one-time bishop of Rome;
b. to have existed in all the centuries since Christ;
c. that every one of her members admits exactly the same essential doctrines;
d. to be Catholic, or universal;
e. to speak with a voice of true authority in the name of God." [156]

Regarding whether a person outside the Catholic Church can be called a Christian, St. Athanasius said: "...in addition to these arguments, let us also examine the tradition, teaching, and faith of the Catholic Church from the beginning, which is nothing other than what the Lord gave, and the Apostles preached, and the Fathers preserved. On this the Church is founded, and whoever falls away from it can no longer be nor be called a Christian." [157]

When our beliefs conflict with what God has revealed in Scripture or with the teachings of His Church, we must discard them and adopt what God revealed; like discarding errors and bad habits and replacing them with truths and good habits in order to become better persons.[158] We must practice Holiness. "Holiness is living in intimate, loving communion with God. More specifically, holiness is observing the two great commandments of love of God and neighbor, avoiding sin, leading a life of virtue, and abiding in sanctifying grace. None of this is possible without the Holy Spirit in your life" (Fr. Donald Calloway, MIC).

Since there are so many religions in the world, including thousands of "Christian" ones, many people tend to think one is not better than the others. So, if all of them will take us to Heaven, then Christ's death has no value whatsoever and that is not true. Since Jesus was - and is - both man and God in one Person, the religion He established, Catholicism, is the one and only true religion on Earth. No religious leader is above or equal to Jesus because Jesus is God and they're not. No one can go to Heaven except through Jesus Christ (see Acts 4:12; Jn 14:6). It is true that everyone is entitled to their own religious beliefs, but that does not make them true.

**Liberal vs. Conservative**

The 21st century leftist liberal tends to dislike following laws (especially moral laws), authority figures, traditions, religious beliefs, avoids self-sacrifice, and in their desire for change to achieve their objectives will resort to anarchy if necessary. Modern conservatives are the opposite. They respect authority figures, are no strangers to self-sacrifice, practice some form of religion (mainly Christian), and support law enforcement, the military, and the rule of law. This is why you will never see a public demonstration of conservatives with signs that say "Defund the Police," or "Down with the Rule of Law," or "We want Communism!" These are signs we are now seeing on our streets, on a regular basis, held by leftist liberal demonstrators. Not good, not good at all.

Unlike their predecessors, most modern American liberals are allied with the liberal left (left-wing) and conservatives with the right (right-wing). In American politics, the majority of Democrat politicians are now allied with the anti-American liberal progressive left due to heavy communist infiltration and indoctrination, while Republicans are allied with the pro-American conservative right. These are the two main groups in modern American politics. Liberals believe it is the duty of the government to alleviate social ills and solve society's problems. "A liberal is someone who feels a great debt to his fellow man, which debt he proposes to pay off with your money" (G. Gordon Liddy). Conservatives believe in personal responsibility, in the empowerment of the individual to solve society's problems. Thus, most liberal Democrats believe in big government while most conservative Republicans believe in limited government. Although there are some exceptions to this rule, this is generally the case.

Leftist liberals tend to be rebel-minded with disdain for the law and authority figures and have little to no patriotism; characteristics that are normally associated with adolescents. Not all, but most tend to be selfish, self-centered, arrogant, and irreligious while Conservatives are law-abiding, God-fearing citizens who are proud of their country. This type of pride is one example of true pride, which is good, while arrogance is false pride, which is not good. Although most leftist liberals obey local and federal laws (to avoid imprisonment), they do so out of necessity and not for love of the law. This is not to say that all conservatives are angels, for none are perfect, have bad habits to deal with, and are sinners just like liberals are. But deep inside, conservatives respect the law, try their best to follow it, and are God-fearing, patriotic people. Modern leftist liberals, however, are not. Interestingly, this applies to religion as well.

First of all, Christ was – and is – the consummate right-wing conservative; Satan, the consummate leftist liberal rebel. Many liberals try to justify their positions by saying that Christ was a rebel, a revolutionary, but that is not quite true. Christ was not - and is not - a rebel. Being against evil, injustice, cruelty, and for God, His Law, and the Commandments is not rebellious. In fact, it is quite the opposite. And in regards to being a revolutionary, that He truly was, but in the conservative, law-abiding, God-fearing sense: to bring about fundamental change in the true worship of God, for the good and benefit of the people. Christ was – and is – absolute Goodness and absolute Truth. Jesus Himself said, "Do not think that I have come to abolish the law and the Prophets; I have come not to abolish them but to fulfil them" (Mt 5:17).

A True revolution is for the rule of law and good of the people; a False revolution is for the opposite: for the benefit of the oppressors. Want to abolish illegal immigration? Remove the dictators in those countries and the people will have no reason to leave! The American Revolution of 1775-76 was for the good of the American people. The Russian communist revolution of 1917-23 was to the detriment of the people. Communism is totalitarian. It takes away God-given human rights; it controls, silences, exploits, and oppresses the people. A constitutional, democratic federal republic, like the system in the USA, is the best political system in the world:

"of the people, by the people, and for the people." Many liberals will say, "Your truth is not my truth," as if truth is not absolute and only relative. [159] Truth does not belong to anyone; it's independent of anyone. So, ask: "Don't you believe in absolutes?" And when the liberal answers, "No, I don't," ask: "Are you absolutely sure?" This is "Checkmate!" Yes, my liberal friends, we are all on the same "Boat," but we all won't have the same destination! You can be absolutely sure of that. Ignoring the truth will lead to ruin.

It has been my observation that the reason why some senior citizens retain a liberal mindset is because they don't like being old. They wear young people's clothes and even get tattoos to "feel" young; to blend in with them and be accepted by them. But this attempt is futile, for once they look in the mirror, all self-deceptions of youth disappear and the reality of old age stares back at them in derision. "The shock of sorrow comes only to those who think this world is fixed and absolute, that there is nothing beyond. They think everything here below should be perfect. Hence, they ask questions: 'Why should I suffer? What have I done to deserve this?' Maybe you did nothing to deserve it. Certainly, Our Lord did nothing to deserve His Cross. But it came, and through it, He went to His glory" (Venerable Fulton Sheen).

You can't be a progressive leftist liberal and also a Christian, and much less, a Catholic. Like oil and water, they don't mix. Leftist liberalism is diametrically opposed to the teachings of the Catholic Church. True conservatism is not. Leftist liberals who decide to follow Christ will discover the absolute need to become a conservative in order to be Catholic: a true Christian. I know this all too well because it happened to me! as well as to many of my friends. You can't "protest" against the very Church Christ founded and also call yourself a Christian, and you can't call yourself a Catholic and maintain a leftist liberal mindset. The two don't mix! Moreover, a high IQ and/or a special education are not needed to become a

Christian: "…Christianity is an education itself" (C. S. Lewis, *Mere Christianity*, p. 78), especially Catholic Christianity. If you ask: "Can one be a conservative and not Catholic?" The answer is: "Yes, of course, but an incomplete one." To truly follow Christ one must **obey** His commandment to remain united to Him: being and remaining a practicing member of His one and only Catholic Church, which is totally conservative; and to be a true conservative one must be Catholic. "So for one who knows the right thing to do and does not do it, it is a sin. […] For the time is coming when people will not endure sound teaching, but having itching ears they will accumulate for themselves teachers to suit their own likings, and will turn away from listening to the truth and wander into myths" (James 4:17; 2 Tim 4: 3-4).

Composer Gustav Mahler once said: "Tradition is not the worship of ashes, but the preservation of fire," and the preservation of fire is a great metaphor for modern conservatism whose goal is to preserve the best of the past and apply it to the present in order to ensure a better life for future generations. In regards to obedience, Jesus set the example for all of us by obeying the Father's Will and suffer death in order to redeem the human race: "In the days of his flesh, Jesus offered up prayers and supplications, with loud cries and tears, to him who was able to save him from death, and he was heard for his godly fear. Although he was a Son, he learned obedience through what he suffered; and being made perfect he became the source of eternal salvation **to all who obey him**" (He 5:7-9). Why obey Christ? See Jn 3:36.

Father Leslie Rumble, Catholic priest and apologist, was asked one day why he spoke so sarcastically of other religions when defending the Catholic Faith, and then told him that "God is love." Fr. Rumble replied, "Inquirers put their religious theories before me and if they are illogical I say so, giving my reasons for saying so. This is not sarcasm, above all since I respect the sincerity of those whose theories are mistaken. Nor is it unkind. If you saw a sick man taking not the medicine prescribed by the doctor but some other drink by mistake, would it be kindness to keep quiet just to spare him the confusion of realizing his mistake? Whilst love may excuse the man who makes a mistake, it cannot say that the mistake is not a mistake. I deny that truth is error, or that error is truth. But I make every allowance for those who mistake error for truth." [160]

Many intelligent, smart and reasonable people are not aware that Catholicism is the only true religion on Earth because they haven't taken the time to study the world's religions and their origins, but once they do, it will become very clear. Now some will say: "What if you are wrong about Catholicism being the only true religion?" And my answer would be, "I cannot be wrong, because Christ taught this to be true, and since He is God, I know God does not lie and knows what He is talking about." The point is not that I might be wrong, but that it is impossible for God to be wrong. That is why I follow only Him and the Catholic religion He established.

Why is being and remaining "One" so important to God? If His Church is going to remain in existence to pass the Good News from generation to generation without errors worldwide, it must remain united to Him as One. Otherwise, it will detach itself from the Vine, teach errors, and wither away like a broken branch. That is why there is only one True Religion: the Holy Catholic Church. God could not have it any other way! St. Paul wrote about this: "There is **one** body [Church] and **one** Spirit, just as you were called to the **one** hope that belongs to your call, **one** Lord, **one faith**, **one** baptism, **one** God and Father of us all" (Eph 4:4-6) [my emph.]. The "Oneness" of God is mirrored in the "Oneness" of His Church on Earth: One God, One Faith, One Church. Pretty simple! If there were 10 Gods, there would be 10 faiths, but there is only One God, so there is only One Faith,

One Church. (For a complete description of the Church, please read Pope Paul VI's "LUMEN GENTIUM.")

God made it very simple: all is ONE. We are the ones who complicate things! We say, "There must be more than one way to get to Heaven! I'm sure God will accept this way and that way; this religion and that religion (religious pluralism). And I know He'll accept me into Heaven even though I don't go to church because I know He loves me and understands me." [161] And the answers are, "No, there is only one way to Heaven: through Christ, His Son." And "No, He does not accept other ways that try to go around His Son's death and Church." And "Yes, He loves you, but do you love Him enough to obey His commands? Yes, He understands you, but do you understand Him?" If you don't, you will ruin it for yourself and you'll have no one else to blame but yourself. Take the time to learn the truth! God's Truth. Your Eternal Happiness depends on it! Since God is Goodness and Love, He loves the good and the true, not the evil and the false.

In the second half of the selected passages on pp. 209-10, Jesus is praying to the Father for His assistance in helping His Apostles to stay united as one for the sake of the Church, one body of believers, on one Mission: to spread the one Good News of Salvation only through Him without fail and without errors of any kind, so that His teachings will survive the weathering of the years without being changed or modified in any way. This way, those who hear His Good News and teachings for the first time will hear them just as if they were sitting right in front of the Lord Himself. Sad enough to say, Protestants are like branches that have detached themselves from the Vine. They've created their own churches, modified teachings of Christ in the Bible, spread lies about Mother Church, and caused/cause confusion, doubts, division, and diversions. Protestantism is a cancer that continues to spread worldwide. In all actuality, this is the Devil's work, not God's work: to confuse, create doubt, and divide.

Now someone I'm sure will say, "This is preposterous! Protestants are not practicing Satanism!" But remember, one can be doing the Devil's work without knowing it! And if you're not united to Christ and His only Church, you're taking a tremendous risk; and moreover, you're not a True Christian: a member of His Mystical Body of believers on Earth. Fr. Tabit once told me, "Protestants are in the 'spirit' of Christ, but none of them are members of the 'Body' of Christ; only Catholics are members of His Mystical Body: i.e., the Catholic Church He founded." So, in regards to His Church, the only Church Jesus founded that would bring His Good News to the world from generation to generation until the end of time: that Salvation (going to Heaven after death) is only possible through Him and only through Him alone, this only Church would obviously have to be One, not many. One single Body of believers united to Christ in order to avoid errors, subtractions, additions, or misinterpretations of His teachings. The Church is all that mankind needs and longs for: it is good, it is true, and it is beautiful: All in one Church! And it will take us to Heaven after death to meet and live with God forever. It is all there!

"Scattered about the entire earth, your mother the Church is tormented by the assaults of error. She is also afflicted by the laziness and indifference of so many of the children she carries around in her bosom as well as by the sight of so many of her members growing cold, while she becomes less able to help her little ones. Who then will give her the necessary help she cries for if not her children and other members to whose number you belong?" (St. Augustine)

## Faith Without Works Is Dead

Back to my Protestant friends who believe in Salvation through faith alone. St. James hits the nail on the head here on this topic. (Martin Luther didn't like James and it is easy to see why.) "What does it profit, my brethren, if a man says he has faith but has not works? Can his faith save him? If a brother or sister is poorly clothed and in lack of daily food, and one of you says to them, Go in peace, be warmed and filled, without giving them the things needed for the body, what does it profit? **So faith by itself, if it has no works, is dead**. But someone will say, You have faith and I have works. Show me your faith apart from your works, and I by my works will show you my faith. You believe that God is one; you do well. Even the demons believe and shudder. Do you want to be shown, you foolish fellow, that faith apart from works is barren? Was not Abraham our father justified by works, when he offered his son Isaac upon the altar? You see that faith was active along with his works, and faith was completed by works, and the Scripture was fulfilled which says, Abraham believed God, and it was reckoned to him as righteousness; and he was called the friend of God. You see that a man is justified by works and not by faith alone. And in the same way was not also Ra'hab the harlot justified by works when she received the messengers and sent them out another way? For as the body apart from the spirit is dead, **so faith apart from works is dead**" (Jas 2:14-26) [my emph.].[162] It is interesting to note that the majority of the Ten Commandments are based on works. What does that tell you?

Here's an example that shows the importance of works. You are driving and see a sign that says, "SPEED LIMIT – 45 MPH." Since you are going 60, you slow down to 45, and not just to avoid a ticket, but because you have faith *in* the law and also love *for* the law. Your "works," your "action" to slow down is proof of this. In the same manner, if you don't obey God's Commandments by your **actions**, your faith in Him will not be complete; in fact, it will be worthless! ("I never knew you; depart from me, you **evildoers**." Mt 7:23.) The Commandments regulate mostly our "actions" and keeps them in check, because as a fallen race, our "actions" need "regulating." So, when we combine proper and moral actions with our faith in God, that's when faith becomes alive. Our

Blessed Mother Mary told the servants at the Wedding at Cana: "Do whatever He [Jesus] tells you" (Jn 2:5), and she tells all of us the same thing. When we obey the teachings of the Catholic Church, we are obeying Christ: "He who hears you hears me, and he who rejects you rejects me, and he who rejects me rejects him who sent me" (Lk 10:16).

Common sense tells us that faith must be followed by good and moral actions in order to "prove" we have faith. The old saying, "Actions speak louder than words" is one example that actions are decisively important in the spiritual life. Jesus' own words tell us: "If you love me, you will keep my commandments" (Jn 14:15). Keeping the Commandments can only be done through actions, through works, and not only through faith. St. Francis is credited with saying: "Go out and preach the Gospel, and if necessary, use words." Whether he actually said this or not does not really matter; the sentence is priceless for it teaches the superiority of actions over words. This is not to say words don't matter, because they do; a single word from a judge can send a person to the executioner. But our actions are more important, and we will be judged by God more for what we have done than for what we have said: "For the Son of man is to come with his angels in the glory of his Father, and then he will repay every man **for what he has done**" (Mt 16:27). (See Mt 25:31-46; 2 Cor 5:10; Rev 22:12) [my emph.].[163] A true Christian is proven by what he does, by his actions. St. Paul was well aware of this fact when he wrote, "Therefore, my beloved, as you have always obeyed, so now, not only as in my presence but much more in my absence, **work out your own salvation with fear and trembling**; for God is at work in you, both to will and to work for his good pleasure. […] For it is **not the hearers of the law** who are righteous before God, but **the doers of the law who will be justified**" (Phil 2:12-13; Rom 2:13) [my emph].

These passages from St. Paul clearly state that Salvation (going to Heaven after death) is something we have to continually strive for and work on in this life, because one can live a life of holiness, and then on the death bed, refuse to repent and forfeit Eternal Life in Heaven. And the reverse is also true: one can lead a life of sin and debauchery, but then sincerely repent on the death bed and go to Heaven! "Truly, I say to you, the tax collectors and the harlots go into the kingdom of God before you" (Mt 21:31). No repentance for mortal sins at death leads to Hell. Protestants are taught that Salvation is only possible through "faith alone," but that is not true; that is not what Christ and His Apostles taught. Certain passages in St. Paul's letter to the Romans are given by Protestants as proof that they are right (their "Roman Road"):

"For we hold that a man is justified by faith apart from works of law. Or is God the God of Jews only? Is he not the God of Gentiles also? Yes, of Gentiles also" (Rom 3:28-29).

What Protestants don't know, what they are not taught by their pastors, either out of ignorance or some other reason, is that Martin Luther added the word "alone" to the above passage from Romans when he translated it into German so that it would read "by faith **alone**" in order to support his "anti-works" agenda. This is what Protestants now have in their Bibles. But the word "alone" does not appear here in the original Catholic Greek text or in the later translated Latin Vulgate. The "works of law" St. Paul is referring to here is circumcision, the 613 Jewish commandments (the mitzvot), the many Kosher laws, celebrating Jewish feasts, and so on. So, when he asked, "Or is God the God of Jews only?" He is asking, "Is God a God for only the Jews, or is He the God of all humanity?" And the answer is: "He's the God of all humanity."

As I mentioned in Chapter 2, St. Paul wrote to the Galatians that circumcising Gentile converts to Christianity was not necessary; converts did not have to obey this OT law that became obsolete with Christ. Circumcision was the sign of the Old Abrahamic Covenant; Baptism is the sign of the New Covenant instituted by Christ. Circumcision is what St. Paul is referring to when he says "works of law," but he is also referring to other Jewish legal practices that became obsolete and unnecessary to both Gentile and Jewish converts to "The Way" (Catholicism). Contrary to what Protestants say about Catholics, the Catholic Church has always taught that nothing we can do will get us into Heaven apart from Christ. Christ's death on the Cross opened the closed Gates of Heaven for all mankind, but not all will enter Heaven; many will be "saved" but many will not. This is what Christ meant when He said at the Last Supper, "This is my blood of the [new] covenant, which is poured out for **many**" (Mk 14:24. See Mt 20:28; 26:28); and again, "For **many** are called, but few are chosen" (Mt 22:14) [my emph.]. Although Christ's Redemption offers Salvation (Heaven) to all mankind through His One and only Church, the Catholic Church, not all will freely accept this invitation to eternal life in Heaven after death.

The reason why not all will accept God's invitation to the "Wedding Feast" in Heaven is because many will choose Hell over Heaven; they will not want to spend Eternity in Heaven with God and all those "goody-goodies" that live there. One elderly man told exorcist Father Lampert that he preferred going to Hell and spend eternity with "the demons he had come to know and befriended in this life" [164] instead of going to Heaven (see Mt 22:1-14). "He who created us without our help will not save us without our consent" (St. Augustine). Those who believe in Christ and "prove it" by **obeying** what He commanded will indeed enter Heaven, and His Commands are only two: (1) Love God with all your heart, soul, mind, and strength; and (2) love your neighbor as yourself. All the other commandments are fulfilled in these two (Mt 22:37-40). Question: "If we are saved through faith alone, how will we know we have true faith?" Answer: "By our behavior, by our 'works'." Jesus said we'd go to Heaven if we love God and neighbor (Lk 10:25-28), and what is the best way to do that? Through what we do: our actions and "works." We can only prove our love for God by obeying the Commandments He gave us, and we can only prove our love for our neighbors by treating them as we would want to be treated by them. Thus, love for God and neighbor require and are dependent on our actions, not our faith, so our faith, true faith, can only be proven through our actions, our works.

The word "alone," interestingly enough, **does** appear in The Letter of James where he says quite the opposite: "Was not Abraham our father justified by works, when he offered his son Isaac upon the altar? You see that faith was active along with his works, and faith was completed by works, and the Scripture was fulfilled which says, Abraham believed God, and it was reckoned to him as righteousness; and he was called the friend of God. You see that a man is justified by works **and not by faith alone.** And in the same way was not also Ra'hab the harlot justified by works when she received the messengers and sent them out another way? For as the body apart from the spirit is dead, so **faith apart from works is dead**" (Jas 2:21-26) [my emph.]. In the early Church, when the Apostles and disciples went forth to preach the Good News of Jesus Christ to all the nations, many people did not like these men with their new teachings and rituals because they challenged the ones they had been used to and were comfortable with, some of which had been a part of their culture for many generations. Since they were told to get rid of their old pagan beliefs and gods and adopt the new Christian teachings and worship only the one True God, many did not like this new idea and the men who brought it to them, so they executed the Christian messengers, not unlike the Jews who stoned to death their Prophets in Jerusalem (Lk 13:34). All of the Apostles were martyred, except St. John who lived to a ripe old age.

The very simple Catholic teachings that there is only one God and therefore only one Faith, one True Church and vehicle through which the Good News is to be preached throughout the world to avoid error, misconceptions and misinterpretations of the Salvation Message given to mankind by God through Christ, these simple Catholic teachings were not going to be accepted by everyone because people were going to have to make a very important personal decision in their lives: keep their present beliefs and present way of life, or get rid of them, adopt these new Christian teachings and change their way of life to accord with them. This is not an easy thing to do for many people with the moral corruption, materialism and secularism that pervades our modern society. Even though Catholicism is a very simple way of life, it is not an easy way of life. This is perhaps the main reason why there are tens of thousands of religions in the world today, because Catholicism is too strict and too hard to follow when compared with other religions, including Protestant denominations which are neither stricter nor more loyal than the Church is to the teachings of Christ. Moreover, another reason the Church is not very popular is because it is too "old-fashioned" and will not "change with the times" to embrace "new" social norms that conflict with Catholic teaching. However, if one truly wants to follow Christ and reap the eternal rewards of doing so in the next life, one must follow the Catholic Church: the one and only True Church that Jesus established 2000 years ago for our eternal benefit and happiness.

Two thousand years after Jesus walked this Earth, many people still do not believe that Jesus is God; they think He was just another human person like you and me so why follow only him? However, proof that Jesus was and is God is the fact that He claimed to be God (Jn 4:26) and proved it by the power He had over the laws of nature shown in the recorded miracles He performed. Think of the importance of His Church this way: imagine that you discover the cure for cancer, so you open up a clinic to cure people who have cancer and many people come to you to be cured. In fact, so many come that you can't handle all of them, so you open other clinics nationwide in order to meet the needs of all those people. Then, someone comes along who does not have your cure, opens a bunch of clinics and advertises the same cure at his locations, but people who go there are not being cured like at your places; some feel better for a while, others for a longer time, but none are being cured and they all eventually die because they are not receiving the actual cure for cancer that you alone possess. The Holy Catholic Church has the "Cure" for death: Eternal Life in Heaven after death through Jesus the Christ. No other church or religion has it. Not one! [165]

One major problem with all protestant denominations is the tampered bibles they are using. The original Bible was compiled by the Roman Catholic Church and finished c. 397 A.D. Protestant bibles have passages that have been edited and modified – many removed – to fit a Protestant agenda, particularly an anti-Catholic agenda, and interpretations of Christ's teachings given by anti-Catholic preachers are wrong, misleading and often deliberately designed to portray His only Church as flawed and guilty of serious crimes that She is innocent of. [166] It is no secret that members of the Catholic Church, including clergy, have committed serious crimes, but they did so against Church teaching. The Catholic Church does not teach or support criminal behavior. Protestants are not receiving the "Cure": absolution for their sins from the priest followed by the body, blood, soul, and divinity of Jesus Christ in the Holy Eucharist at Mass. Christ explicitly said:

"**Receive the Holy Spirit. If you forgive the sins of any, they are forgiven; if you retain the sins of any, they are retained**. [...] I am the living bread which came down from heaven; if any one eats of this bread, he will live forever; and the bread which I shall give for the life of the world is my flesh. The Jews then disputed among themselves, saying, How can this man give us his flesh to eat? So Jesus said to them, Truly, truly, I say to you, unless you eat the flesh of the Son of man and drink his blood, you have no life in you; he who eats my flesh and drinks my blood has eternal life, and I will raise him up at the last day. For my flesh is food indeed, and my blood is drink indeed. He who eats my flesh and drinks my blood abides in me, and I in him. As the living Father sent me, and I live because of the Father, so he who eats me will live because of me. This is the bread which came down from heaven, not such as the [manna the] fathers ate and died; he who eats this bread will live forever. This he said in the synagogue, as he taught at Caper'na-um. [...] After this many of his disciples drew back and no longer walked with him. Jesus said to the Twelve, Will you also go away? Simon Peter answered him, Lord, to whom shall we go? You have the words of eternal life; and we have believed, and have come to know, that you are the Holy One of God" (Jn 20:22-23; 6:51-59, 66-69).

First of all, Jesus wants us to confess our sins to a priest for several reasons, and one is the humility required for that. The person who says, "I will confess only directly to God" is speaking out of arrogance. One cannot call the White House and talk directly to the president but to an agent who has been hired for that; similarly, Jesus "hired" priests (Jn 20:22-23) to hear the confessions of sinners, but it is Jesus who provides the forgiveness for those sins. Those who truly love Jesus will obey His commands in this regard with humility.

Secondly, a number of other Scriptural teachings given by Christ to His Apostles to hand down from generation to generation have either been modified, watered down, or misrepresented by Protestants. This is no small matter. Thus, the actual true teachings of Christ are only being taught and handed down by the Catholic Church, His True Church, and not by the Protestants. There is no church or religion on

Earth, except the Holy Catholic Church, where one can go and receive forgiveness for our sins and also the actual body, blood, soul and divinity of Christ in the Eucharist, God Himself, for spiritual nourishment and union with Him. These facts alone should induce all Protestants, Jews, and non-Catholics to rush to the nearest Catholic Church and convert immediately! None of the Protestant churches, Jewish synagogues, Hindu or Buddhist temples, nor anyone else, has the Holy Eucharist to give to their followers. Many claim the Eucharist is only a "symbol," that Jesus was speaking symbolically and did not mean His actual body and blood. Do the above words spoken by Christ, that are right there in the Bible, sound like He is talking about a symbol? No they don't. John Calvin's "Short Treatise on The Holy Supper" has misled some Catholic theologians to think he believed in the real presence of Christ in the Eucharist, but that is not so. Calvin taught that it was a "spiritual" presence and not the Catholic "physical" presence of body and blood.

At the Last Supper, Jesus changed the bread into His body and gave His Apostles His **actual** body to eat, and then changed the wine into His blood and gave His Apostles His **actual** blood to drink, because He had told them earlier this is what they needed: "… he took bread, and when he had given thanks he broke it and gave it to them, saying, 'This is my body which is given for you. Do this in remembrance of me.' And likewise the chalice after supper, saying, 'This chalice which is poured out for you is the new covenant in my blood' " (Lk 22:19-20).

The Protestant Reformation that took place in the 16th century, responsible for tens of thousands of different "Christian" denominations worldwide now, was the biggest blow Satan has given to the Catholic Church in its entire history, but it did not destroy His Church as Christ predicted: "….and the gates of Hades shall not prevail against it" (Mt 16:18). It is still going strong and will remain in existence until the End of Time. FACT: There are no traces of Lutherans, Baptists, or any other Protestants before 1500 A.D. TAKE NOTE! Look at this: the only "Christian" religion that was handing on the teachings of Christ from generation to generation and baptizing believers, just as Christ commanded 2000 years ago, from 33 A.D. to the 16th century when the Catholic monk Martin Luther [167] began the Protestant Reformation, was the Catholic Church. There were no others! This means that for roughly 1500 years, the only Christian religion that was proclaiming the Good News of Jesus Christ was the Catholic Church. This absolute truth proves without a doubt that the Roman Catholic Church, with Peter as its first Pope, truly was – and still is – the **original** Church founded by Christ **Personally**; the One Church we are **not** supposed to separate from: "…the branch cannot bear fruit by itself, unless it abides in the vine" (Jn 15:4); nor abandon: "remain united to me" (Jn 15:4); and the One we are supposed to listen to: "He who hears you hears me, and he who rejects you rejects me, and he who rejects me rejects him who sent me" (Lk 10:16).

The "Christian" teachings propagated by the thousands of Protestant denominations that have sprouted from the Protestant Reformation are like "incomplete maps" with missing streets, signs, and compass points, including signs pointing in the wrong direction! How can anyone get to Heaven with these faulty maps! That's why many good people are lost, including the pastors themselves, because of the errors they teach.[168] Would you send your child to a school that teaches 2+2=7 and 10+10=50? Of course not! Then why would anyone attend a church that is teaching serious errors? An interesting point many Protestants are not aware of, children who are baptized in the name of the Triune God with plain water in Protestant churches are technically Catholics and will remain Catholics until they reach "the age of reason and adopt Protestantism," if that is what they want to do, [169] because Christian Baptism is a Catholic Sacrament, it is not Protestant.

Protestants are not true Christians. Many are attempting to do Christian things, but that does not make them true Christians. Father Rumble made it clear when he said: "A true Christian accepts the complete teaching of Christ and does all that he commands. And all is accepted on the authority of Christ, not on the authority of one's own human judgment. A self-made religion built upon a personally approved selection from the teaching of Christ does not give us the Christian religion … Protest as much as you like against individual abuses in the Church, but no man has the right to set up a new Church." [170]

Roman Catholicism has stood the test of time and survived countless demonic onslaughts, even those from within, and continues to survive to this day. Some mistakenly condemn the Catholic Church because of the clerical sexual abuse scandal, but those individuals who did those terrible things were not following the teachings of the Church; you can't condemn a store like WALMART, for example, if some of its employees were guilty of committing crimes. Bela Dodd admitted to placing over a thousand communist men in Catholic seminaries in the late 30s, many of whom were homosexuals; that explains the majority, if not all, of the scandals. Catholicism was established by God in the Person of Jesus Christ. Jesus could have exhorted His followers to continue practicing Judaism, but as the Bible clearly shows, He established a brand new Church: a "Catholic" one.

## Catholics - God's New Chosen People?

As already stated, the Jews of Christ's time did not realize that Jesus was God, the Messiah foretold by the Prophets, because they were expecting an "earthly messiah" to free them from the Romans. [171] The Jews did not know (and still do not) that God was going to replace their religion and their status as

"God's Chosen People" with Catholicism and Catholics, but that is what happened. The Jews still believe they are God's **only** Chosen people, and although they remain God's Chosen people [172] (Rm 9:4-5; CCC, 839), Catholics are also God's Chosen People: for believing that Jesus is the Messiah and for spreading the Good News worldwide that salvation is only attained through Him. It was not God who abandoned the Jews; the Jews abandoned God by rejecting the Messiah He sent through them (see Acts 18:5-7). Jesus made it very clear at the Last Supper when He told His Apostles, "This chalice which is poured out for you is the **new covenant in my blood**" (Lk 22:20) [my emph.]. There is no room for doubt here. This New Covenant Jesus established through His sacrificial death on the cross was not only with the Jews, but with all mankind: Jews and Gentiles, one human race.

When the Jews say that God would not allow the Covenant He made with Abraham to be replaced with another one (and many do say this), they forget that God respects our free will and allows us not only to sin by idolatry, by murder, by theft, by fornication, and by adultery, but also by many other sins we commit day in and day out. Likewise, God allowed His Chosen People to freely reject His Son when He sent Him to Earth to redeem the human race lost to sin. So again, it was not God who abandoned the Jews, but the Jews who abandoned God in the person of Jesus the Christ: they failed to recognize the Heavenly Messiah and had Him crucified for blasphemy. This is why God, in the person of Jesus, established a brand New Covenant with all mankind, both Jews and Gentiles alike, and a New Religion: Roman Catholicism, the Universal Faith for all peoples, and therefore, faithful Roman Catholics are also His Chosen People: chosen to preach the Good News to the world.

If the Jews had realized that Jesus was the Son of God, the foretold Messiah, and had not forced the Romans to execute Him, the Redemption of mankind would not have taken place; at least, not then. So, from an eagle's point of view, from the top down, God knew that the Jews were going to reject Jesus, have Him executed, and not follow His teachings, and He knew this before He created the universe. Thus, God knew that He would have to start a new religion in order to inform the world, generation after generation, of the Good News of His coming. Even though God knew what the Jews were going to do to His Christ, He did not force them to do it, or cause them to do it. They did this through their own free will. Foreknowledge does not cause future events. Jesus knew Judas would betray Him, but He did not force him or cause him to do it.

Think about this for a moment. First of all, why were the Jews God's Chosen people? Was it because God loved them more than everyone else He had created? Of course not, for God loves all persons equally. Even though God chose to reveal Himself to mankind through the Jews to let the whole world know that there is only one God, not many (as everyone else thought there was then), and this absolute fact was written down in the Hebrew Holy Scriptures, this was a secondary reason. The main reason why the Jews were considered God's Chosen People is because God chose to bring to Earth His only Son, the Heavenly Messiah, through the Jewish people to redeem mankind. He could have picked the Africans, or the Chinese, or the Indians, the Egyptians, the Aztecs, the Eskimos, even the Romans, but He did not. He alone knows why He picked the Jews through whom He would bring His only Son into the world. So why did God choose them? God only knows! Perhaps because they were the least of all.

## The Need For A New Religion

Secondly, what did the Jews do to the promised Heavenly Messiah when He finally came? Since they failed to realize Jesus was the Heavenly Messiah, sent by God the Father, they urged and instigated Pontius Pilate to crucify Him because He claimed to be God. Undoubtedly, the chief priests (the Sadducees), the Pharisees, the Elders, and the scribes were

NOT going to go out into the world - after Christ's Death and Resurrection - and preach the Good News: the Gospel of Salvation only through Jesus Christ. It is very obvious, as recorded in Scripture, that they would not have done that - and in fact did not do that. Moreover, they still hated the followers of Christ, the "Christians" as they were called then, after His Resurrection, and even made up lies about Jesus not rising from the dead ! (Mt 28:11-15.) They even persecuted and stoned to death some of the first Christians (Acts 6:8-15; 7:1-60). Saul, a Pharisee, who later became known as St. Paul, was one of those in charge of the persecutions and stonings (Acts 8:1-3).

And if that is not enough, after the Apostles were put in prison by Cai'aphas and the Pharisees because they were attracting a large crowd – like Jesus had done – with their healings and expelling of demons, an angel came, released them from prison, and told them to go preach at the Temple, and when they were discovered and returned to Cai'aphas, he told them: "We strictly charged you not to teach in this [Jesus'] name, yet here you have filled Jerusalem with your teaching and **you intend to bring this man's blood upon us**.... they beat them and charged them not to speak in the name of Jesus" (Acts 5:28, 40) [my emph.]. After instigating Pilate repeatedly to crucify Jesus, even telling him: "His blood be on us and on our children!" (Mt 27:25), Cai'aphas now claims they are innocent of Jesus' blood? I can't imagine a more irresponsible, cowardly, patently false and egregious thing to say! Jesus was so right when He called them all those names: "Woe to you, scribes and Pharisees, hypocrites! for you are like whitewashed tombs, which outwardly appear beautiful, but within they are full of dead men's bones and all uncleanness. So you also outwardly appear righteous to men, but within you are full of hypocrisy and iniquity" (Mt 23:27-28).

A clarification here is in order regarding Judaism. The reader should not assume that I am promoting antisemitism when I stated that Judaism became obsolete with the coming of

Christ and was supplanted by Catholicism as the religion through which salvation is to be obtained. Antisemitism is prejudice against or hatred of the Jewish people, which is quite different. "Semites" refers to certain peoples, notably Jews (Arabs are also Semites). Judaism however, is a religion, not a people. Please take note. Jesus came to establish a NEW Covenant with all mankind and seal it with HIS Blood, not with the blood of an innocent animal (see Heb 9:11-15), and consequently, also a brand NEW religion, a new Church, whose members, the "New Chosen people" so to speak, would spread out into all parts of the world and preach the Good News of Salvation through Him for the Eternal Benefit of mankind. Thus, Catholicism became the New and True Religion to follow from Christ forward. The OT Judaic Covenants were supplanted by Christ's New Covenant (see Heb 8:6-13).

Further evidence that Christ established a new religion, when Christ told His Apostles "I **will** build **my Church**" (Mt 16:18), this obviously meant a NEW Church, a NEW religion, because Judaism with its Second Temple and synagogues already existed and had been established for quite some time. So, the "Church" Jesus was building was a Brand New One, [173] a Universal one. Since the Jews rejected Jesus, He saw the need to prescribe new doctrines and new modes of worship and that meant a new religion. (Catholicism is the "portal" through which one can enter Heaven after death.) This is why Judaism was no longer to be followed by anyone with the coming of Christ, and this included the Jews. After Christ's Ascension, the Apostles went to the Temple and told the Jews to convert to the new religion (Acts 3:1-26; 4:1-4), and Jesus had forewarned them that they would be beaten in the synagogues for trying to convert the Jews to the new religion (Mk 13:9; Acts 5:40-42). Some say, "Just because we reject Jesus doesn't mean we also reject the Father in Heaven," but they are wrong, for Jesus said: "He who hears you hears me, and he who rejects you rejects me, and **he who rejects me rejects him who sent me**" [the Father] (Lk 10:16) [my emph.]. And in John we find: "....the

Father loves the Son, and has given all things into his hand. He who believes in the Son has eternal life; he who does not **obey** the Son shall not see life, but the wrath of God rests upon him. […] He who does not honor the Son does not honor the Father who sent him" (Jn 3:35-36; 5:23) [my emph.]. Jesus Himself said: "…no one comes to the Father, but by me" (Jn 14:6). Many Jewish authorities believed in Jesus: "Nevertheless many even of the authorities believed in him, but for fear of the Pharisees they did not confess it, lest they should be put out of the synagogue: for they loved the praise of men more than the praise of God" (Jn 12:42-43).

It isn't easy to determine exactly when the Pharisees came into existence, but in "Antiquities of the Jews," Book 13, Chapter 5, § 9, Josephus mentions them when Jonathan Maccabeus sent ambassadors to the Romans (c. 150 B.C.), so they had existed for about 200 years or so by the time Jesus was born. The Pharisees were not priests. The Sadducees were the priests, and also the wealthy nobility. The Sadducees were very friendly with and "in bed" with the Romans; they even allowed the Romans to appoint a new High Priest every year, a position that was supposed to be for life according to Jewish tradition. The Pharisees, on the other hand (the name means "separated ones"), were working class lay people who separated themselves to avoid adopting Greek customs like the Sadducees were doing. As mentioned in Chapter 4 (p. 73), Antiochus IV Epiphanes imposed Hellenistic practices on the Jews and made Judaism illegal executing violators. Wanting to keep Judaism intact and free from Hellenism, they formed a group for this purpose and called themselves Pharisees. They even put a "Fence around the Torah" to protect those teachings from corruption.

Again, it was the Sadducees, scribes, and especially the Pharisees who were mainly responsible for instigating the crowd at Christ's arrest which ultimately forced Pilate to crucify Him even though Pilate had repeatedly declared He was innocent. Moreover, these groups were the first to persecute the first Christians. Saul (aka St. Paul) was a Pharisee and was very much involved in this initial persecution. Scripture mentions him being present at the martyrdom of St. Stephen, the first Christian martyr, and persecuting other Christians (Acts 7:58; 8:1, 3). Interesting to note, Jesus sided somewhat with the Pharisees to the point where He even told His disciples to follow only their teachings but not what they do (Mt 23:3). Cai'aphas, High Priest of the Sanhedrin, who ordered the arrest of Jesus, and Annas, his father-in-law, were both Sadducees. Both parties, the Pharisees and the Sadducees, had their own reasons for wanting to get rid of Jesus, and both parties conspired and worked together to have Him executed. The Sadducees did not believe in the supernatural: the devil, the Resurrection of the Dead, miracles, angels, demons, immortality of the soul, etc., and were not interested in the Prophets, including their messianic prophecies.

One day, Jesus told the people in the Temple the following parable; a parable that describes how He was going to be treated by the Pharisees and the chief priests, and even by the scribes, the ones who taught the Torah to the people.

"And he began to tell the people this parable: 'A man planted a vineyard, and leased it to tenants, and went into another country for a long while. When the time came, he sent a servant to the tenants, that they should give him some of the fruit of the vineyard; but the tenants beat him, and sent him away empty-handed. And he sent another servant; him also they beat and treated shamefully, and sent him away empty-handed. And he sent yet a third; this one they wounded and cast out. Then the owner of the vineyard said, 'What shall I do? I will send my beloved son; it may be they will respect him.' But when the tenants saw him, they said to themselves, 'This is the heir; let us kill him, that the inheritance may be ours.' And they cast him out of the vineyard and killed him.

What then will the owner of the vineyard do to them? He will come and destroy those tenants, and give the vineyard to others.' When they heard this, they said, 'God forbid!' But he looked at them and said, 'What then is this that is written: 'The very stone which the builders rejected has become the cornerstone'? Everyone who falls on that stone will be broken to pieces; but when it falls on any one it will crush him' " (Lk 20:9-18; see Acts 13:46-52; 18:5-7).

## The Holy Sacrifice Of The Mass

The most important prayer we can offer to God our Father in Heaven is the Holy Sacrifice of the Holy Catholic Mass. There is no other prayer greater than this one. The reason for this is because the Catholic Mass is "a re-presentation, memorial, and effective application of the merits [we] gained by Christ. […] The same Christ who offered himself once in a bloody manner on the altar of the cross is present and offered in an unbloody manner" [174] in the Holy Sacrifice of the Catholic Mass. An often overlooked yet very important part of the Mass is during the Offertory: "Pray, brethren, that my sacrifice **and yours** may be acceptable to God, the almighty Father." Here, at this time, we unite our sufferings, hardships, prayers, thanks, trials, and even our accomplishments with Christ's sacrifice and offer them to our Father in Heaven. The Holy Eucharist is then given to the faithful at the end of the Mass for their spiritual nourishment.

"Calling to mind" the Passover meal Christ had with His Apostles, which is how most Protestants regard the Last Supper (as only a "reminder" of this meal) is not the same or equivalent to the Holy Sacrifice of the Holy Catholic Mass where the Eucharistic bread and wine miraculously become the actual body, blood, soul, and divinity of Jesus Christ and is eaten by the faithful who are in the state of grace. This miracle only takes place in all Catholic Masses and not in Protestant services or during any other religious events of other religions. God Almighty becomes present, in the person of Jesus Christ, on Earth. In St. Ignatius of Antioch's "Epistle to the Smyrnaeans" (Ch. 7), he says: "They abstain from the Eucharist and from prayer, because they confess not the Eucharist to be the flesh of our Saviour Jesus Christ, which suffered for our sins…" St. Ignatius wrote this in 110 A.D.!

As stated, the Roman Catholic Mass is a "re-presentation" of the Holy Sacrifice that Jesus made for us on the Cross; the Holy Sacrifice that restored the broken relationship between the human race and God. In other words, "we" humans don't make Christ's Sacrifice present at any event by simply calling the Last Supper to mind, or by regarding it as only "a reminder" of the Passover meal as Protestants do, but rather it is God's Grace that makes the body, blood, soul, and divinity of Christ truly present in the Eucharist on all the altars during Mass in all the Catholic churches around the world. It is not we who do this, but God who does this. And even after everyone leaves the Catholic church after Mass ends, Christ is still present there in the left over consecrated hosts that are kept in the tabernacle. God Almighty, present in the person of Christ, in all the Catholic churches worldwide! Is this real? Is this true?

Those who have doubts regarding the Holy Eucharist being the actual body, blood, soul and divinity of Christ, incontrovertible scientific evidence of the Eucharist miraculously turning into human flesh is given in "A Cardiologist Examines Jesus," by Dr. Franco Serafini. Here, the examined flesh contains blood, white blood cells, red blood cells undergoing autolysis, hemoglobin, leukocytes, and in fact, the flesh itself is still alive! These are miracles God gives to mankind in order to draw souls to His Holy Mother Church. Other miracles with the same purpose are listed in the book "The Incorruptibles" by Joan Carroll Cruz. Here, Catholic saints who have passed away, some of them hundreds of years ago, were found to be without corruption and appear to be only sleeping after exhumation.

Since the Eucharist is the very body, blood, soul, and divinity of God in the Person of Jesus Christ, it is therefore the most valuable item on Earth! And best of all, we can obtain it free of charge with only one condition: we must be a member of the Catholic Church in "good standing," in the "state of grace" : free of grave (mortal) sin. Nothing else can compare in value; not money, jewels, real estate, or power. The special value of the Eucharist is given to us by Christ Himself:

"So Jesus said to them, Truly, truly, I say to you, unless you eat the flesh of the Son of man and drink his blood, you have no life in you; **he who eats my flesh and drinks my blood has eternal life, and I will raise him up at the last day.** For my flesh is food indeed, and my blood is drink indeed. **He who eats my flesh and drinks my blood abides in me, and I in him**. As the living Father sent me, and I live because of the Father, so **he who eats me will live because of me**. This is the bread which came down from heaven, not such as the [manna the] fathers ate and died; he who eats this bread will live for ever. This he said in the synagogue, as he taught at Caper'na-um" (Jn 6:53-59) [my emph.].

There are striking parallels between the Old Covenant God made with the Israelites through Moses as mediator at Mt. Sinai and the New and Eternal Covenant God made with the entire human race through Jesus Christ at the Last Supper. One is, Moses led the Israelites from slavery in Egypt through forty years of suffering and trials in the Desert and finally to the Promised Land in Canaan, and Christ, through His sacrificial death on the Cross, leads those who believe in Him–and are united to Him–from suffering and slavery to sin and death in this world through the Door of Death to Eternal Bliss in the Promised Land in Heaven. Moses is the harbinger of Christ; Christ is the **Way**, the **Truth**, and the **Life** (Jn 14:6).

Another parallel is in the Book of Exodus. Here we find: "And Moses took half of the blood and put it in basins, and half of the blood he **threw against the altar.** Then he took the book of the covenant, and read it in the hearing of the people; and they said, 'All that the LORD has spoken we will do, and we will be obedient.' And Moses took the blood and **threw it upon the people**, and said, 'Behold the **blood of the covenant** which the LORD has made with you in accordance with all these words' " (Ex 24:6-8) [my emph.].

The parallel to this is found in the Last Supper and in the Roman Catholic Mass. In Matthew we find: "Now as they were eating, Jesus took bread, and blessed, and broke it, and gave it to the disciples and said, 'Take, eat; this is my body.' And he took a chalice, and when he had given thanks he gave it to them, saying, 'Drink of it, all of you; for this is my **blood of the covenant**, which is **poured out** for many for the forgiveness of sins' " (Mt 26:26-28). And in Luke we find: "And he took bread, and when he had given thanks he broke it and gave it to them, saying, 'This is my body which is given for you. Do this in remembrance of me.' And likewise the chalice after supper [i.e., not part of the meal], saying, 'This chalice which is **poured out** for you is **the new covenant in my blood'** " (Lk 22:19-20; see Heb 9:15-22) [my emph.].

Towards the middle of the Roman Catholic Mass, the priest, acting "in persona Christi," in the Person of Jesus Christ, will recite a very special prayer, the **epiklesis**, the prayer of Consecration. At this time, the Eucharist on the altar miraculously becomes the body, blood, soul, and divinity of Jesus in substance, not in appearance. The words of the epiklesis, a combination of the above words from Matthew and Luke, spoken by Christ at the Last Supper, are:

"At the time He was betrayed and entered willingly into His Passion, He took bread and giving thanks, broke it, and gave it to His disciples saying: 'Take this all of you and eat of it. For this is my body, which will be given up for you.' (The Host is elevated for all to see ) In a similar way, when supper was ended, He took the Chalice, and once more giving thanks, He gave it to his disciples saying, 'Take this, all of you, and drink from it, for this is the chalice of my blood, the blood of the New and Eternal Covenant, which will be poured out for you and for many, for the forgiveness of sins. Do this in memory of me.' " (The Chalice is elevated for all to see )

At this particular time, the altar symbolically becomes Calvary at the very moment when Jesus died, and the bread and wine become the actual body, blood, soul, and divinity of Jesus through the miraculous process of transubstantiation while still keeping the appearances of bread and wine. It is important to understand that the body of Christ is not IN the Eucharist, but rather it IS the Eucharist, and the same with the wine: it IS the blood of Christ.

Just like His mother Mary, St. John, and the others at the foot of the Cross, we join ourselves to His Sacrifice at this time in the Mass. We enter into the Mystery of His Holy Sacrifice for mankind. This is the most important part of the Roman Catholic Mass. Jesus is offering Himself for us on the altar just as He offered Himself for us on the Cross. It does not matter if we are halfway around the world where the Mass is being said in a foreign language we don't understand. The Holy Sacrifice of the Mass is there and we enter into His Mystery. Jesus is truly there in the Eucharist, and we are there to partake of Him for our spiritual nourishment and union with Him. It is a "Mystery" God revealed to us.

We can clearly see here the parallels between the Old Covenant God made with the Israelites where Moses took the blood from the sacrificial animal and threw it against the altar, and compare this with the New and Eternal Covenant Christ made with mankind by shedding His blood during His Passion and Crucifixion on the Altar of Calvary. When Moses took the rest of the sacrificial blood and threw it upon the people, saying: "Behold the blood of the covenant which the LORD has made with you," this can be compared with Christ taking the chalice **after supper** (i.e., not part of the meal) and telling His Apostles, "Drink of it, all of you; for this is my blood of the covenant," speaking, of course, about the New and Eternal Covenant with the human race. It is of utmost importance when we partake of the Eucharist, commonly referred to as "Holy Communion," that we are in the worthy state of grace; i.e., free of mortal sin(s). Taking communion when not in the state of grace is a mortal sin in itself. A mortal sin is a grave and serious sin committed against either God or against another person that eradicates the sanctifying grace in the soul which makes a person unworthy to receive Holy Communion until the mortal sin is confessed to a priest and absolution is received from God through the priest in the Sacrament of Penance (Confession).

In his letter to the community at Corinth in Greece, a large city that had many shrines to pagan gods where immoral entertainment and living were commonplace, St. Paul wrote: "For I received from the Lord what I also delivered to you, that the Lord Jesus on the night when he was betrayed took bread, and when he had given thanks, he broke it, and said, This is my body which is for you. Do this in remembrance of me. In the same way also the chalice, after supper, saying, This chalice is the new covenant in my blood. Do this, as often as you drink it, in remembrance of me. For as often as you eat this bread and drink the chalice, you proclaim the Lords death until he comes. Whoever, therefore, eats the bread or drinks the cup of the Lord in an unworthy manner [not in the state of grace] will be guilty of profaning the body and blood of the Lord. Let a man examine himself, and so eat of the bread and drink of the cup. For anyone who eats and drinks without discerning the body eats and drinks judgment upon himself" (1 Cor 11:23-29).

Regarding the Eucharist, there is a very interesting passage in Exodus 25:30: "And you shall set the bread of the Presence on the table before me always." What is this "bread of the Presence"? The bread of the Presence, also called showbread or shewbread, was very special bread placed on a special table, made from acacia wood and overlaid with gold, which was kept in the tabernacle: the portable temple the Israelites used during their time in the desert after the Exodus from Egypt. The recipe for making and handling this bread is found in the Book of Leviticus:

"And you shall take fine flour, and bake twelve cakes of it; two tenths of an ephah shall be in each cake. And you shall set them in two rows, six in a row, upon the table of pure gold. And you shall put pure frankincense with each row, that it may go with the bread as a memorial portion to be offered by fire to the LORD. **Every sabbath day** Aaron shall set it in order before the LORD continually on behalf of the sons of Israel as a covenant for ever. And it shall be for Aaron and his sons, and they shall **eat it in a holy place**, since it is for him a most holy portion out of the offerings by fire to the LORD, **a perpetual debt**" (Lv 24: 5-9) [my emph.].

The Table for the bread of the Presence, together with the bread, were also kept in the First and Second Temples after they were built. Worthy of note, the talmudic **halakhah** prescribes that the loaves were to be of un-leavened bread [175] just like the bread that is used to make Eucharistic hosts for Roman Catholic Masses; hosts that miraculously become the body, blood, soul, and divinity of Christ. The frankincense served with the bread symbolized God. It appears that the bread of the Presence from the time of Moses was a symbolic precursor of the Eucharist: "the living bread which came down from heaven" (Jn 6:51), the body, blood, soul, and divinity of Christ, the **complete** Christ. This clearly shows how God the Father was lovingly making preparations – from the time of Moses – for the coming of His Son to not only save us from our sins through His Sacrifice on the Cross, but also to give us His body, blood, soul, and divinity for our Spiritual Nourishment: to give us Life, **Real** Life in us (see Jn 6:53).

It should now be clear how important it is to be Roman Catholic: to benefit from the Sacraments Jesus instituted: to go to Confession regularly in order to have our sins forgiven; to attend the Holy Sacrifice of the Mass at least once a week on Sundays in order to enter into the Mystery of Christ's Sacrificial Offering and unite our sufferings with His; and to receive Holy Communion so as to "live forever" through Christ, with Christ, and in Christ. A quick word on the miracle of Transubstantiation: the host turning into the body, blood, soul, and divinity of Jesus Christ during Mass.

## Transubstantiation

As mentioned earlier in other pages, the consecrated hosts given to practicing Catholics in a state of grace at the end of the Mass is the actual body, blood, soul, and divinity of Jesus Christ. This, of course, is a miracle that was begun and instituted by Jesus Christ at the Last Supper (see Last Supper). But Jesus had prepared His Apostles to receive this special and miraculous food from Him at the Last Supper *before* that event took place. The first time Jesus mentions the eating of His flesh and drinking of His blood is in John 6:35-69, right after He miraculously fed five thousand people with only five barley loaves and two fish (Jn 6:1-14). Here, Jesus tells His Apostles and disciples: "unless you eat the flesh of the Son of man and drink his blood, you have no life in you; he who eats my flesh and drinks my blood has eternal life, and I will raise him up at the last day" (Jn 6:53-54). Jesus said this "in the synagogue, as he taught at Caper'na-um" (Jn 6:59). At this time, many of His disciples left Him because this teaching was too hard for them to accept (Jn 6:66), even though "they were about to come and take him by force to make him king" (Jn 6:15). As also mentioned earlier, some consecrated hosts have been miraculously transformed into living human flesh, and this has been proven, beyond the shadow of a doubt, by the most rigorous, meticulous, and professional scientific analyses available in the world (see pages 101, 239). The word "transubstantiation" was chosen by the Council of Trent in 1551 to accurately describe the process by which the hosts become the body, blood, soul, and divinity of Christ. Here, three miracles take place at the same time. (1) The "substance" of bread changes into the "substance" of Christ's body, blood, soul, and divinity. (2) The "properties" of bread remain intact (still looks like bread). (3) The "properties" of Jesus' body, blood, soul, and divinity do not appear (are invisible). The change is in the "substance" and not in the properties thereof. Thus, "transubstantiation" takes place. Just before He ascended into Heaven, Christ commanded His Apostles to, "Go therefore and make disciples of all nations, baptizing them in the name of the Father and of the Son and of the Holy Spirit, teaching them to observe all that I have commanded you; and behold, **I am with you always**, to the close of the age" (Mt 28:19-20) [my emph.]. Thus, through His Church, Jesus in the Eucharist can come and live **with** us and **in** us. Wow!

### Did Jews Offer Sacrifices To Roman gods?

An interesting thought came to my mind as I was finishing this book, "If many of the early Christians were turned into human torches, fed to the lions, brutally tortured, grilled to death on hot irons, crucified, stabbed, beheaded, drowned, mauled with iron rakes, shot through with arrows, and who knows how many other tortures and forms of execution they were victim to by the Romans for refusing to offer sacrifices to their pagan gods, were the Jews also obligated to offer sacrifices to them too? I don't recall reading in Scripture accounts of Jews being treated this way. How come? This question had never crossed my mind before nor had I ever heard it asked before, so I decided to look into this since refusal to worship the gods of the Roman State was equivalent to treason, a crime punishable by death. Which brought up another question, namely, why didn't Pilate command Jesus to offer sacrifice to a Roman god? His refusal would have given Pilate just reason to execute Him. Moreover, this would have switched the guilt of His execution from the Jews to the Romans which may have produced a different set of consequences. Evidently, it was not meant to be this way.

By the time Christ entered the world, the Jews had ceased the practice of child sacrife and only sacrificed animals, fowl, plants and wine as mandated by Jewish Law, and the Romans did the same according to their laws which gave support to the very lucrative business of raising and selling these items solely for the purpose of sacrifices. But Christianity threw a big wrench into this business: so many people were becoming Christians that purchasers of these items were diminishing in large numbers since these types of sacrifices were non-existent in Christianity. This eventually became a BIG problem and was VERY bad for "business." Yet another reason to hate the Christians (see Acts 19:23-27)

There were occasional clashes between the Romans and the Jews due to differing political and religious views, but the Jews were respected – **to a certain degree** – by the Romans and were legally exempt, specifically under Julius Caesar, from having to offer sacrifices to Roman pagan gods. In fact, Caesar considered Judaism to be superior over the Eastern religions that had been brought to Rome over the years, but Cicero considered Judaism "superstitio," a deviant form of religion. According to Tertullian, Judaism, unlike Christianity, was given the title "religio licita" ("Apologia," xxi), which means "legal religion," and that meant they could practice their religion without interference which included not offering sacrifices to pagan gods. Julius Caesar's enmity toward Pompey for defiling the Temple's Holy of Holies after conquering Jerusalem won him great favor among the Jews. The number of Jews in Caesar's army during the Pompeian wars was quite significant even though they were exempt from military service, and in his court and councils the Jews were very influential when it came to political and financial matters. The great historical significance of Caesar's good relations with the Jews perhaps reached its highest after his successful military Alexandrian campaign in Egypt between 48 and 47 B.C., after which Caesar granted many privileges and favors to the Jews and gave Judea the right of "status clientis," the greatest autonomy that a country under Roman rule could be given. Here are a few of the decrees of the consuls during the rule of Julius Caesar favoring the Jews ("Jewish Encyclopedia," Caesar, Caius, Julius):

Sept. 19, 49 B.C.: Report on the public proceedings at Ephesus concerning the exemption of the Jews of Asia Minor from military service on account of their religion, and the decree in this sense of the consul Lucius Lentulus ("Ant." xiv. 10, § 19).

46-45 B.C.: Admonitory letter of the proconsul Publius Servilius to the magistrate of Miletus that the Jews should not be disturbed in the execution of their religious customs (ib. § 21).

46-45 B.C.: Decree of the Sardians, upon the representation of the pretors, granting the Jews religious liberty, setting apart for them a place for public worship, and even directing those that have charge of the provisions of the city to "take care that such sorts of food as they esteem fit for their eating may be imported into the city" (ib. § 24).

These decrees show Caesar's unquestionable generosity and consideration toward the Jews and identifies them as an important component of the Roman Empire; one, however, whose days were numbered. After the Roman destruction of Jerusalem in 70 A.D. led by the future Emperor Titus, the Jewish nation ceased to exist from there forward, but Emperor Vespasian made no changes to the prestigious religious status given to the Jews primarily by Caesar with only one exception: the tribute-money sent by the Jews to the Temple at Jerusalem was from there forward to be sent to the Roman coffers. Although the mighty Roman Empire declared war on the innocent early Christians and put to death thousands of them in a brutal and merciless way, including St. Peter the first Pope, St. Paul, and many of the Apostles and disciples, the Church eventually won and planted the Vatican flag firmly in Rome. This is why and where Roman Catholicism gets its name, and why it is centered in Rome.

## The Jewish Curse on the Christians

Towards the end of the 9th century A.D. at the invitation of Gamaliel II, Pharisee and High Priest (nasi) of the Sanhedrin, Samuel ha-Katan composed the prayer, "Birkat ha-Minim," asking God to curse the Christians: the "minim" or "Nozerim" (Nazarenes; see Acts 24:5), the "heretical enemies" of the Jews and Judaism (the first Christians were converted Jews). The Birkat ha-Minim was inserted in the "Eighteen Benedictions" and appears in the Amidah, the core prayer that observant Jews recite three times a day. The following is an example of the prayer/curse as found in a Palestinian siddur from the Cairo Genizah: "For the apostates let there be no hope. And let the arrogant government be speedily uprooted in our days. Let the nozerim and the minim be destroyed in a moment. And let them be blotted out of the Book of Life and not be inscribed together with the righteous. Blessed art thou, O Lord, who humblest the arrogant" (Schechter).[176]

## Speaking In Parables and The Road To Emma'us

(Seeing and Hearing)

"And he said, Go, and say to this people: 'Hear and hear, but do not understand; see and see but do not perceive' " (Is 6:9). There is an interesting link between Jesus speaking in parables to the crowds and the Road to Emma'us incident, and it has to do with Jesus being the Heavenly Messiah and not the Earthly messiah the Jews had been waiting for. In regards to the parables, in the Gospel of Matthew we find:

"Then the disciples came and said to him, 'Why do you speak to them in parables?' And he answered them, 'To you it has been given to know the secrets of the kingdom of heaven, but to them it has not been given' " (Mt 13:10-11). The main teaching here is that the "secrets" Jesus is talking about is He Himself. That God the Father would send to Earth His Son to redeem the human race was a "secret" of Heaven, a secret contained in a veiled way in the prophecies of the OT Prophets, but now, the "secret" is standing right in front of them! In person! "That is; With the hearing ye shall hear words, but shall not understand the hidden meaning of those words; seeing ye shall see My flesh indeed, but shall not discern the divinity."[177]

"For to him who has will more be given, and he will have abundance; but from him who has not, even what he has will be taken away. This is why I speak to them in parables, because seeing they do not see, and hearing they do not hear, nor do they understand. With them indeed is fulfilled the prophecy of Isaiah which says: 'You shall indeed hear but never understand, and you shall indeed see but never perceive' " [Is 6:9] (Mt 13:12-14).

In this passage, Jesus is saying that "him who has," that is, he who has faith and believes Jesus is the Son of God, the Heavenly Messiah (and not the Earthly messiah), more faith will be given to him, but he who does not have that Faith, even the little faith he does have will have it taken away because he is not worthy of it. The Jews are seeing and hearing the Heavenly Messiah, but they are not aware of that fact because they were not expecting him to be the Son of God in human form due in large part to the false messianic teachings of the Pharisees. "Whoso has the desire and the zeal, to him shall be given all those things which are of God; but whoso lacketh these, and does not contribute that part that pertains to him, to him neither are the things which are of God given, but even those things that he hath are taken from him; not because God takes them away, but because he hath made himself unworthy of those that he has." [178]

"Or, To the Apostles who believe in Christ, there is given, but from the Jews who believed not on the Son of God, there is taken away, even whatever good they might seem to have by nature. For they cannot understand anything with wisdom, seeing they have not the head of wisdom." [179] "For by reason of the darkness of His discourse, they being blinded did not understand the Lord's sayings, and not understanding them, they did not believe on Him, and not believing on Him they crucified Him" [180] (see Jn 12:37).

"These things then which the Apostles saw and heard, are such as His presence, His voice, His teaching. And in this He sets them before not the evil only, but even before the good, pronouncing them more blessed than even the righteous men of old. For they saw not only what the Jews saw not, but also what the righteous men and Prophets desired to see, and had not seen. For they [the righteous and Prophets] had beheld these things only by faith, but these [Apostles and others] by sight, and even yet more clearly. You see how He identifies the OT with the New, for had the Prophets been the servants of any strange or hostile Deity, they would not have desired to see Christ." [181]

"For this people's heart has grown dull, and their ears are heavy of hearing and their eyes they have closed, lest they should perceive with their eyes, and hear with their ears, and understand with their heart, and turn for me to heal them. But blessed are your eyes, for they see, and your ears, for they hear. Truly, I say to you, many Prophets and righteous men longed to see what you see, and did not see it, and to hear what you hear, and did not hear it" (Mt 13:15-17).

Jesus is saying in this passage that the hearts of the Jews had become "dull": not on fire and "burning" for the Lord anymore, and their ears are "heavy of hearing": they don't listen to God and don't obey Him, and "their eyes they have closed": they failed to understand the Messianic prophecies because they were reduced to nationalistic aspirations by the Pharisees, and all of these are now preventing them from "seeing" (the "log" in their eye) and recognizing the True and Heavenly Messiah that is right in front of them, speaking to them in person (see Acts 28:25-31). The righteous men and Prophets of old once longed for the privilege and opportunity to have seen and heard the Messiah in person as they all are seeing and hearing Him now. "Or, He is speaking of the blessedness of the Apostolic times, to whose eyes and ears it was permitted to see and to hear the salvation of God, many Prophets and just men having desired to see and to hear that which was destined to be in the fullness of times." [182]

In regards to the Road to Emma'us incident, in the Gospel of Luke we find:

"That very day two of them were going to a village named Emma'us, about seven miles from Jerusalem, and talking with each other about all these things that had happened. While they were talking and discussing together, Jesus himself drew near and went with them. But their eyes were kept from recognizing him. And he said to them, 'What is this conversation which you are holding with each other as you walk?' And they stood still, looking sad. Then one of them, named Cle'opas, answered him, 'Are you the only visitor to Jerusalem who does not know the things that have happened there in these days?' And he said to them, 'What things?' And they said to him, 'Concerning Jesus of Nazareth, who was a **prophet** mighty in deed and word before God and all the people, and how our chief priests and rulers delivered him up to be condemned to death, and crucified him. **But we had hoped that he was the one to redeem Israel**. Yes, and besides all this, it is now the third day since this happened. Moreover, some women of our company amazed us. They were at the tomb early in the morning and did not find his body; and they came back saying that they had even seen a vision of angels, who said that he was alive. Some of those who were with us went to the tomb, and found it just as the women had said; but him they did not see ' And he said to them, '**O foolish men, and slow of heart to believe all that the Prophets have spoken!** Was it not necessary that the Christ should suffer these things and enter into his glory?' **And beginning with Moses and all the Prophets, he interpreted to them in all the Scriptures the things concerning himself**. "So they drew near to the village to which they were going. He appeared to be going further, but they constrained him, saying, 'Stay with us, for it is toward evening and the day is now far spent.' So he went in to stay with them. When he was at table with them, he took the bread and blessed and broke it, and gave it to them. And their eyes were opened and they recognized him; and he vanished out of their sight. They said to each other, '**Did not our hearts burn within us while he talked to us on the road, while he opened to us the Scriptures?**' And they rose that same hour and returned to Jerusalem; and they found the Eleven gathered together and those who were with them, who said, 'The Lord has risen indeed, and has appeared to Simon!' Then they told what had happened on the road, and how he was known to them in the breaking of the bread" (Lk 24:13-35) [my emph.].

The first thing to notice here is the word "**prophet**," that they considered Jesus a "prophet mighty in deed." This proves they were not aware that He was God in the flesh, the Son of God. And the second thing to notice here is, "**we had hoped that he was the one to redeem Israel**." The "redeeming of Israel" was synonymous with the liberation from Roman Rule led by the expected Earthly messiah. This is substantial proof that these two disciples – together with who knows how many others – were hoping that Jesus was going to be the expected Earthly messiah that would free Israel from Roman rule and domination. St. Thomas Aquinas confirms this point here: "For they expected that Christ would redeem Israel from the evils that were rising up among them **and the Roman slavery**" (Catena Aurea, St. Luke, p. 775, Theophyl; see Acts 1:6) [my emph.].

Jesus tells them how foolish they are for not understanding and "believing" the actual contents of the Messianic prophecies that spoke about a Heavenly Messiah and not an Earthly messiah. This is why Jesus "interpreted" and explained the Scriptural prophecies to them: to make them understand that the Earthly messiah the Jews were expecting, the one even they themselves had hoped Jesus was, was a gross misinterpretation of the Messianic prophecies: a reduction to nationalistic aspirations. After Jesus gave them the correct interpretation of the prophecies, that He was not the Earthly messiah they had hoped He was ("…we had hoped that he was the one to redeem Israel"), their "hearts burned" within them by having the correct interpretation of the Scriptures and then knowing who Jesus **truly** was: the True Messiah and Son of the Living God who came to redeem the world, and not just the Jews. They also realized that Jesus, the one the Jews rejected and crucified, was indeed the foretold Heavenly Messiah and not the Earthly messiah the Pharisees had erroneously led the Jews to expect: a Pharisaic pseudo-messiah many Jews are sadly still waiting for to this day, and one that is never going to come, because

Jesus Christ was AND IS the Prophesied Messiah who already came, completed His Mission, and went Home to our Father in Heaven to intercede for us daily.

It is interesting to note that these two persons on the road to Emma'us recognized it was Jesus "in the breaking of the bread" (Lk 24:31). How can this be? Cle'opas was not at the Last Supper when Jesus "Broke the Bread" for the first time, and the other individual with him was not an Apostle, for Scripture says that they both "returned to Jerusalem; and they found the Eleven gathered together and those who were with them" (24:33). Since it was only the Apostles who were with Jesus at the Last Supper when He Broke the Bread and instituted the Holy Eucharist for the first time, how did these two, who were not present at the Last Supper, put together the breaking of the bread with Jesus only three days later on the day of Resurrection? The answer may be that being disciples, they learned about the "Breaking of the Bread" from the Apostles sometime after the arrest of Jesus and before they started their Journey of Discovery on the Road to Emma'us. Moreover, while they were all together discussing all this in Jerusalem, Jesus appeared to them **again** and likewise "opened their minds to understand the Scriptures" (24:45). Clearly, Jesus was making sure they all understood that He was the prophesied Heavenly Messiah who came to redeem mankind and not just the Jews. But this "understanding" took some time, for in Acts 1:6, just before Jesus ascended into Heaven, the Apostles asked Him: "Lord, will you at this time restore the kingdom to Israel ?" (Free them from the Romans.) Therefore, they **still** did not understand what His Holy Mission on Earth was. Thank God He is so Loving and Patient. Very, very Loving and Patient.

It appears that Jesus' divinity remained a secret from the time of His birth and well into His public ministry when He was in His early 30s, and most likely never performed miracles as a child, as an adolescent, or even as an adult prior to His public ministry except perhaps in the private company of His parents, Mary and Joseph. This is somewhat confirmed by the fact that when Jesus read the Scriptures in the synagogue in Nazareth where He grew up, they all wondered, "Where did this man get this wisdom and these mighty works? Is not this the carpenter's son?" (Mt 13:54-55). In other words, "Isn't he just like one of us, an ordinary person?" Evidently, His parents kept His divinity a secret and for good reason, yet Mary knew He possessed supernatural powers as revealed at the Wedding at Cana (Jn 2:1-12). Further proof of this well-kept secret is also found in the "Walk to Emmaus" in the Gospel of Luke. Here, one of the two walking on the road is named Cle'opas, and Cle'opas refers to Jesus as a "prophet mighty in deed and word" (Lk 24:19). According to various sources, Cle'opas was the "brother" of Joseph, the legal father of Jesus who raised Him from birth. So, if Cle'opas, a close family member, did not know that Jesus was a divine Person, it's because Joseph and Mary did not reveal this to their family members, and much less, to anyone else. (Prophets were not divine Persons.) It was very important to keep Jesus' divinity a secret while He was growing up. In this light, it is now easy to see why Mary got upset with the boy Jesus after spending three days looking for Him and finally finding Him in the Temple (Lk 2:48), perhaps Mary and Joseph were very worried that His divinity would be discovered without them there to prevent the exposure of that secret; one they had kept for so long. In v. 51, it says that after they found Him, Jesus "was obedient to them," most likely after they reminded Him of the importance of keeping that secret. In fact, Jesus, as an adult, kept this secret for quite some time, gradually revealing it to His Apostles. Incredible as it sounds, many still don't know He is God! Still a secret?

Before I close this book, I need to make something very clear. Jesus was never an enemy of Rome. He never broke any Roman laws. Pilate, governor of Judaea, had Him crucified because the Pharisees, Sadducees, scribes, and the crowd they incited demanded His execution because He claimed to be the Son of God, a serious blasphemy punishable by death, and only the Romans had the "authority" to execute a person; the Jews did not. If you'll remember (on page 114), when Jesus enters Jerusalem to willingly accept His execution, a great crowd welcomed Him with great joy, and some called Him "the King of Israel." I also mentioned here that the term "King of Israel" was precisely the type of individual who fits the description of the Earthly messiah the Jews had been waiting for to free them from Roman rule. But this was a serious error, because Jesus' Mission, the Mission of the awaited Heavenly Messiah, was not to free the Jews from Roman rule, but to restore the broken relationship between man and God and redeem the entire human race through His sacrificial death on the Cross. Some books and magazines (even some that are Catholic) claim that Jesus **was** an enemy of Rome because some of the Jews called Him king, and that is why the Romans, afraid of an insurrection, crucified Him. However, nothing could be further from the truth; and the proof is found in Scripture. As I state on page 152, Pilate repeatedly declared Jesus innocent, saying: "**I find no crime in him**," and also said, "I am innocent of this **righteous man's** blood" (Mt 27:24). Secondly, Jesus Himself told Pilate: "My kingship is not of this world" (Jn 18:36). If the governor said Jesus was innocent, it's because he did not see Him as a threat, to him or to Rome. One thing that influenced Pilate to authorize His crucifixion is that "a riot was beginning" to form (Mt 27:24) and feared an insurrection might follow, but one not led by Jesus, but by the Pharisees, Sadducees, and scribes! The **real** troublemakers.

## The Supernatural Within Catholicism

Miraculous and supernatural occurrences within the Catholic Church date back to its founding by Jesus Christ in 33 A.D., not to mention the miracles that Jesus Himself performed as found in Scripture. One that was very important for the Church was the conversion of Saul (St. Paul) on his way to Damascus to persecute Christians, and this one is a real biggie because St. Paul became a founding pillar of the Church. Another example, some Christians (not all) who were chosen by Roman Emperors to provide "entertainment" for the crowds in the Colosseum by being devoured by lions and wild beasts had to be executed by other means because the animals refused to harm them and laid down beside them, and the list goes on. Many books have been written about these and other supernatural phenomena within Catholicism; the exorcism of demons, including Satan, from possessed people is another. Earlier in this book, I mentioned the miracles of the Holy Eucharist turning into human flesh (pp. 101, 239), which is the most important of all the miracles within the Church. I also mentioned the Incorruptibles (p. 239), saints who have died but have not decomposed; they look like they are just sleeping. I must here mention the apparitions of our Blessed Mother, Mary, mother of Jesus, who has appeared in many places around the world with the same message from Heaven for us: repent, sacrifice, pray, and follow her Son. The most notable of these apparitions are: Guadalupe, Mexico (1531), Lourdes, France (1858), and Fatima, Portugal (1917). As I mentioned earlier, all of these supernatural miracles have been – and are – given to us by God in order to draw souls to His Holy Mother Church. As far as I know, no other religion on Earth–including Protestantism–has any evidence of supernatural occurrences within it that have been scientifically documented like those within the Catholic Church. This, of course, is God's way of leading us to follow His one and only Church, for the salvation of our souls, and not some other man-made religion. There is no other way. Jesus Himself said: "I am the way, and the truth, and the life; no one comes to the Father [in Heaven], but by me" (Jn 14:6).

Since it is a historical fact that the Catholic Church is the "religion" founded by God Himself in the Person of Jesus Christ, it is therefore only through the Church that we are able to establish a real, personal, and ongoing relationship with God/Jesus and follow only Him and His teachings through Mother Church in order to enjoy Eternal Life in Heaven after death. I sincerely hope this book will be of some help to you. Let us pray that all non-Catholics will come into the Church so we can all be One. The Triune God wants everyone to go to Heaven, and proof of this is in Jesus Christ Himself, the Lamb of God who died for all mankind. May God bless all of you and keep you in His Loving Care.

"Now Paul and his company set sail from Pa'phos, and came to Perga in Pamphyl'ia. And John left them and returned to Jerusalem; but they passed on from Perga and came to Antioch of Pisid'ia. And on the sabbath day they went into the synagogue and sat down. After the reading of the law and the Prophets, the rulers of the synagogue sent to them, saying, Brethren, if you have any word of exhortation for the people, say it. So Paul stood up, and motioning with his hand said: Men of Israel, and you that fear God, listen. The God of this people Israel chose our fathers and made the people great during their stay in the land of Egypt, and with uplifted arm he led them out of it. And for about forty years he bore with them in the wilderness. And when he had destroyed seven nations in the land of Canaan, he gave them their land as an inheritance, for about four hundred and fifty years. And after that he gave them judges until Samuel the prophet. Then they asked for a king; and God gave them Saul the son of Kish, a man of the tribe of Benjamin, for forty years. And when he had removed him, he raised up David to be their king; of whom he testified and said, I have found in David, the son of Jesse, a man after my heart, who will do all my will. Of this man's posterity God has brought to Israel a Savior, Jesus, as he promised. Before his coming John had preached a baptism of repentance to all the people of Israel. And as

John was finishing his course, he said, What do you suppose that I am? I am not he. No, but after me one is coming, the sandals of whose feet I am not worthy to untie. Brethren, sons of the family of Abraham, and those among you that fear God, to us has been sent the message of this salvation. For those who live in Jerusalem and their rulers, because they did not recognize him nor understand the utterances of the Prophets which are read every sabbath, fulfilled these by condemning him. Though they could charge him with nothing deserving death, yet they asked Pilate to have him killed. And when they had fulfilled all that was written of him, they took him down from the tree, and laid him in a tomb. But God raised him from the dead; and for many days he appeared to those who came up with him from Galilee to Jerusalem, who are now his witnesses to the people. And we bring you the good news that what God promised to the fathers, this he has fulfilled to us their children by raising Jesus" (Acts 13:13-33). Paul's words, like Christ's, enraged the Jews who eventually plotted to kill him (Acts 23:12), but also like Jesus, who was found innocent by Pilate, tribune Claudius Lysias declared that Paul was innocent of wrongdoing and did not deserve death or imprisonment (Acts 23:29). Nevertheless, Paul was eventually martyred by beheading during Nero's reign c. 67 A.D.

After Christ's Ascension into Heaven, Peter healed a man who was lame from birth and then addressed the Jews who had cried out to Pilate to crucify Jesus: "Men of Israel, why do you wonder at this, or why do you stare at us, as though by our own power or piety we had made him walk? The God of Abraham and of Isaac and of Jacob, the God of our fathers, glorified his servant Jesus, whom you delivered up and denied in the presence of Pilate, when he had decided to release him. But you denied the Holy and Righteous One, and asked for a murderer to be granted to you, and killed the Author of life, whom God raised from the dead. To this we are witnesses. And his name, by faith in his name, has made this man strong whom you see and know; and the faith which is through Jesus has given the man this perfect health in the presence of you all. And now, brethren, **I know that you acted in ignorance, as did also your rulers.** But what God foretold by the mouth of all the Prophets, that his Christ should suffer, he thus fulfilled. Repent therefore, and turn again, that your sins may be blotted out, that times of refreshing may come from the presence of the Lord, and that he may send the Christ appointed for you, Jesus, whom heaven must receive until the time for establishing all that God spoke by the mouth of his holy Prophets from of old" (Acts 3:12-21) [my emph.] (see Acts 2:29-36).

"In giving us his Son, his only Word (for he possesses no other), he [God the Father] spoke everything to us at once in this sole Word – and he has no more to say [ … ] because what he spoke before to the Prophets in parts, he has now spoken all at once by giving us the All Who is His Son. Those who now desire to question God or receive some vision or revelation are guilty not only of foolish behavior but also of offending him by not fixing their eyes entirely on Christ and by living with the desire for some other novelty." (St. John of the Cross, "The Ascent of Mount Carmel." 22.3, 22.4, 22.5.)

"Where is the wise man? Where is the scribe? Where is the debater of this age? Has not God made foolish the wisdom of the world? For since, in the wisdom of God, the world did not know God through wisdom, it pleased God through the folly of what we preach to save those who believe. For Jews demand signs and Greeks seek wisdom, but we preach Christ crucified, a stumbling block to Jews and folly to Gentiles, but to those who are called, both Jews and Greeks, Christ the power of God and the wisdom of God. For the foolishness of God is wiser than men, and the weakness of God is stronger than men. For consider your call, brethren; not many of you were wise according to the flesh, not many were powerful, not many were of noble birth; but God chose what is foolish in the world to shame the wise, God chose what is weak in the world to shame the strong, God chose what is low and despised in the world, even things that are not, to bring to nothing things that are, so that no flesh might boast in the presence of God. He is the source of your life in Christ Jesus, whom God made our wisdom, our righteousness and sanctification and redemption; therefore, as it is written, Let him who boasts, boast of the Lord" (1 Cor 1:20-31).

When I stated earlier that Jesus established a New Religion, Catholicism, the True Religion to follow from Christ forward in order to merit Salvation (going to Heaven), this is all true. However, keep in mind that Catholicism and Judaism are intimately linked since Catholicism is the "perfection" of Judaism. This is why Catholicism embodies many Judaic elements within it. The Jews erroneously believed the Messiah was coming to save only them when He was actually coming to redeem the entire human race. Those who accept this truth and join the Church He established are known as Catholics. But this doesn't mean those who practiced and are practicing Judaism will not be saved, for St. Paul said: "…a hardening has come upon part of Israel, until the full number of the Gentiles come in, and so all Israel will be saved […] For the gifts and the call of God are irrevocable" (Rom 11:25, 26, 29).

In the first "visitation," Satan came to Earth to destroy the holy relationship between God and His children; in the second Visitation, an angel came to announce the restoration of that relationship through Christ with Mary's co-operation. "Fear not, for I have redeemed you; I have called you by name, you are mine" (Is 43:1).

"To use this life well is the pathway through death to everlasting life." St. John Almond.

* * *

## Endnotes

1. See *Where We Got The Bible (WGB)*, Henry G. Graham, p.17.
2. *Catechism of the Catholic Church (CCC)*, 669, 751, 789, 792; *Radio Replies (RR)*, Fr. Leslie Rumble, # 1, p. 17; # 78, p.65; see *WGB*, p. 170.
3. See *RR*, # 78, p. 65.
4. Ibid., # 108, p. 79.
5. *CCC*, 613-14.
6. *In The Beginning (ITB)*, Dr. Gerard M. Verschuuren, p. 20.
7. www.thoughtco.com/georges-lemaitre-3071074.
8. *Big Bang*, Singh, Simon (2010). Ch. 8, Part 12; Ch. 9, Part 1-2.
9. See G. Lemaître, *The Primeval Atom – An Essay on Cosmogony*, New York-London, D. Van Nostrand Co, 1950.
10. catholicscientists.org/catholic-scientists-of-the-past/georges-lemaitre.
11. *ITB*, pgs. 57, 58, 68.
12. Ibid., p. 69.
13. Ibid, p. 67.
14. Ibid. pgs, 67, 97.
15. Ibid. p. 82.
16. www.catholicscientists.org/idea/monsignor-georges-lemaitre-originator-of-big-bang-theory.
17. *ITB*, pgs. 8-9.
18. Ibid., pgs. 8, 79, 81, 100, 131.
19. Ibid., p. 79.
20. Ibid., p. 80.
21. Ibid.
22. Ibid., p. 82.
23. Ibid., see p. 83.
24. See *The Privileged Planet*, Guillermo Gonzalez, Jay Richards.
25. *Cosmology and Controversy: The Historical Development of Two Theories of the Universe*, Kragh, Helge, p. 55.
26. *CCC*, 390, 391.
27. Ibid.

28. Ibid., 396-421.
29. Gn 3:6.
30. Gn 3:22; see *CCC*, 376.
31. See *Theology and Sanity (TS)*, Frank Sheed, p. 184; see *CCC*, 376, 1008.
32. *ITB,* p. 80-83.
33. *TS,* pgs. 174-76, 185-86, 275; Jn 1:12.
34. Ibid.
35. *Fr. Mitch Pacwa, SJ, talks about "Bible difficulties" and religion,* with Robert J. Hutchinson. www.youtube.com/watch?v=TnSm6SpP1aA/: (Time 40:20).
36. *The Real Story*, Sri and Martin, pgs. 25-29.
37. See *Why Does God Permit Evil?*, Dom Bruno Webb, pp. 89-137.
38. *Exorcism: The Battle Against Satan and His Demons,* Fr. Vincent P. Lampert, pgs. 50-51, 104.
39. Ibid., pgs. 29, 31, 66.
40. Ibid., p. 77.
41. Ibid., p. 105.
42. See *www.whiteestate.org.*
43. *RR*, # 58, p. 52.
44. *Pocket Catholic Dictionary (PCD)*, John A. Hardon, S.J., p. 5.
45. Gn 11:10-24.
46. Gn 6:11-22.
47. Gn 5:1-29.
48. Gn 9:28.
49. Gn 11:27.
50. Gn 12:4-5.
51. Gn 10:6.
52. Gn 13:2.
53. Gn 12:19-20.
54. Gn 13:12-13.
55. Gn 17:10-14.
56. Gn 15:8-21.
57. Gn 17:5.
58. Gn 17:24.
59. Gn 18:16-33; 19:1-29.

60. *Radio Replies,* # 97, p. 74.
61. Ex1:1-7.
62. Gn 41:37-45.
63. Ex 13:19.
64. Num 20:6-13; Dt 32:48-52; 34:1-7.
65. 1 Sm 10:1.
66. Ibid., 17:1-51.
67. Ibid., 31:1-6; 2 Sm 2:4.
68. 1 Kgs 4:34.
69. Ibid., 11:1-43.
70. Ibid., 11:3.
71. Ibid., 11:43.
72. www.jewishvirtuallibrary.org/judaism-s-rejection-of-original-sin; www.jewishvirtuallibrary.org/jews-for-jesus.
73. *A Catholic Introduction To The Bible (CIB), Volume I, The Old Testament*, John Bergsma, Brant Pitre, pgs. 517-18.
74. See *RR*, # 125, p. 87.
75. *Antiquities of the Jews (AJ)*, Flavius Josephus, Book XIV. Ch.14 v.4; 13:1; www.livius.org/articles/person/herod-the-great/; www.jewishvirtuallibrary.org/herod.
76. *AJ*., XVII. 9.
77. Ibid., 10:5-7.
78. www.livius.org/articles/person/quinctilius-varus/.
79. *AJ*, XVII. 10:5-7; www.livius.org/articles/religion/messiah/messianic-claimant-3-athronges/; www.livius.org/articles/person/herod-archelaus/.
80. *AJ*, XVIII. 1:1, 6; www.livius.org/articles/religion/messiah/messianic-claimant-4-judas-the-galilean/.
81. www.focusonjerusalem.com/thefallofjerusalem.html.
82. www.jewishvirtuallibrary.org/shimon-bar-kokhba; www.livius.org/articles/concept/roman-jewish-wars/roman-jewish-wars-8/.
83. Ibid.
84. *First Apology*, St Justin Martyr, 31:6.
85. www.livius.org/articles/concept/roman-jewish-wars/roman-jewish-wars-8/.
86. Ibid.

87. https://en.wikipedia.org/wiki/Bethlehem.
88. www.jewishvirtuallibrary.org/the-bar-kokhba-revolt-132-135-ce.
89. www.livius.org/articles/concept/roman-jewish-wars/roman-jewish-wars-8/.
90. *St. Jerome Chronicles, 228th Olympiad*, p. 283. 17b.
91. www.jewishvirtuallibrary.org/shabbetai-zvi-false-messiah-judaic-treasures.
92. Ibid.
93. www.jewishvirtuallibrary.org/pharisees-sadducees-and-essenes.
94. *(CIB),* pgs. 890, 900-01.
95. www.jewishvirtuallibrary.org/the-messiah.
96. *Seven Prophets and the Culture War*, A. Havard, pp. xiv-xv.
97. See *CCC*, 490-94.
98. See Lk 3:23.
99. www.jewishvirtuallibrary.org/anthropomorphism.
100. Mt 16:16.
101. Gn 17:1-8; 22:16-18; Ex 3:7-10.
102. *Hebrew Chronicle: From Adam to Moses,* Eusebius, 40.
103. *Messiah in Rabbinic Thought*, www.jewishvirtuallibrary.org/messiah.
104. Rv 5:5.
105. Lk 1:34-35.
106. Lk 1:26-35.
107. Lk 10:16; Jn 12:49.
108. Mt 26:30.
109. See "St. Jerome's Comm. on Galatians," #79.
110. See *TS,* p. 299.
111. *Eucharistic Miracles*, Joan Carroll Cruz; *Unseen*, Ron Tesoriero, *A Cardiologist Examines Jesus*, Dr. Franco Serafini.
112. See *TS* , p. 269.
113. See *CCC*, 595-97.
114. See *The Fourth Cup*, Scott Hahn.
115. See *TS,* p. 274; see *Catena Aurea (CA)*, Vol II, St Mark, p. 30. Bede.

116. www.ncregister.com/search?q=when+Jesus+died.
117. Dt 7:6; 14:2; see *CCC*, 62-64.
118. www.britannica.com/topic/chosen-people.
119. www.jewishvirtuallibrary.org/the-quot-chosen-people-quot.
120. See *RR*, # 136, p. 93; # 141, p. 95; # 147, p. 98; # 148, p. 99; # 475, p. 242; # 476, p. 243; # 482, p. 245; # 512, p. 257.
121. https://reason2bcatholic.com/2021/06/29/saints-alive-solemnity-of-saints-peter-and-paul/.
122. Gn 22:1-2.
123. Gn 22:14.
124. www.jewishvirtuallibrary.org/sacrifices-and-offerings-.
125. Ibid.; *Nm* 19:1-10.
126. Jn 18:33, 36.
127. *St. Jerome Chronicles, 204th Olympiad*, p. 260. 3c.
128. *CCC*, 709.
129. www.youtube.com/watch?v=X0atBTyMK8w (Time. 28:05).
130. See *Works on the Spirit*, Athanasius/Didymus, p. 57f.
131. See *RR*, # 374-75, p. 203; # 376, p. 204; # 379, p. 205; # 380, p. 206.
132. *RR*, # 142, p. 96.
133. See *CA,* Luke, p. 169. Bede; *CA,* Luke, p. 170. Bede; see 1 Cor 2:6-9.
134. www.jewishvirtuallibrary.org/the-messiah.
135. *CA*, Vol II, St Mark, p. 30. Theophyl.
136. www.catholic.org/saints/saint.php?saint_id=376.
137. *CA*, Vol II, St Mark, p. 29. Theophyl.
138. *The Messianic Secret*, William Wrede. Cambridge: James Clarke & Co., 1971.
139. *RR*, # 221, p. 136.
140. See *RR*, # 124, p. 87.
141. See *CCC*, 770-71; see *RR*, # 176, p. 112; # 216, p. 135; #s 219-228, pgs 136-39.
142. *PCD*, p. 64.
143. *CCC*, 849; see Jn 6:53-56.

144. See *RR*, # 149, p. 99; # 151, p. 100; # 153, p. 100; # 154, p. 101.
145. See *RR*, # 119, p. 83.
146. See *RR*, # 475, p. 242.
147. Mt 17:1-13; Mk 9:2-13; Lk 9:28-36.
148. See *CCC*, 172; see Eph 4:4-6, 12-13.
149. See *RR*, # 476-78, p. 243; # 479-80, p. 244.
150. See *RR*, # 177-78, p. 113; # 338, p. 187.
151. See *RR*, # 46, p. 45; # 49, p. 47; # 58-59, pgs. 52-53; # 61, p. 55.
152. See *RR*, # 323, p. 180; # 325, p. 181; # 326-27, p. 182; # 328, p. 183; # 338, p. 187.
153. *RR*, # 154, p. 101; # 168, p.106; # 173, p. 110; # 176, p. 112; # 338, p. 187; # 361, p. 199.
154. See *RR*, # 49, p. 47.
155. See Lk 17:2; *RR*, # 185, p. 116; # 192, p. 120.
156. *RR*, # 223, p. 137.
157. See *Works on the Spirit*, Athanasius/Didymus, p. 96.
158. See *RR*, # 85, p. 69.
159. See *RR*, 149, p. 99.
160. *RR*, # 206, p. 127.
161. See *RR*, # 147, p. 98; # 151, p. 100; # 153, p. 100.
162. See *RR*, # 119, p. 83.
163. See *RR*, #s 475-80, pgs. 242-44.
164. *Exorcism: The Battle Against Satan and His Demons,* Fr. Vincent P. Lampert, pg. 96.
165. See *RR*, # 223, p. 137; # 226, p. 138; # 231, p. 141; # 291, p. 165; # 313, p. 175.
166. See *RR*, # 192-93, p. 120; # 323, p. 180; # 338, p. 187.
167. See *RR*, #s 117 & 118, pgs. 187-88.
168. See *RR*, # 82, p. 67; # 151, p. 100; # 154, p. 101.
169. See *RR*, # 208, p. 128.
170. *RR*, # 190, p. 119; # 180, p. 114.
171. See *RR*, # 125, p. 87; see # 144, p. 96.
172. See NOSTRA AETATE, His Holiness Pope Paul VI, 1965.
173. See *RR*, # 123, p. 86; # 124, p. 87; # 125, p. 87.

174. *PCD*, p. 248.
175. www.jewishvirtuallibrary.org/shewbread-or-showbread.
176. www.jewishvirtuallibrary.org/birkat-ha-minim; www.jewishencyclopedia.com/articles/10846-min.
177. *CA*, Volume 1, St. Mt., Part 1, p. 486. Gloss.
178. *CA*, Volume 1, St. Mt., Part 1, p. 485. Chrys.
179. *CA*, Volume 1, St. Mt., Part 1, p. 485. Jerome.
180. *CA*, Volume 1, St. Mt., Part 1, p. 488-89 Aug.
181. *CA*, Volume 1, St. Mt., Part 1, p. 490. Chrys.
182. *CA*, Volume 1, St. Mt., Part 1, p. 489. Hilary.

# Index

## A

## B

## C

## D

## E

## F

## G

## H

# I

# J

## K

## L

## M

## N

## O

## P

# Q



# R

# T

## U

## V

## W

## X, Y



## Z

# RELIGIOUS TRUTH
# HOW OLD IS YOUR CHURCH?

**LUTHERAN** – Martin Luther

If you are a Lutheran, your Protestant religion was founded in 1528 by Martin Luther, a corrupt, egocentric and morally depraved excommunicated rogue Catholic monk who broke away from the Catholic Church in 1517 and became one of the protestant "reformers" responsible for the intrinsically heretical "religious" movement known today as the Protestant Reformation, and specifically, Lutheranism.

While translating the New Testament from Greek into German while hiding from the public in a castle, the Wartburg (thanks to Frederick the Wise), Luther added the word "alone" to Romans 3:28 in order to justify his "faith alone" (***sola fide***) heretical protestant doctrine, thereby excusing himself, as well as his followers, from having to follow moral conduct as prescribed by the Catholic Church. He thereafter erroneously declared that human beings were "justified," that is, saved from going to hell by faith in Christ *alone*, that man was hopelessly corrupt due to original sin, and that all his good works, even those done from charitable or pious motives, were grave sins and were of no use toward salvation. Luther therefore concluded that following God's Commandments and living a moral life doing good for others, as Christ Himself instructed, was actually unimportant, unnecessary, and unrewarding, and that only faith in Christ alone would take you to Heaven no matter what you did here on Earth, whether good or bad. Luther's first German translation of the Bible omitted 16 OT books and 9 NT books primarily to support his "anti-works" *sola fide* doctrine and also his other heretical doctrine ***sola scriptura***: that the Bible and not the Pope is the ultimate authority.

(NOTE: The original Bible is a Catholic Book.) Modern Protestant Bibles are still missing 7 books, some versions even more; not to mention illicit additions and deletions within them.

According to Luther, Redemption meant being justified by faith (trust) in Christ alone, whereby the sinner is considered pleasing to God without any co-operation on the sinner's part. Luther's disagreements with Catholic Church teachings on these matters led him to "protest" against the Church, which eventually led him to start his own brand of religion, ultimately becoming known as Lutheranism. Many people who were weak in their faith and morals at the time believed in Luther and became his followers. It is firmly recorded in history that Luther was a victim of melancholia, sensual attacks, and, according to Luther himself, diabolical obsession. He attacked Erasmus for upholding free will, and in his "Servitude of the Will," advocated determinism. Luther's teachings and unbridled writings had been fanning the fire of the peasants' growing discontent, resulting in the *Peasants' War* of 1525. He sounded a warning, but too late, and throwing in his lot with the princes, he eloquently exhorted them "to slaughter the peasants like dogs."

Luther married an ex-Bernardine nun, Katharina von Bora, both intentionally breaking the vows of celibacy they had taken when they entered the religious life; he fathered six children with her. Not surprisingly, Luther's "protest," inspired others to do the same: to break away from the Catholic Mother Church and start their own "Christian" church, most notably, Ulrich Zwingli in Switzerland and John Calvin in France. But those who followed Luther's example at first, and who had the most to benefit from by following him were kings, princes, noblemen, and the like, for these had wanted to get their hands on Church property for a long time. Some of them stormed Catholic monasteries and churches, looted and then burned them, even raped the nuns, and executed many of the priests, monks, and nuns. All this, and much more, eventually led to what is known today as the "Protestant Reformation," the supposed "reform" of Catholicism, which in turn gave birth to "Protestantism": the proliferation of small churches, each professing their own brand of Christianity, without being united to Christ's original Church, the Roman Catholic Church. Luther was excommunicated by Pope Leo X on January 3rd, 1521 for being a heretic, and rightly so. The destructive effects of Luther's "protest," together with those of the others who also protested, followed his example, and also started their own brand of "Christianity" are still being felt to this day around the globe. As of this writing, there are hundreds of thousands of protestant denominations worldwide.

**CHURCH OF ENGLAND** – King Henry the VIII

If you belong to the Church of England, your Protestant religion was founded by King Henry the VIII in the year 1532. Interestingly enough, at one point in his life, King Henry worked hard against Martin Luther in defense of the Seven Sacraments, the Mass, and the papal supremacy of the Catholic Mother Church, which won for him the title "Defender of the Faith," conferred on him by Pope Leo X. But his desire for a male heir to his throne, combined with lust for sexual pleasure with a young woman, Anne Boleyn, caused him to break away from the Mother Church and establish his own church, the church of England, starting in 1532. Henry had been married to his brother's widow, Catherine of Aragon, a woman of Spanish nobility, and she had bore him a daughter, who later became Queen Mary. But Henry wanted a son – a son that would become King of England one day.

After having immoral relations with Elizabeth Blount and Mary Boleyn, Anne's older sister, Henry became obsessed with violent passion for young Anne, who at the time was only in her late teens or early twenties, but Anne denied him sexual favors and basically told him: "either make me Queen or you get nothing!" Henry quickly started proceedings to get his marriage annulled but these failed, so divorce was then next on the list. Claiming that his marriage to Catherine was actually not legal, Henry tried to persuade Cardinal Wolsey to grant him a divorce so he could marry Anne, but the Cardinal would not grant it to him. Henry eventually married Anne (while still being legally married to Catherine), but Anne bore him another daughter. Henry soon began to lust for another young woman, Jane Seymour, and had Anne beheaded so he could marry Jane. Consequently, Henry eventually opened the doors to his new church, the Church of England, and placed himself as the head of it. No one was going to tell him what was morally right or wrong anymore!

Incidentally, contrary to popular belief, Henry never liked Martin Luther or any of the other "reformers" and never adopted any of their protestant heretical doctrines. In fact, King Henry VIII did not adopt protestant doctrines because his break with Rome was driven by political and not theological motives; i.e., to secure an annulment and a male heir, not to reform Catholic doctrine. As a staunch, traditional Catholic, he upheld Latin mass, transubstantiation, and priestly celibacy, even burning reformers for heresy while establishing himself as head of the Church of England.

**PRESBYTERIAN** – John Knox (devout Calvinist)

If you are a Presbyterian, your protestant religion was founded by John Knox in Scotland in the year 1560, a product of the Protestant Reformation which was largely begun by Ulrich Zwingli, Martin Luther and John Calvin. Their ultimate authority is their General Assembly.

**CONGREGATIONALIST** – Robert Brown (Calvinist)

If you are a Congregationalist, your protestant religion was originated by Robert Brown. Robert Brown organized his first separatist congregation in Norwich, England, around 1580 and later formalized his views in books published in Middelburg, Netherlands, in 1582. Congregationalists do not believe in organized unity. Members' beliefs differ in what faith is.

**BAPTIST** – John Smyth (Mennonitic)

If you are a Baptist, you owe the tenets of your protestant religion to John Smyth who launched it in Amsterdam in 1609 by breaking with Puritan Separatism to establish a "believer's church." Baptists forbid infant baptism.

**DUTCH REFORMED** – Jonas Michaelius (Calvinist)

If you are of the Dutch Reformed church, your protestant religion was started by Jonas Michaelius in New York in 1628.

**METHODIST** – John and Charles Wesley

If you are a Methodist, your protestant religion, a revival movement within the Church of England, was launched by John and Charles Wesley in London, England in 1739. Methodists have no creed, no "method" to express their Christian beliefs and shun Catholic dogmas. The Methodist protestant religion is a blend of High-Church Anglican structure, pietist heart-religion, and Arminian theology.

**UNITARIAN** – Theophilus Lindley

If you are Unitarian, Theophilus Lindley founded your protestant religion in London in 1774. They reject the Holy Trinity calling it "irrational" and "unscriptural."

**EPISCOPALIAN** – SamuelSeabury

If you are an Episcopalian, your protestant religion is a mixture of Anglicanism, Calvinism, and Arminian perspectives. It is an off-shoot of the Church of England and was founded by Samuel Seabury in the American colonies in 1784.

**MORMON** – Joseph Smith

The Church of Mormon was not considered by Joseph Smith, its founder, as a reformed protestant denomination because he declared that God the Father and Jesus appeared to him in 1820 when he was 14 and instructed him not to join any existing religions; that they were going to "restore" the original Church they had established through him because it had been "lost" after the death of the Apostles and had not existed for 1,800 years. Mormonism practices baptism of the dead, rejects original sin, and teaches that Jesus was a human who became God (reverse Catholicism) and that we too can become Gods.

**SEVENTH DAY ADVENTISTS** – James White, Ellen G. White, and Joseph Bates

If you belong to the Seventh Day Adventists, your protestant religion was founded in 1860 by Ellen G. White, Joseph Bates, and Hiram Edson.

**SALVATION ARMY** – William Booth

Originally started as a Wesleyan-Methodist revival movement, if you worship with the Salvation Army, your protestant religion began with William Booth, an English Methodist preacher, in London in 1865.

**CHRISTIAN SCIENTIST** – Mary Baker Eddy

If you are a Christian Scientist, you look to 1879 as the year in which your protestant religion was born and to Mrs. Mary Baker Eddy as its founder. Denies the divinity of Christ.

**ROMAN CATHOLIC** – Jesus Christ

If you are a Roman Catholic, your religion, the True, authentic, and original Christian religion on Earth, was founded around the year 33 A.D. by Jesus Christ Himself, the Son of God the Father, with Peter as its first Pope (Mt. 16:18). The Pope continues – to this day – to be the head of the Church, His Church, on Earth, just as Jesus ordained it 2,000 years ago, "...and the gates of Hell shall not prevail against it" (Mt 16:18).

## Why have Religion? And why go to Church?

God created the universe, planet Earth, and the human race. We are therefore indebted to God for all He has given to us, including our existence, and religion is the means or vehicle commonly used to worship God and give Him thanks. There are many religions in the world and all of them were established by human beings except one: the Roman Catholic religion, established by God Himself in the person of Jesus Christ c. 33 A.D. Although all other religions give thanks to God in one way or another - some have even brutally sacrificed human beings to appease God, much to His displeasure – it is only through Catholicism that true worship and thanks are justly given to God by following the instructions He gave us personally through Christ. Religion is our "debt" to God, and through it we give to God what we owe Him: thanks and appreciation. Catholics worship God and give Him thanks in appreciation mainly in two ways: privately and publicly, and we do this through the religion He gave us. Catholics do this privately by praying to Him regularly, and publicly by going to Mass at a Catholic church at least once a week on Sundays. Just as we are obligated to justly pay our debts to others, all of us are obligated to justly pay our debts to God, and Catholics do this regularly through Catholicism and its Church founded by God Himself in the person of Jesus Christ, the Holy Roman Catholic Church. Most importantly, it is only the Catholic religion, the original Christian religion established by God Himself through Jesus Christ that teaches the truth about the human race, death, and life after death. The relationship between mankind and God was broken by the first humans because they sinned, but God restored it through Christ by His death on the Cross. So, it is only through Jesus Christ and His **One, Holy, Catholic and Apostolic** Church that salvation: living with God in Heaven after death, can be attained, and not through any other man-made religion on Earth.

# LIST OF ROMAN CATHOLIC POPES

1. St. Peter (33-67)
2. St. Linus (67-76)
3. St. Anacletus (76-88)
4. St. Clement I (88-97)
5. St. Evaristus (97-105)
6. St. Alexander I (105-115)
7. St. Sixtus I (115-125) Also called Xystus I.
8. St. Telesphorus (125-136)
9. St. Hyginus (136-140)
10. St. Pius I (140-155)
11. St. Anicetus 155-166)
12. St. Soter (166-175)
13. St. Eleutherius (175-189)
14. St. Victor I (189-199)
15. St. Zephyrinus (199-217)
16. St. Callistus I (217-222)
17. St. Urban I (222-30)
18. St. Pontain (230-35)
19. St. Anterus (235-36)
20. St. Fabian (236-50)
21. St. Cornelius (251-53)
22. St. Lucius I (253-54)
23. St. Stephen I (254-257)
24. St. Sixtus II (257-258)
25. St. Dionysius (260-268)
26. St. Felix I (269-274)
27. St. Eutychian (275-283)
28. St. Caius (283-296) Also called Gaius.
29. St. Marcellinus (296-304)
30. St. Marcellus I (308-309)
31. St. Eusebius (309 or 310)
32. St. Miltiades (311-14)
33. St. Sylvester I (314-35)

34. St. Marcus (336)
35. St. Julius I (337-52)
36. Liberius (352-66)
37. St. Damasus I (366-83)
38. St. Siricius (384-99)
39. St. Anastasius I (399-401)
40. St. Innocent I (401-17)
41. St. Zosimus (417-18)
42. St. Boniface I (418-22)
43. St. Celestine I (422-32)
44. St. Sixtus III (432-40)
45. St. Leo I The Great (440-61)
46. St. Hilarius (461-68)
47. St. Simplicius (468-83)
48. St. Felix III (II) (483-92)
49. St. Gelasius I (492-96)
50. Anastasius II (496-98)
51. St. Symmachus (498-514)
52. St. Hormisdas (514-23)
53. St. John I (523-26)
54. St. Felix IV (III) (526-30)
55. Boniface II (530-32)
56. John II (533-35)
57. St. Agapetus I (535-36) Also called Agapitus I.
58. St. Silverius (536-37)
59. Vigilius (537-55)
60. Pelagius I (556-61)
61. John III (561-74)
62. Benedict I (575-79)
63. Pelagius II (579-90)
64. St. Gregory I The Great (590-604)
65. Sabinian (604-606)
66. Boniface III (607)
67. St. Boniface IV (608-15)
68. St. Deusdedit (Adeodatus I) (615-18)
69. Boniface V (619-25)
70. Honorius I (625-38)

71. Severinus (640)
72. John IV (640-42)
73. Theodore I (642-49)
74. St. Martin I (649-55)
75. St. Eugene I (655-57)
76. St. Vitalian (657-72)
77. Adeodatus (II) (672-76)
78. Donus (676-78)
79. St. Agatho (678-81)
80. St. Leo II (682-83)
81. St. Benedict II (684-85)
82. John V (685-86)
83. Conon (686-87)
84. St. Sergius I (687-701)
85. John VI (701-05)
86. John VII (705-07)
87. Sisinnius (708)
88. Constantine (708-15)
89. St. Gregory II (715-31)
90. St. Gregory III (731-41)
91. St. Zachary (741-52)
92. Stephen II (752)
93. St. Paul I (757-67)
94. Stephen III (768-72)
95. Adrian I (772-95)
96. St. Leo III (795-816)
97. Stephen IV (816-17)
98. St. Paschal I (817-24)
99. Eugene II (824-27)
100. Valentine (827)
101. Gregory IV (827-44)
102. Sergius II (844-47)
103. St. Leo IV (847-55)
104. Benedict III (855-58)
105. St. Nicholas I (the Great) (858-67)
106. Adrian II (867-72)

107. John VIII (872-82)
108. Marinus I (882-84)
109. St. Adrian III (884-85)
110. Stephen V (885-91)
111. Formosus (891-96)
112. Boniface VI (896)
113. Stephen VI (896-97)
114. Romanus (897)
115. Theodore II (897)
116. John IX (898-900)
117. Benedict IV (900-03)
118. Leo V (903)
119. Sergius III (904-11)
120. Anastasius III (911-13)
121. Lando (913-14)
122. John X (914-28)
123. Leo VI (928)
124. Stephen VII (929-31)
125. John XI (931-35)
126. Leo VII (936-39)
127. Stephen VIII (939-42)
128. Marinus II (942-46)
129. Agapetus II (946-55)
130. John XII (955-63)
131. Leo VIII (963-64)
132. Benedict V (964)
133. John XIII (965-72)
134. Benedict VI (973-74)
135. Benedict VII (974-83)
136. John XIV (983-84)
137. John XV (985-96)
138. Gregory V (996-99)
(John XVI was an antipope from 997-98)
139. Sylvester II (999-1003)
140. John XVII (1003)
141. John XVIII (1003-09)
142. Sergius IV (1009-12)

143. Benedict VIII (1012-24)
144. John XIX (1024-32)
145. Benedict IX (1032-45) He appears on this list three separate times, because he was twice deposed and restored.
146. Sylvester III (1045) Considered by some to be an antipope.
147. Benedict IX (1045)
148. Gregory VI (1045-46)
140. Clement II (1046-47)
150. Benedict IX (1047-48)
151. Damasus II (1048)
152. St. Leo IX (1049-54)
153. Victor II (1055-57)
154. Stephen IX (1057-58)
155. Nicholas II (1058-61)
156. Alexander II (1061-73)
157. St. Gregory VII (1073-85)
158. Blessed Victor III (1086-87)
159. Blessed Urban II (1088-99)
160. Paschal II (1099-1118)
161. Gelasius II (1118-19)
162. Callistus II (1119-24)
163. Honorius II (1124-30)
164. Innocent II (1130-43)
165. Celestine II (1143-44)
166. Lucius II (1144-45)
167. Blessed Eugene III (1145-53)
168. Anastasius IV (1153-54)
169. Adrian IV (1154-59)
170. Alexander III (1159-81)
171. Lucius III (1181-85)
172. Urban III (1185-87)
173. Gregory VIII (1187)
174. Clement III (1187-91)
175. Celestine III (1191-98)
176. Innocent III (1198-1216)

177. Honorius III (1216-27)
178. Gregory IX (1227-41)
179. Celestine IV (1241)
180. Innocent IV (1243-54)
181. Alexander IV (1254-61)
182. Urban IV (1261-64)
183. Clement IV (1265-68)
184. Blessed Gregory X (1271-76)
185. Blessed Innocent V (1276)
186. Adrian V (1276)
187. John XXI (1276-77)
188. Nicholas III (1277-80)
189. Martin IV (1281-85)
190. Honorius IV (1285-87)
191. Nicholas IV (1288-92)
192. St. Celestine V (1294)
193. Boniface VIII (1294-1303)
194. St. Benedict XI (1303-04)
195. Clement V (1305-14)
196. John XXII (1316-34)
197. Benedict XII (1334-42)
198. Clement VI (1342-52)
199. Innocent VI (1352-62)
200. Blessed Urban V (1362-70)
201. Gregory XI (1370-78)
202. Urban VI (1378-89)
203. Boniface IX (1389-1404)
204. Innocent VII (1404-06)
205. Gregory XII (1406-15)
206. Martin V (1417-31)
207. Eugene IV (1431-47)
208. Nicholas V (1447-55)
209. Callistus III (1455-58)
210. Pius II (1458-64)
211. Paul II (1464-71)
212. Sixtus IV (1471-84)
213. Innocent VIII (1484-92)

214. Alexander VI (1492-1503)
215. Pius III (1503)
216. Julius II (1503-13)
217. Leo X (1513-21)
218. Adrian VI (1522-23)
219. Clement VII (1523-34)
220. Paul III (1534-49)
221. Julius III (1550-55)
222. Marcellus II (1555)
223. Paul IV (1555-59)
224. Pius IV (1559-65)
225. St. Pius V (1566-72)
226. Gregory XIII (1572-85)
227. Sixtus V (1585-90)
228. Urban VII (1590)
229. Gregory XIV (1590-91)
230. Innocent IX (1591)
231. Clement VIII (1592-1605)
232. Leo XI (1605)
233. Paul V (1605-21)
234. Gregory XV (1621-23)
235. Urban VIII (1623-44)
236. Innocent X (1644-55)
237. Alexander VII (1655-67)
238. Clement IX (1667-69)
239. Clement X (1670-76)
240. Blessed Innocent XI (1676-89)
241. Alexander VIII (1689-91)
242. Innocent XII (1691-1700)
243. Clement XI (1700-21)
244. Innocent XIII (1721-24)
245. Benedict XIII (1724-30)
246. Clement XII (1730-40)
247. Benedict XIV (1740-58)
248. Clement XIII (1758-69)
249. Clement XIV (1769-74)
250. Pius VI (1775-99)

251. Pius VII (1800-23)
252. Leo XII (1823-29)
253. Pius VIII (1829-30)
254. Gregory XVI (1831-46)
255. Blessed Pius IX (1846-78)
256. Leo XIII (1878-1903)
257. St. Pius X (1903-14)
258. Benedict XV (1914-22)
259. Pius XI (1922-39)
260. Pius XII (1939-58)
261. Blessed John XXIII (1958-63)
262. Paul VI (1963-78)
263. John Paul I (1978)
264. John Paul II (1978-2005)
265. Benedict XVI (2005-2013)
266. Francis (2013-2025)
267. Leo XIV (2025-

# THE FALLACY of REINCARNATION
(For Catholics and other Christians)

**REINCARNATION**: The belief that a person's immortal soul enters another living or non-living entity after death.

The belief in reincarnation has been held by various pagan man-made religions for perhaps thousands of years. Although its origin is really not important for this particular study, it is commonly believed to have originated in the Eastern religions such as Hinduism, Buddhism, Jainism, Shinto, and Sikhism, perhaps even more. But as I said, this is really not important to prove the following point of this analysis.

Let's suppose that reincarnation is possible and true; that the same soul of a person has reincarnated into only one other human body and therefore lived two separate and distinct lives on this beautiful planet we live in, planet Earth.

Now, during this person's first lifetime, he lived a very worldly life with little or no regard for anything or anyone else. He was a very wealthy man, and because of this, he never lacked a single thing and enjoyed the comforts and worldly pleasures that only money can buy. He never married for fear that women would take his wealth, and instead had more lovers than the grains of sand on the seashore. (I bet some of you wish you had a life like this!) In addition, he either killed or had someone else kill other human beings, from time to time, in order to keep his wealth and worldly power which never bothered him one bit. Then one day, quite unexpectedly, he died without repenting of his many sins, and because of his "bad karma," when his soul left his body, it entered a second body, also of a male.

This time however, this same soul in this new second body eventually became a Roman Catholic monk, a very holy and religious monk. He fed and gave drink to the hungry and thirsty on a daily basis. He took in strangers all the time and helped them with their troubles. He made clothes for those who were naked and had none. He also cared for the sick on a daily basis and even visited those who were in prison to give them comfort and friendship. Then one day, quite unexpectedly, he had a heart attack while sewing clothes for the needy and died.

Coincidentally, the world ends and Judgment Day comes the very second he dies. The next thing he knows, his soul is standing in front of God Almighty facing Judgment. But there is a problem here, a very serious one indeed! Jesus looks at him and says: "Well, in your first life, you didn't do so well. In fact, you were a terrible person. And because you did not repent for the sins you committed at death, some of which were extremely horrible, the penalty is Hell for all Eternity. However, in your second life, you were a living saint, and the reward for such a saintly life is Eternal Life in Heaven. What, then, am I going to do with you? The two bodies you used on Earth are waiting for resurrection to be reunited with you once again, but you can only have one body for all Eternity, not two. What now?"

This, of course, is only a story to illustrate why reincarnation is not an actual reality but only a mythical idea that was invented by a very imaginative person. But don't fool yourself into believing that since this is only a story, it therefore may not be actually true in real life and reincarnation may in fact be something that truly happens when a person dies. Nothing could be further from the actual truth. It is a fallacy and does not really happen in actual life.

To all who are Catholic, and to those who are not but consider themselves to be "Christian," the belief in reincarnation is incompatible with the teachings of Christ and His Holy Church. To those who firmly believe in life after death and the Final Judgment of mankind at the end of the world, reincarnation is not only contrary to common sense and reason, it is also quite impossible to say the least. Otherwise, imagine the poor soul who has used 10, 20 100, or perhaps thousands of bodies and then faces judgment by God at the End of Time! What a nightmare that would be! All those bodies lined up waiting for the soul to enter them and animate them once again, but there's only one soul for all of them! It is totally ridiculous, illogical, and senseless.

In Revelation 2:10-11, we find the following:

"Do not fear what you are about to suffer. Behold, the devil is about to throw some of you into prison, that you may be tested, and for ten days you will have tribulation. Be faithful unto death, and I will give you the crown of life. He who has an ear, let him hear what the Spirit says to the churches. He who conquers shall not be hurt by the second death."

A "second death?" What does that mean? Maybe reincarnation is true! Not quite. Let's take another look at Revelation, this time at 20:6:

"Blessed and holy is he who shares in the first resurrection! Over such the second death has no power, but they shall be priests of God and of Christ, and they shall reign with him a thousand years."

Some of you may be thinking, "First, a 'second death' and now a 'first resurrection'? You mean there's going to be two deaths and two resurrections?" Before we get really confused, let's take a look at what the Navarre Bible Commentary (NBC) says about this:

"According to this interpretation, the 'first resurrection' should be understood in a spiritual sense; it is **Baptism**, which regenerates man and gives him new life by freeing him from [Original] sin and making him a son of God. The second resurrection is the one which will take place at the end of time, when the body is brought back to life and the human being, body and soul, enters into everlasting joy (NBC, Rev, p. 141, my emph.).

But what about the "second death"? Let's go back to Revelation once more and find out.

"Then I saw a great white throne and him who sat upon it; from his presence earth and sky fled away, and no place was found for them. And I saw the dead, great and small, standing before the throne, and books were opened. Also another book was opened, which is the book of life. And the dead were judged by what was written in the books, **by what they had done**. And the sea gave up the dead in it, Death and Hades gave up the dead in them, **and all were judged by what they had done**. Then Death and Hades were thrown into **the lake of fire. This is the second death, the lake of fire**; and if any ones name was not found written in the book of life, he was thrown into the lake of fire.... And he said to me, It is done! I am the Alpha and the Omega, the beginning and the end. To the thirsty I will give water without price from the fountain of the water of life. He who conquers shall have this heritage, and I will be his God and he shall be my son. But as for the cowardly, the faithless, the polluted, as for murderers, fornicators, sorcerers, idolaters, and all liars, their lot shall be in the lake that burns with fire and brimstone, **which is the second death**" (Rev 20:11-15; 21:6-8, my emph.). Again, let's take a look at what the NBC says about all this:

The "flight of earth and sky" mean that they disappear (for even non-rational created things have been contaminated by sin: see Rom 8:19ff) to make way for a new heaven and a new earth (21:1; see 2 Pet 3:13; Rom 8:23).... "Second death": a reference to irreversible, enduring, condemnation [in Hell]…. Therefore, we should be vigilant, as St. Augustine taught: "Everyone fears physical death; **but few fear the death of the soul** […]. Mortal man strives not to die; so, should not the man destined to live eternally strive not to sin?" (In Ioann. Evang., 49, 2; NBC, Rev, pp. 142, 45, 147) [my emph.]. So, now we know what the second death is: eternal punishment in the Lake of Fire, which is Hell, reserved for those who are wicked, evil, polluted, and corrupt; all the unrighteous who have actually condemned themselves through their own freely made choices and actions, not anyone else's.

This scripturally proves, once and for all, that there are only two (2) deaths: the first one, when our bodies will die here on Earth, which is only temporary, and the second one, when the condemned are sent to Hell for all eternity.

Every human person will undergo two judgments: the first is called the Particular Judgment, where one is judged by God immediately after death, and the second is called the Last Judgment or Final Judgment which will take place at the end of the world with all humanity assembled as one before God. When St. Paul said: "And just as it is appointed for men to die **once**, and after that comes judgment" (Heb 9:27), he is here talking about the first one, the Particular Judgment, after which the person's soul is either condemned and goes to Hell, or is rewarded with Heaven but has to go to Purgatory for a final cleansing before entering Heaven, or goes directly to Heaven if it is in a perfect state of holiness. There are only three destinations for the soul after death (only one physical death): either Hell, Purgatory, or Heaven. So, to answer the famous question, "Where do we go from here?" The answer is:

**"IT ALL DEPENDS ON YOU!"**

We are all called to be saints. And with God's Mercy, Love, and Grace, we can be. All In Time!

## FAITH - What Is It, And How Do We Get It?

The general and simple meaning of faith is confidence or trust in someone or something often without full or visible proof, and when it comes to faith in God, paragraph 153 of the Catechism of the Catholic Church (CCC) states: *Faith is a gift of God, a supernatural virtue infused by him.* "Before this faith can be exercised, man must have the grace of God to move and assist him; he must have the interior helps of the Holy Spirit, who moves the heart and converts it to God, who opens the eyes of the mind and 'makes it easy for all to accept and believe the truth.'" (*DV* 5; cf. DS 377; 3010.)

If faith is then a gift *of* God, and therefore *from* God, and not something we acquire through our intelligence or reason, why are there so many people without it? In other words, why doesn't God give the gift of faith to everyone? That way, everyone will believe in Him and most likely will also love their neighbor and get along with everyone resulting in little or no violence and evil in the world. So, why doesn't God give the gift of faith to everybody? It is logical to believe that the world would be a much better place to live in if God gave this gift to everyone. Doesn't God love everyone He creates? Doesn't He want all that is good for all of us? Doesn't He want us to live in a peaceful and loving world without evil? So why doesn't He give the gift of faith to everyone so we can have that? I believe the answer lies in the free will we are created with.

All of us have a soul, and the soul has two faculties: the intellect and the will. Through the intellect, we know, we understand, we see. What do we see? What is there. And through the will, we love, we choose, we decide, and then we act. Therefore, since it is through the will that we choose and decide what to do, that is why it is called "free will," because we are totally free to choose what we want, and then make the decision to get it or to do it. Every human being is born with free will. The Merriam-Webster dictionary lists free will as the "freedom of humans to make choices that are not determined by prior causes or by divine intervention." This means that all the choices we make in life, we make them all by ourselves. Unless someone forces us (which is rare), no one makes us or forces us to make the choices we make in life, not even God ("divine intervention") makes us or forces us to make them. We have the "ability" to think, choose and do whatever we want to do. God gives this ability to all of us. It is called "free will." We are not robots who follow a specific program in life; we are totally *free* to think and do whatever we want to think and do.

So, what does free will have to do with faith and why God does not give faith to everyone? Since we are created by God with free will and it is us – and no one else – who makes the choices we make in life, we must *freely* ask God to *give* us this gift of faith, because if He gave it to us without our consent, without we wanting it, even though it would be for our own good, He would be forcing us to have it and that would violate the free will He created us with, and God cannot do that. Sounds logical so far? Some may ask: "Why wouldn't all of us want such a valuable gift? Don't we all want to believe in God and get along with everyone else?" And the answer is no, not all people want to believe in God or get along with everyone else. Everyone wants to be able to *choose* what they want to believe and who or what they like. That is the essence of free will: to be able to *choose* what we want, and when it comes to faith, we must *ask* God to give it to us. If we don't, we won't get it! It is that simple. Jesus said: "Ask, and it will be given [to] you; seek, and you will find; knock, and it will be opened to you. For every one who asks receives, and he who seeks finds, and to him who knocks it will be opened" (Mt 7:7-8).

Now, since God truly knows what we truly want, for no one can fool Him, and since God does not want to force anything on us that we truly do not want (even if it is for our own good), we must ask God for this gift of faith from our heart, with sincerity and heartfelt certainty that we truly want it, and have the confidence that God will indeed give it to us because we truly want it. It is then, and only then, that God will give us the gift of faith. Now this may not happen right away, even though we may want it right away. God only knows the correct time to give this precious gift to us, so we must be patient if we do not receive it right away, always trusting in Him that He will give it to us when it is the right time for us to receive it. In short, God will not give a person faith if that person truly does not want it. The same, by the way, is true for forgiveness. The Catholic Church teaches that if a person truly repents for his/her sins at the moment of death (no matter what religion they followed), that person will go to Heaven - with a possible stopover in Purgatory. However, if that person is not truly sorry and does not ask God *freely and sincerely* for forgiveness at the moment of death, Hell will be the destination after death (CCC 1033). God will not force faith or forgiveness on anyone because He is bound to respect and honor the free will He gives to all. God does not force anyone to love Him or to hate Him. Only we can do that through the free will He gave us. So, what are *you* waiting for? Lacking in faith? Ask God, from your heart, to give you the gift of faith. And turn away from your sinful life. Walk no further on the road that leads to destruction. Turn away from sin and walk on the Road of Holiness, the one less traveled, the one that leads to Eternal and Everlasting Life.

## "THE STRAIGHT AND NARROW ROAD"

There is a path in Life that's called,
'The Straight and Narrow Road.'
Not easy to achieve, I know,
As attempts of mine have showed.
Not hidden or invisible,
But hard to see it clearly,
'cause the path that twists which rivals it,
Impairs the sight severely.
Of both the friend and foe alike,
With promises of riches,
Adventures, pleasures, strange delights,
The sky becomes the limit!
Its cordial, sweet and bitter,
Will rob the soul of sight,
And blindly you will go, a babbler,
Into the Dark of Night.

* * *

But the Straight will not deceive you,
Like its twisted rival does.
Its Love and Care are always True,
And guided from above.
Ever close, not far away,
It will support the heavy load,
Of friend and foe if they should walk,
The Straight and Narrow Road.

Juan Novo (C) 2015

## "EL CAMINO REAL"

En la vida si existe, un Camino Real!

Es un Camino recto y dificil de lograr.

Sin embargo no es oculto, pero si es ilusorio,

Pues hay otro parecido que entretiene el mirar,

Del amigo y enemigo, con promesas de tesoros,

De delicias y aventuras; arrebatos sin frenar.

Dulce-amargo su cordial, embriagando ciegos ojos,

Este otro parecido nunca falla de ruinar.

* * *

Pero el recto nunca engaña, como si el serpentino!

Infinito es su paciencia, y su amor: Siempre Leal.

Al alcance – no rechaza, ni el amigo o enemigo,

Y los llama a regresar, hacia el Camino Real.

Juan Novo (C) 1994

December 25th, 1994

# THE TEN COMMANDMENTS
(The Decalogue)

1. I am the Lord your God: You shall not have strange Gods before me.

2. You shall not take the name of the Lord your God in vain.

3. Remember to keep holy the Lord's Day.

4. Honor your father and mother.

5. You shall not kill.

6. You shall not commit adultery.

7. You shall not steal.

8. You shall not bear false witness against your neighbor.

9. You shall not covet your neighbor's wife.

10. You shall not covet your neighbor's goods.

## BIBLIOGRAPHY

1. *The Didache Bible, with commentaries based on the Catechism of the Catholic Church.*

2. *Theology and Sanity*, Frank Sheed.

3. *Exorcism: The Battle Against Satan and His Demons*, Fr.Vincent P. Lampert.

4. *The Self Does Not Die*, Rivas, Dirven, and Smit.

5. *Witnesses To Mystery*, Gorny, Rosikon.

6. *Radio Replies*, Fr. Leslie Rumble.

7. *Eucharistic Miracles, The Incorruptibles* , Joan Carroll Cruz.

8. *The Real Story*, Edward Sri, Curtis Martin.

9. *Seven Prophets and the Culture War*, Alexandre Havard.

10. *A Cardiologist Examines Jesus*, Dr. Franco Serafini.

11. *In The Beginning*, Dr. Gerard M. Verschuuren.

12. *Catena Aurea*, St. Thomas Aquinas.

13. *Where We Got The Bible*, Henry G. Graham.

14. *A Catholic Introduction To The Bible, Volume I, The Old Testament*, John Bergsma and Brant Pitre.

15. *Catechism Of The Catholic Church*, Libreria Editrice Vaticana.

16. *The Privileged Planet*, Guillermo Gonzalez, Jay Richards.

## ABOUT THE AUTHOR

Juan Novo was born in Habana Cuba seven years before the communist Castro regime took totalitarian control of this burgeoning island paradise and turned it into an isolated, run down specter of her former glory. He came to the U.S.A. unaccompanied when he was nine years old through "Operation Pedro Pan," a clandestine operation that succeeded in rescuing over 14,000 unaccompanied Cuban minor children from communist indoctrination and control by the communist Castro regime. The operation, which ended with the Cuban Missile Crisis in 1962, was run and directed by Monsignor Bryan O. Walsh of the Catholic Welfare Bureau in Miami, Florida.

By the time he was nineteen, Juan had become a professional musician and was making a living as a percussionist playing music in the San Francisco area under contract to Warner Brothers Studios in a band called "Fat City." In 1976, he graduated from Spokane Falls Community College with degrees in both music theory and musical instrument repair and has been practicing the repair trade for the past 50 years.

Mr. Novo founded the Research and Development Committee for the National Association of Professional Band Instrument Repair Technicians (NAPBIRT) in 1983, and it was here where he was "bit" for the first time by the "investigative writing bug." Juan ended up publishing a work entitled "The Grenadilla Story," an in-depth investigative study of African Blackwood, an African hardwood that has been used to make woodwind musical instruments for over a century. The report revealed the precious wood was at the edge of extinction which led to successful replanting programs years later. Mr. Novo has written technical repair and restoration articles published in the Association's trade journal, "TechniCom." His work with musical instruments has been featured in several TV specials, and articles about him and his work have appeared in both foreign and domestic newspapers, magazines and periodicals. Although Juan switched careers and entered the musical instrument repair field full time in 1977, he continued to play percussion as a hobby and has performed in concerts with Jazz legends such as the late Dizzy Gillespie and Ira Sullivan.

Since 1983, Mr. Novo has been making professional model Grenadilla wood mouthpieces for the metal concert flute which are played by both amateur and professional flutists worldwide. Between 1981 and 1984, Mr. Novo was awarded two U.S. patents on musical instrument designs. One of these, patent # 4,685,373, is for the transparent FANTASIA flute he invented in 1984: a professional grade transparent flute that is illuminated with colored lights during performance. The first such instrument, built in 1985, was commissioned by the late Julius Baker, principal flautist for the New York Philharmonic Orchestra. This instrument was later purchased by the late New York Latin-Jazz flutist Dave Valentin and is featured in one of his albums entitled, "Light Struck." The FANTASIA flute made U.S. Patent history, for it was the first illuminated musical wind instrument to be awarded a patent by the U.S. Patent Office. As a result, a new division had to be created for it and it remains to this day the only such instrument in its class.

In the late 80s, Juan served for a time as editor of the "Sunshine Jazz Messenger," the newsletter for Miami's Sunshine Jazz Organization, and in 1990, his Grenadilla flute mouthpiece, played by Dave Valentin, was featured in the soundtrack of the film "Havana" starring Robert Redford. This present book, "A Race Redeemed," is Mr. Novo's latest and most important investigative work, according to him. Juan is a practicing Catholic, a member of the Knights of Columbus, and an avid student of Catholic theology and philosophy. He now works part time for a company that is devoted to music education for children.

GOD'S CREATION – IN THE BEGINNING

THE GARDEN OF EDEN

AFTER ORIGINAL SIN

BANISHMENT FROM EDEN

BLIND SODOMITES GROPING FOR LOT'S DOOR

THE DESTRUCTION OF SODOM AND GOMORRAH

THE BINDING OF ISAAC

THE EXODUS FROM EGYPT

THE ANNUNCIATION

THE NATIVITY OF THE LORD

THE LAST SUPPER

THE GARDEN OF GETHSEMANI

THE ARREST OF JESUS

THE TRIAL OF THE CHRIST

THE DEATH OF THE MESSIAH

THE RETURN FROM CALVARY

THE RESURRECTION OF THE MESSIAH

PENTECOST

THE HOLY TRINITY

GOD'S NEW CHOSEN PEOPLE

www.ingramcontent.com/pod-product-compliance
Lightning Source LLC
La Vergne TN
LVHW020503100826
845148LV00003B/692
*9798888706893*